YOU CAN TEACH YOUR CHILDREN MATH

MICHAEL M. FEEMSTER

Silversmith Press–Houston, Texas
www.silversmithpress.com

ISBN 978-1-967386-48-2 (Softcover Book)

To the parents concerned with the education of their children and want to do something about it.

CONTENTS

INTRODUCTION

I have been tutoring or teaching Math since I was eighteen years old. I have been successful explaining math concepts to people who have had difficulties with the subject.

For many students and adults, math is something mysterious that only a very few people will ever understand. It is seen as something strange and complex, which causes immense frustration when trying to learn it.

I have spoken with several high school students and adults about their experiences and aggravations about the subject. Students just want to get the experience over with so that they can graduate and adults want to do as little math as possible in their lives.

I have had friends who are now parents complain to me that they are unable to help their children with elementary school math. They feel helpless with the new way that math is being taught. These parents also understand that the world is changing. Old jobs are disappearing, never to return; but new jobs are appearing. These jobs did not exist a generation ago. The gatekeeper to many of these new jobs is math skills.

Fields in science, technology, engineering and math, often referred by the acronym STEM are where the growth and innovation in new jobs will be concentrated. Without strong math skills, jobs in these fields will be closed off to many young people. Sadly, many young people make a decision to avoid math at a young age.

Over the years I have come to realize that the way bureaucrats in education force teachers to teach math makes the subject difficult for most people.

I plan to change that.

I wrote this book to help parents teach their children math. The way a parent will teach a child using this book will be very different from the way an elementary school teacher will teach a child math. This has the potential to cause problems because children will tell their parents, "That is not how my teacher says how to do it."

It is necessary to understand that what is important in elementary school is not the grade, but the mastery of the subject matter. The two skills that are absolutely necessary for students to master before entering into an Algebra I class are to know their multiplication facts and how to do operations with positive and negative numbers.

It is common doctrine that students no longer have to memorize their multiplication facts, what was in the past called times tables. The reasoning behind this doctrine is that the use of calculators is widespread and therefore the students can use these calculators to do math problems instead of memorizing their multiplication facts. My experience refutes this argument.

There are several algebra problems that can be easily solved in five to fifteen seconds if the student has mastery over their multiplication facts. If a student does not have mastery of these facts, then the same problems will be more difficult for the student to solve. Such difficulty will result in frustration and despair for the student, which will then cause the student to put in the bare minimum of effort to complete an assignment. The assignment will be complete, but no learning or understanding will take place.

Confidence and curiosity are two neglected aspects by the education establishment of educating children. I usually have to spend more than half of my time in a classroom having to convince students that they have the ability to be successful at math.

By using the techniques in this book, a parent can make math more enjoyable for a child to learn. If parents start before their children begin kindergarten, then their children will be ahead of their peers. Math will no longer be a difficult subject only mastered by a very few, but a subject that is mastered and enjoyed. However, this is not to suggest that if parents start later the benefits of working with their children in mastering mathematics is unattainable. Therefore, I encourage parents to get involved in the education of their children regardless of age.

Parents must understand that there is no such thing as new math. What is new is how teachers are forced to teach math. When parents understand this, then they can concentrate on having their children master the subject matter instead of worrying about math grades in an elementary school math class. Think about this: If a student displays mastery of algebra, geometry and calculus in high school, a university will not reject that student for a poor math grade in elementary school. After all elementary school exists to prepare a young student for the rigors of high school. The modern elementary school way of teaching fails in that regard. It is the goal of this book to help remedy that situation.

In addition to classroom homework, parents can easily spend just ten to fifteen minutes a day working with their children to improve both their competence and their confidence in elementary school mathematical skills. These activities should be conducted in a manner that is enjoyable and stress free as possible.

The timetable for suggested learning is as follows:

Preschool and early elementary:

Teaching Counting
Teaching Addition
Teaching About Even and Odd
Teaching Subtraction

Middle elementary:

Teaching Multiplication
Teaching Number Recognition to One Million
Teaching Measurements
Teaching Rounding
Teaching Division

Late elementary:

Teaching Order of operationsTeaching Area and perimeter

Teaching Factors and multiples
Teaching Divisibility rules
Teaching Prime and Composite Numbers
Teaching Prime Factorization
Teaching Greatest Common Factor
Teaching Least Common Multiple
Teaching Fractions
Teaching Decimals
Teaching Central Tendency
Teaching Exponents
Teaching Ratios
Teaching Unit Rates
Teaching Proportions
Teaching Percents
Teaching the Metric System
Teaching Scientific Notation
Teaching Positive and Negative Numbers
Teaching Square Roots
Teaching Basic of Circles

It is important for parents not to feel overwhelmed by all of the listed above skills. If the skills are mastered in the proper order, then the next new skill will be relatively easy to master. Everyday practice is the key.

Daily practice is almost always overlooked when it comes to mastery in mathematics. To achieve mastery in athletic endeavors, music proficiency or culinary pursuits will always require practice. The same is true in academics, particularly mathematics. Most students never practice their mathematical skills and as a result lack the confidence and competence needed to become successful in math.

I urge parents to be more involved and take control of the education of their children. For too long their children have been treated as subjects in educational theory by bureaucrats and educational professors looking to make a name for themselves. The result of all of this is that the education of the average child has suffered in the past decades.

With this book parents now have a tool to combat the educational establishment that has wreaked havoc on the lives of our children. I wish the best for all parents who desire a better life and education for their children.

TEACHING COUNTING

Parents and grandparents can begin teaching children mathematics long before the children enroll in kindergarten. This will help take the mystery out of mathematics and get children comfortable working with numbers. The desire is to spark in young children a curiosity about numbers and math that will lead to a lifetime of learning.

As soon as possible the child should be introduced to counting and number recognition. This should be done in a way that is fun and not stressful to the child. In the beginning there does not need to be a set time to do these activities. They are simple and short so these activities can be done at various times throughout the day.

Depending on the age of the child, counting to five or ten can be a starting point. Teach the child his or her age by holding up the proper number fingers. For instance, the child could be asked, "How old are you?" when the child answers, hold up three fingers. Then ask, "What comes next?" When the child answers, "four," hold up four fingers.

A single deck of playing cards can be used to work with a child. It is important to treat this as a play activity so that the child perceives this as fun. Some examples of play could be to have the child count various things around the house and then pick the correct card that matches the number on the card. Simply ask the child, "How many chairs are there?" The child then should pick the card with the correct number.

The important thing is to get the child to recognize a printed number and associate that printed number with a number of things. Thus, the child learns that the figure 5 represents the number five and means five things.

A word processing program such as Microsoft Word® can be used as a game with a child. Set the alignment to center and then set the font size to 300. (The number must be typed in the font size box, because when the drop-down box only goes to 72.

Once this is done type a number and ask the child, "What number is that?" Once the child answers correctly, hit the backspace key and type a new number.

Another activity can be shared when a parent is shopping with the child. Look at the price and ask the child to say the numbers that are on the price tag. For young children all that is necessary is to say the single digits. For example, something that is eighty-nine cents a child need only say, "Eight," and "nine." Any time the child is outside a parent can consistently ask about numbers that appear on signs. When in an elevator tell the child what floor you are going to and ask the child to point to the number. If the parent is willing the child could be picked up and allowed to press the button.

The goal of this initial stage of working with the child is to get the child to master number recognition of numbers from one to ten and to be able to comfortably count from one to ten. Also counting to ten by two can be mastered at this time. Teach the child to count, "Two, four, six, eight, ten," in addition to counting from one to ten. Have the child count several times a day.

Once the child has completely mastered the numbers from one to ten then work should begin to teach the child how to recognize and count numbers up to one hundred. A good technique to use is to take any book that has the pages numbered and count the pages with the child. It may be necessary to teach the child how to count to one hundred by tens before attempting this task.

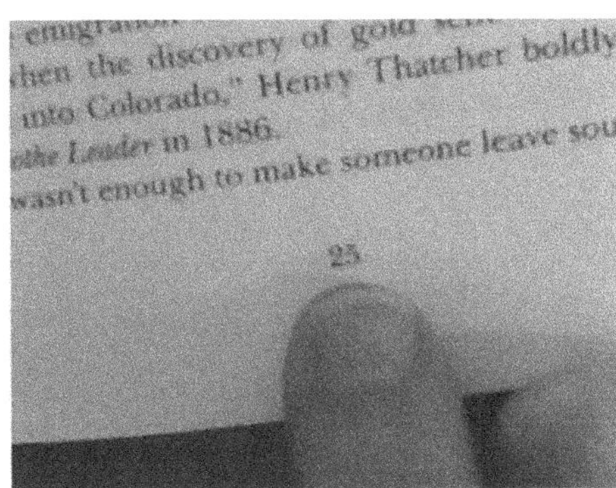

Also, a parent can sit with the child and write a two-digit number on a piece of paper and ask the child what number comes next. For example, write the number seventeen on a piece of paper, (it can be an envelope for a credit card application) ask the child what number comes next, when the child answers, "eighteen," write down the number and then ask what comes next for a short period of time.

Remember, it is important for the child to believe that this is a fun activity that is shared with an adult.

Once the child has mastered counting to one hundred, have the child count to one hundred at least once a week for several weeks. It is a good idea to "show off" this ability to other adult guests, especially grandparents, aunts, and uncles. Do not forget to praise the child for this accomplishment.

TEACHING ADDITION

Once the child has mastered counting from one to one-hundred and recognizing any number from one to one hundred, then it is time to begin teaching the child the basics of addition. It is necessary to get the child to understand what addition is before having the child learn addition facts.

In order to teach the child, the concept of what addition is, it might be necessary to use manipulatives. Manipulatives are any group of small objects that can be counted. Schools often purchase colorful blocks or small plastic figures to help teach young students to basics of addition.

Fortunately, it is not necessary to spend money on manipulatives for teaching addition to young children at home. Pennies, crackers, peanuts, and chewable vitamins are just a few examples of what can be used as manipulatives in the home.

Start with one plus one equals two. Place two manipulatives apart and then hold up one and ask the child, "How many is this?" When the child answers "one," then repeat with the other hand. Once the child answers "one" again then place the two manipulatives together and then ask, "How many?" Once the child answers "two," say, "one plus one equals two."

For now, limit the value of the addends, that is the numbers that are added, to five or smaller. So, the highest sum will be ten because five plus five equals ten. Fingers can also be used. For example, hold up two fingers on one hand and three fingers on the other hand. Hold your hands apart so that the child identifies two and three.

Then move your hands together so that the child sees five fingers and say, "Two plus three equals five."

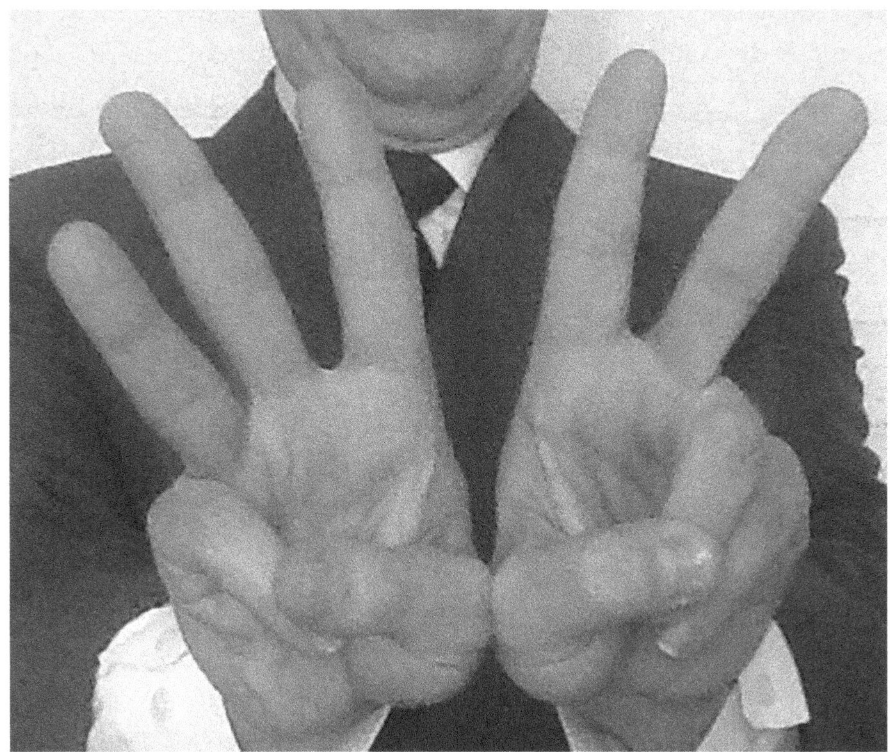

Practice daily with the child for about ten to fifteen minutes. Remember to make the activity fun for the child. Other adults and older siblings can play this game with the child as well.

Once the child is comfortable with the addition of numbers that are five and smaller, work can now begin on mastery of the addition of single digit numbers. This could be done at the pre-school and kindergarten level. The goal is to have the child be able to quickly add any two single digit numbers without having to count. This skill will take several different steps as patience is necessary.

While rote memorization has fallen out of favor with bureaucrats in education in recent years, I believe that some rote memorization is necessary especially with addition facts. However, the techniques that I will describe will combine rote memorization with critical thinking skills.

Begin this process by introducing the child to doubles. These are easy to remember and can practiced frequently and quickly. I have prepared some power points to download to aid in this task.

The first set of doubles will be recited as follows:

$$1 + 1 = 2$$
$$2 + 2 = 4$$
$$4 + 4 = 8$$
$$8 + 8 = 16$$
$$16 + 16 = 32$$
$$32 + 32 = 64$$

Notice that there are only six equations to memorize. Repeating these three times a night in addition to the other activities will solidify these facts in the child's mind.

The next set of doubles to be learned will be all of the single digit numbers and ten.

$$1 + 1 = 2$$
$$2 + 2 = 4$$
$$3 + 3 = 6$$
$$4 + 4 = 8$$
$$5 + 5 = 10$$
$$6 + 6 = 12$$
$$7 + 7 = 14$$
$$8 + 8 = 16$$
$$9 + 9 = 18$$
$$10 + 10 = 20$$

Occasionally quizzing the child during the day should be done in a relaxed and playful manner. Just ask the child, "What's five plus five?" When the child answers, "Ten," praise the child and continue with other daily activities. For instance, if the child is watching a television program, ask the child an addition question during a commercial. Soon answering these addition questions correctly will become second nature to the child.

Instead of purchasing flash cards a simple deck of playing cards can be used for practicing addition with the child. Introduce adding the number one to another number by taking a black ace and making a small deck of just the red numbered cards by removing the red kings, queens and jacks. Place the black ace face up on the table and the flip over the red cards one at a time. If a red five is flipped over ask the child, "What is one plus five?"

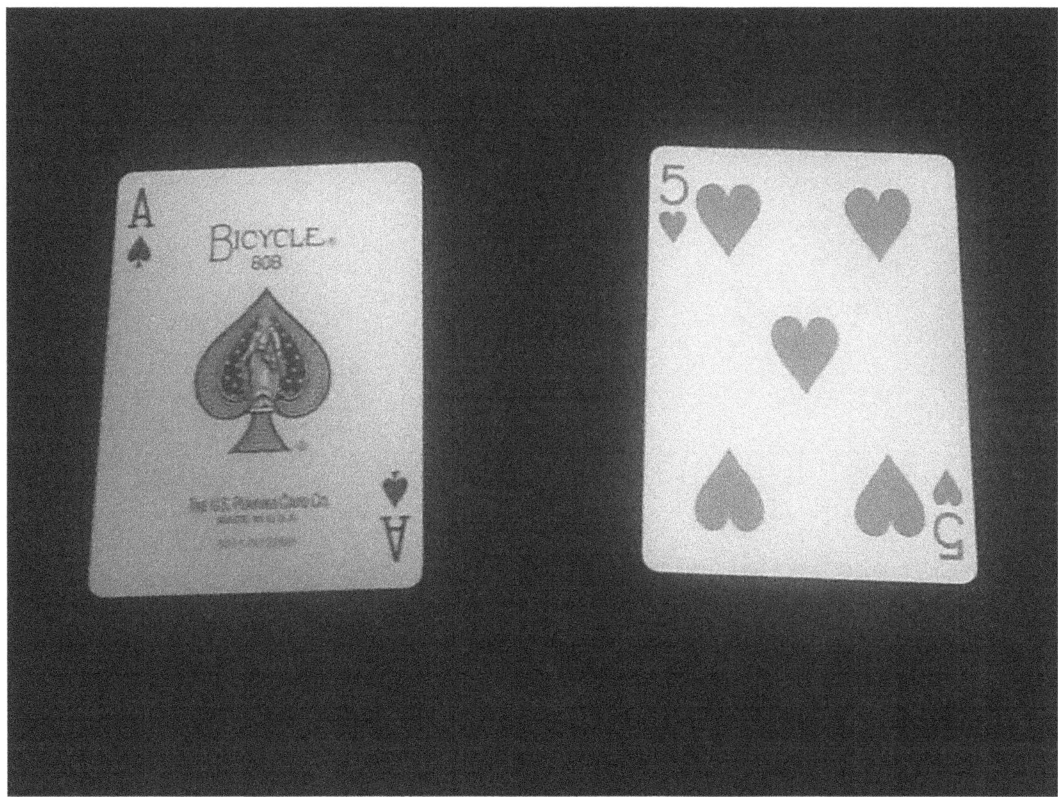

Explain to the child that when one is added to a number the answer will always be increased by one. For instance, one plus five is six and so on. Add this exercise to the daily practice activities and the child should be comfortable with the concept of addition as mastery is eventually achieved.

It is important to make an activity that the child perceives as fun. This can be an activity to be done with grandparents, siblings and possibly babysitters. Always remember to praise the child.

Once the child has mastered adding one to a number, then do the same activity by replacing the one (ace) with a ten. The goal is to have the child quickly add a single digit number to the number ten without having to resort to counting. After the child has mastered both adding one and ten to a single digit number, work with both numbers.

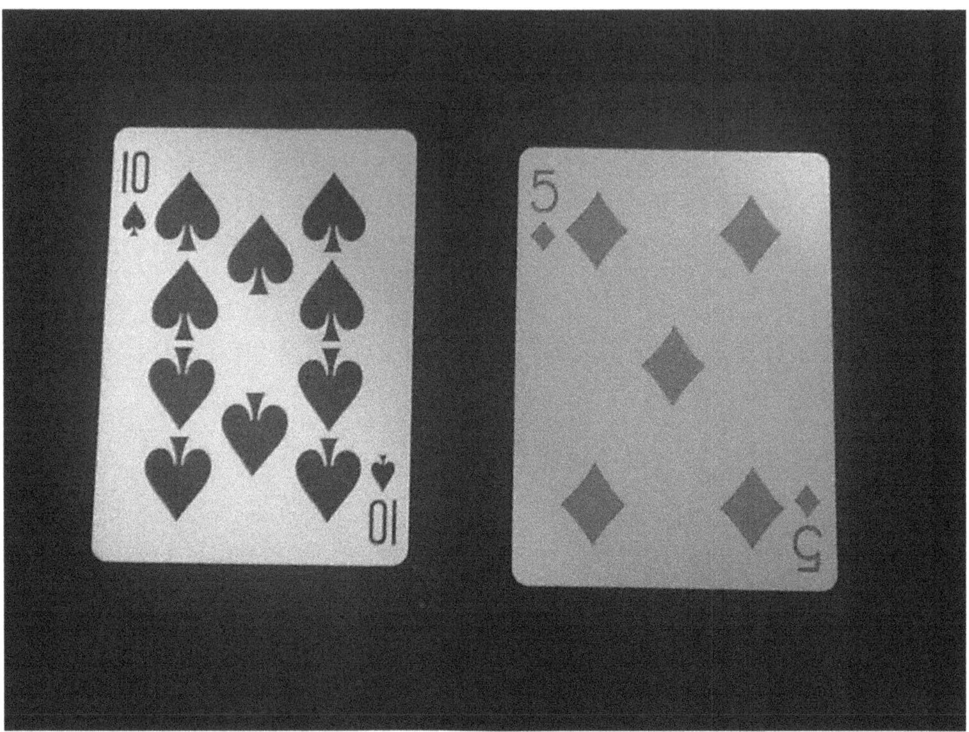

Place a black ace face up on the table and place a black ten directly under the black ace. Shuffle the small deck of red numbered cards and flip them over one at a time, alternate between placing the cards next to the ace and then next to the ten. The goal is to get the child to add the numbers in two seconds or less.

Now it is time to get the child comfortable with using pencil and paper. The parent will print out a worksheet for the child to complete. This activity should not take longer than ten minutes. If the child has achieved mastery in adding single digit numbers by one and ten it should be completed even faster.
The website to use for this is:

themathworksheetsite.com

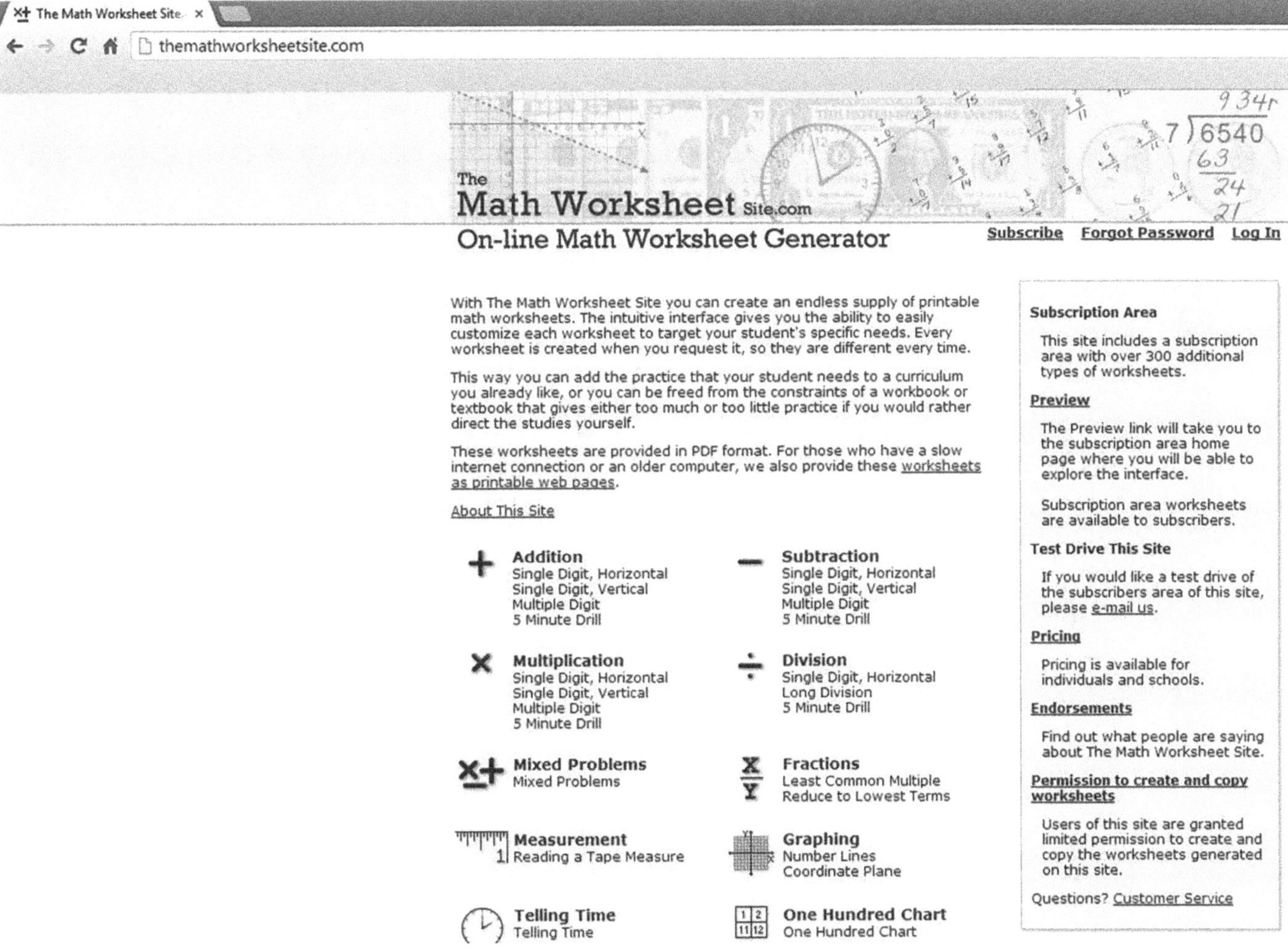

I have found this to be the best site to use for creating math worksheets for practicing basic computational skills.

Look for the addition sign and under it choose the option:

Single Digit, Horizontal

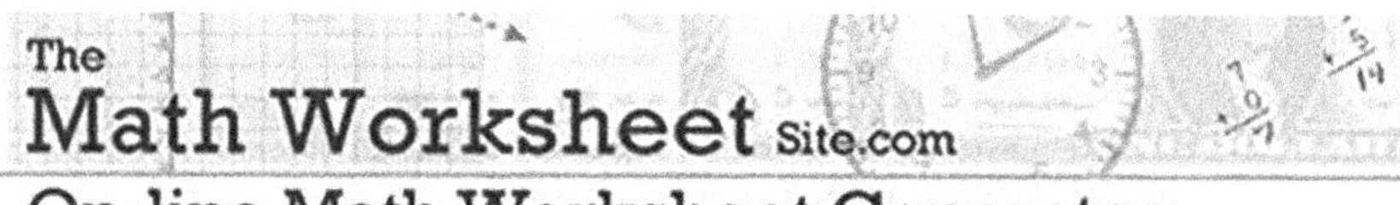

With The Math Worksheet Site you can create an endless supply of printable math worksheets. The intuitive interface gives you the ability to easily customize each worksheet to target your student's specific needs. Every worksheet is created when you request it, so they are different every time.

This way you can add the practice that your student needs to a curriculum you already like, or you can be freed from the constraints of a workbook or textbook that gives either too much or too little practice if you would rather direct the studies yourself.

These worksheets are provided in PDF format. For those who have a slow internet connection or an older computer, we also provide these worksheets as printable web pages.

About This Site

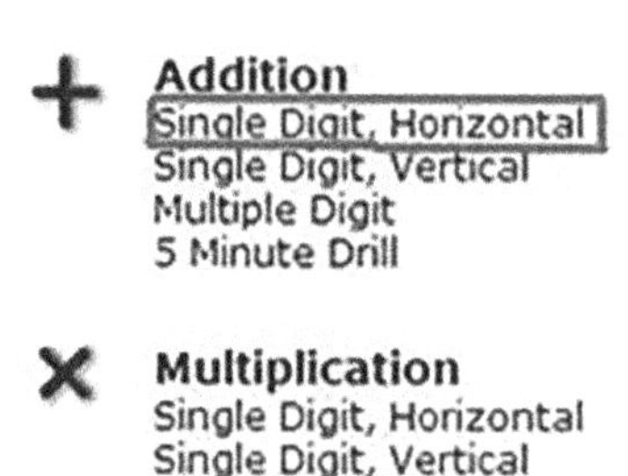

Subtraction
Single Digit, Horizontal
Single Digit, Vertical
Multiple Digit
5 Minute Drill

Division
Single Digit, Horizontal
Long Division
5 Minute Drill

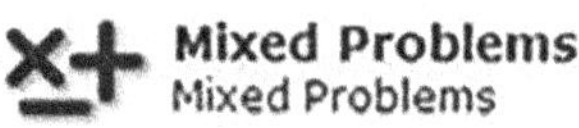

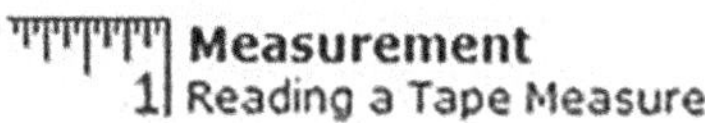

Next select 10 problems
Where it says: "Add these numbers..." select 1 and 10
Where it says: "to these numbers." Select 1 *and* 10 (You need to deselect 0)

The Math Worksheet Site.com

On-line Math Worksheet Generator

Addition: Single Digit, Horizontal

Each problem will have one addend from the selections on the left and one addend from the selections on the right. If there are no addends selected in one of the lists, the numbers 0 through 9 will be used.

Number of problems

- (•) 10 problems
- ( ) 16 problems
- ( ) 20 problems

Add These Numbers...			To These Numbers.		
☐ 0	☑ 1	☑ 2	☐ 0	☑ 1	☐ 2
☑ 3	☑ 4	☑ 5	☐ 3	☐ 4	☐ 5
☑ 6	☑ 7	☑ 8	☐ 6	☐ 7	☐ 8
☑ 9	☑ 10	☐ 11	☐ 9	☑ 10	☐ 11
☐ 12			☐ 12		
All	0-9	Clear	All	0-9	Clear

☐ Include Answer Key

Create It

Now a pdf worksheet will appear that can be printed for the child. It will also be a good time for the child to practice writing his or her name.

At this time introduce the child to the concept of zero. Hold up three fingers on one hand and a fist in the other.

The first is zero so explain that three plus zero equals three. Then explain that if any number is added to zero it does not change. Once the child fully understands the concept of zero, go back to the mathworksheetsite.com and make worksheets that add single digit numbers to one, ten and zero.

Now teach the child the different pairs of numbers that add up to ten. These are as follows:

0 + 10 = 10
1 + 9 = 10
2 + 8 = 10
3 + 7 = 10
4 + 6 = 10
5 + 5 = 10
6 + 4 = 10
7 + 3 = 10
8 + 2 = 10
9 + 1 = 10
10 + 0 = 10

It is important to explain that it does not matter what order the numbers are added. This is called the commutative property of addition. It is not necessary for a preschool child to know the name of this property, just how the property works.

A good exercise is to write the number 10 on an index card or a piece of paper and place a playing card beside it.

Now have the child find the appropriate card that would make the two numbers add up to 10.

This can be repeated with several different cards until the child has mastery. Then just place the paper or index card with 10 down and mix the numbered cards together and have the child pair up cards that add up to 10.

So far, the child should have several addition facts memorized.

0 plus all numbers 1 thru 10	(10 facts)
1 plus all numbers 1 thru 10	(10 facts)
10 plus all numbers 2 thru 10	(9 facts)
Doubles 2 + 2 thru 10 + 10	(9 facts)
Doubles 16 + 16 = 32 and 32 + 32 = 64	(2 facts)
And 2 + 8 = 10, 3 + 7 = 10, and 4 + 6 = 10	(3 facts)

This is 43 addition facts memorized. It is important to practice these facts daily.

Now introduce adding five to single digits numbers. This is where some critical thinking can be introduced to learning addition facts. This is because of an interesting outcome when numbers are added to five. When a number one from four is added to five the sum is a single digit number. When this number is added to five the sum is a double-digit number which has the one's digit the same as the original number.

To illustrate this point, take the number one.

$$1 + 5 = 6$$

The answer is six. Now add five again.

$$5 + 6 = 11$$

The one's digit (1) is the same as the original number that was added to five.

1 + 5 = 6	5 + 6 = 11
2 + 5 = 7	5 + 7 = 12
3 + 5 = 8	5 + 8 = 13
3 + 4 = 9	5 + 9 = 14

Start the child by working with numbers one thru four. Playing cards can be used by taking a black five with a small deck of red cards that contain two aces, twos, three and fours.

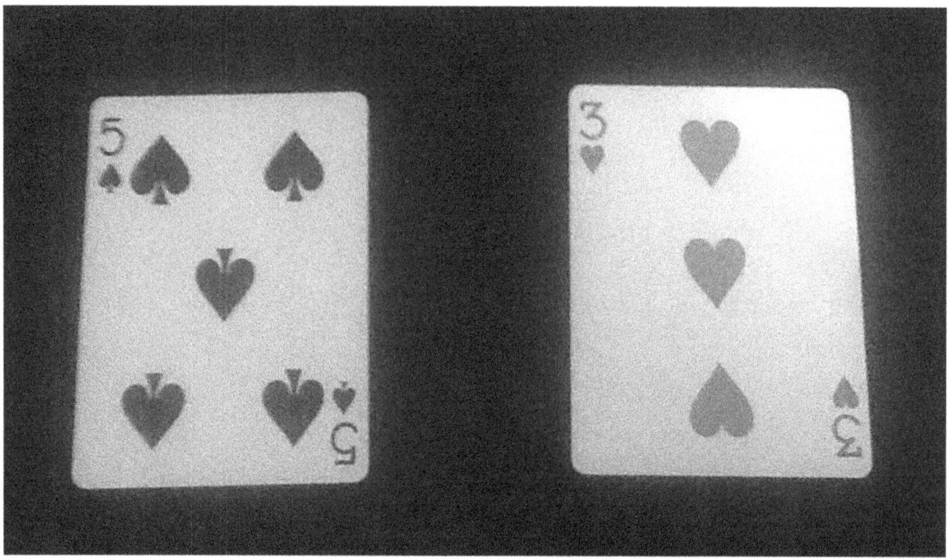

Once the child masters these four facts, work with numbers six, seven, eight and nine. Next a worksheet can be created on themathworksheetsite.com website where 5 is added to numbers 0 thru 10.

At this point it is necessary to teach the child the concept of one less or one fewer. Hold up a hand with four fingers.

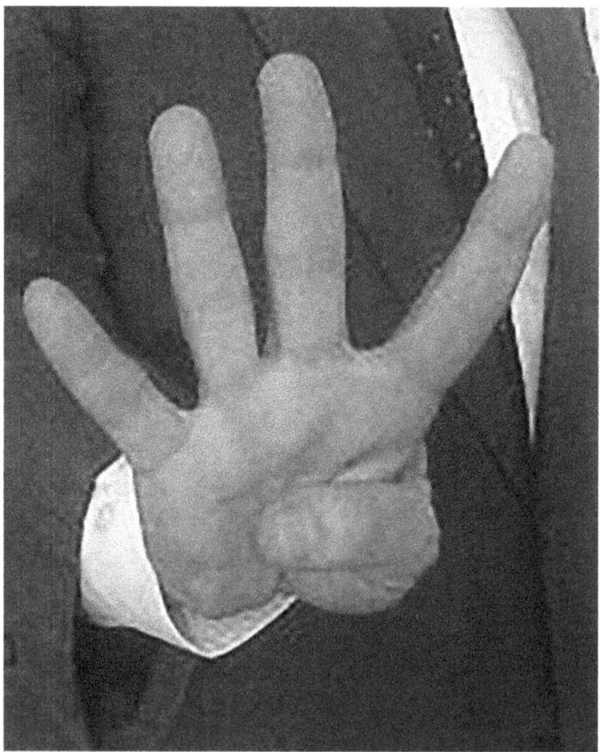

Explain that one less is three, and put a finger down so three fingers are shown.

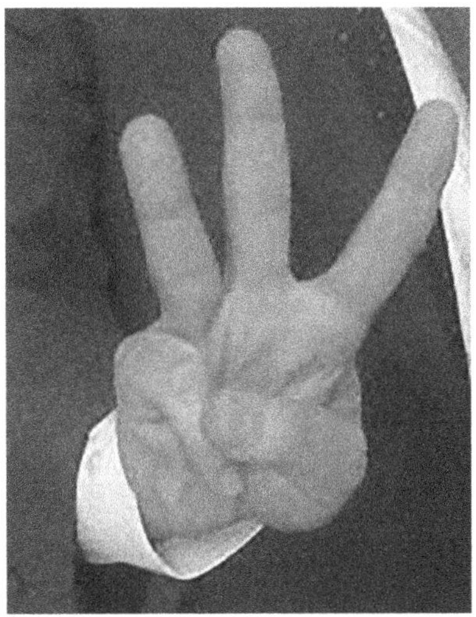

Also use a small number of manipulatives and take one away until the child fully understands this concept.

Now introduce adding nine to a single digit number. Explain to the child that the answer will be one less than when the ten is added to the number. For instance, when six is added to nine the result is one less than when six is added to ten.

Since 10 + 6 = 16
9 + 6 = 15 (one less than 16)

Practice a few times with playing cards where a black nine is added to a shuffled deck of red numbered cards.

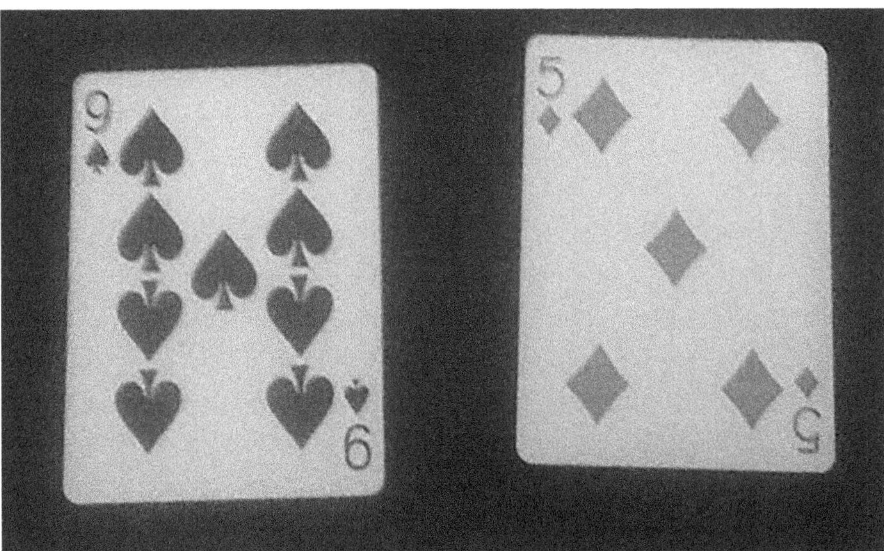

Once this is practiced a few times create worksheets with themathworksheetsite.com website where 9 is added to numbers 0 thru 10.

Once the child has mastered adding nine and ten to single digit numbers, then practice alternating nine and ten black cards with a deck of red numbered cards. Then create worksheets where both 9 and 10 are added to numbers 0 thru 10.

Now the child should have mastered the following:

Doubles

Adding one to a single digit

Adding ten to a single digit

Adding zero to a single digit

Adding five to a single digit

Adding nine to a single digit

Adding to single digit numbers to get a sum of ten

Daily practice is necessary to continue to improve the math skills learned. Practice of addition facts is often ignored by the public education system, so it is very important for the parent to practice daily with the child. Remember the more the child perceives this as a fun and playful activity the more advanced the child's skill in math will become.

Now it is time to work on the two-digit combinations that will result in a sum of eleven. The child should know that 6 + 5 = 11. Explain that six is one more than five so six plus five is one more than five plus five. Teach the child these facts.

9 + 2 = 11 (one more than 9 + 1 = 10)

8 + 3 = 11 (one more than 8 + 2 = 10)

7 + 4 = 11 (one more than 7 + 3 = 10)

6 + 5 = 11 (one more than 6 + 4 = 10)

Now the child can practice with the deck of cards and the number 11. Write the number 11 on an index card or a piece of paper and have the child pair two cards that add up to 11.

The same concept can be used for sums of nine except one less will be used instead of one more, thus:

4 + 5 = 9 (one less than 5 + 5 = 10)

This fact should have been previously mastered by the child adding five to a single digit.

3 + 6 = 9 (one less than 4 + 6 = 10)

2 + 7 = 9 (one less than 3 + 7 = 10)

1 + 8 = 9 (one less than 2 + 8 = 10)

Once again, the child should have 1 + 8 = 9 mastered because it is one added to a single digit. This means there are actually two new addition facts 3 + 6 = 9 and 2 + 7 = 9 that are introduced to the child. Now the math lines game can be used for 9, 10 and 11.

Once this is mastered it is time to work on what could be called one less than the double. To review these are the doubles that the child should be able to mentally add in less than two seconds:

1 + 1 = 2

2 + 2 = 4

3 + 3 = 6

4 + 4 = 8

5 + 5 = 10

6 + 6 = 12

7 + 7 = 14

8 + 8 = 16

9 + 9 = 18

10 + 10 = 20

Now teach the child:

2 + 3 = 5	(one less than 3 + 3 = 6)
3 + 4 = 7	(one less than 4 + 4 = 8)
6 + 7 = 13	(one less than 7 + 7 = 14)
7 + 8 = 15	(one less than 8 + 8 = 16)
8 + 9 = 17	(one less than 9 + 9 = 18)

The addition facts of 4 + 5 = 9 and 5 + 6 = 11 could be included in this but should have been previously memorized and mastered by the child.

Now there are just a few single digit addition facts that the child has not been exposed to in order to master single digit addition. Two of these are 2 + 4 = 6 and 2 + 6 = 8. Once the child has memorized these facts, practice with playing cards using a black 2 with a shuffled deck of red numbered cards.

Begin increasing the number of problems on worksheets created on themathworksheet.com website to 20 and adding 2 and 3 to numbers 0 thru 10. The child should be able to easily complete the worksheet in less than three minutes. Remember to continually praise the child.

Next teach the child 6 + 8 = 14. Recall that 6 + 7 = 13, so teach the child that 6 + 8 is one more than 6 + 7. After that the last fact is 4 + 8 = 12. Once that last fact is memorized then it is necessary to constantly practice single digit addition.

On the mathworksheetsite.com website in the Addition there is a selection titled "5-minute drill." This will create a single sheet of 100 problems for the child to complete. The goal is for the child to complete this task in five minutes.

By this time the child should see this as a fun challenge instead of a stressful chore. Daily practice will strengthen and hone the math skills of the child and work to establish a foundation for building further mathematical knowledge.

Now a deck of cards can be used to make a fun game to be played with the child. To do this make two decks, one of red cards and one of black cards. Remove the face cards from the two decks and shuffle each deck separately. The parent will take one deck and the child the other deck. The parent and child will then turn up a single card. The goal is to be the first player to shout out the sum of the two turned up cards. Give the child a few seconds to add the two cards and say the result. The more the game is played the better the child will become at single digit addition.

It is important to keep practicing single digit addition while the child progresses to more advanced mathematical concepts. The next step is to work with the child on double digit addition. This will be done in two steps. The first step is to have the child add two double digit numbers that does not require carrying or what is now called renaming.

Go back to the themathworksheetsite.com and under the Addition symbol select Multiple Digit.

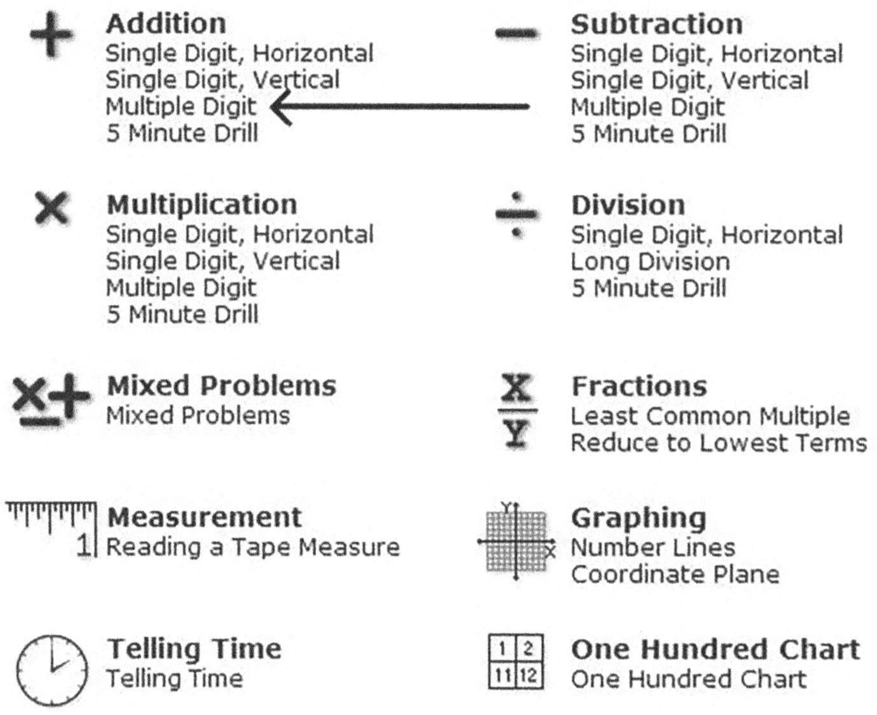

On the page select 2 for Number of Digits and 2 for Number of Addends and finally select the "Without Carrying" bullet.

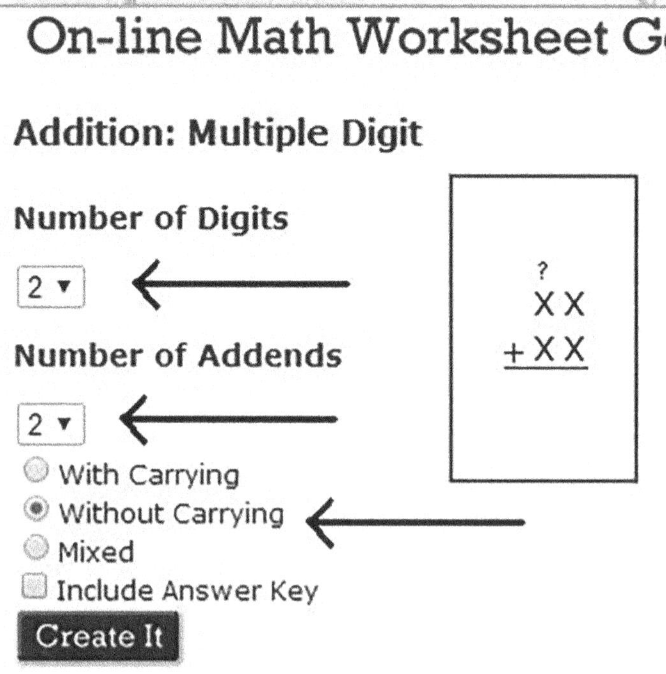

The worksheet created will contain twenty problems. Explain to the child that all that is necessary is to add both pairs of numbers. It is important for the child to understand that the front digit is the tens digit.

For instance, the child sees the problem:

$$\begin{array}{r} 35 \\ \underline{+14} \end{array}$$

The child first completes the ones digits 5 + 4 = 9.

$$\begin{array}{r} 35 \\ \underline{+14} \\ 9 \end{array}$$

Then the child completes the ten's digits 3 + 1 = 4.

$$\begin{array}{r} 35 \\ \underline{+14} \\ 49 \end{array}$$

The answer is 49.

It is important to train the child to always add the one's digit first. That is work back to front. Once the child masters this it is time to teach the concept of carrying.

Before working with the child on the concept of carrying, adding three single digits quickly, where one of these digits is 1 must first be taught. Fortunately, this is simple and can be mastered in a short amount of time.

Example:

$$\begin{array}{r} 1 \\ 5 \\ \underline{+8} \end{array}$$

With this problem have the child add 1 + 5 first to get 6 and then add 6 + 8 to get 14. Vocalize to the child, "" One plus five is six. Six plus eight is fourteen."

After a few more examples such as this the child should understand how to add three single digit numbers. Once this is mastered, work on adding two double digit numbers where carrying is involved, can be taught to the child.

Since the child has mastered adding three single digits, this concept will now be used to introduce the concept of carrying.

Take the problem:

$$\begin{array}{r} 15 \\ \underline{+14} \end{array}$$

When the child completes this the answer will be 29. Now ask the child, "What is one more than 29?" When the child answers, "30," explain that the ten's digit increases by one, (in this case from 2 to 3.)

Now go back to the original problem:

$$\begin{array}{r} 15 \\ \underline{+14} \end{array}$$

Change it to:

$$\begin{array}{r} 16 \\ \underline{+14} \end{array}$$

Since 16 is one more than 15, then 16 + 14 must be one more than 15 + 14. Since 15 + 14 = 29, then 16 + 14 = 30. Once the child understands this, then show the steps on how to solve the problem.

$$\begin{array}{r} 16 \\ \underline{+14} \end{array}$$

The child adds the one's digit. (6 + 4 = 10)

Now explain to the child that the number 10 has two digits, a ten's digit and a one's digit. The one's digit is zero, so place the zero under the 6 and 4.

$$\begin{array}{r} 16 \\ \underline{+14} \\ 0 \end{array}$$

Once the zero is placed, then tell the child that the ten's digit is one and that it will be placed above the ten's digit in 16.

$$\begin{array}{r} 1 \\ 16 \\ \underline{+14} \\ 0 \end{array}$$

Then the child should add the three ten's digits to get 3. (1 + 1 + 1 = 3)

$$\begin{array}{r} 1 \\ 16 \\ \underline{+14} \\ 30 \end{array}$$

Thus 16 + 14 = 30

Now demonstrate a few more problems for the child and use digits other than one for the ten's digit, while at the same time ensuring that the sum of the ten's digit with the carried one will be less than ten.

For example:

```
 37
+58
```

In this case the ten's digits (3 and 5) when combined with the carried 1 (3 + 5 + 1) will result in a sum of 9, which is less than 10.

Add the two one's digits (7 + 8 = 15) and place the 5 under the 8 in the one's digits place.

```
 37
+58
  5
```

Now carry the 1 and write it above the 3 in the ten's place.

```
  1
 37
+58
  5
```

Now add the three digits in the ten's place (1 + 3 + 5) to get 9.

```
  1
 37
+58
 95
```

So 37 +58 = 95.

Next, work with the child on double digit addition where the two numbers will add up to a sum greater than one-hundred. In order to do this, the sum of the two ten's digits must be more than 10. The first few examples should be where no carrying is involved.

Example:

```
 42
+85
```

Have the child add the one's digits (2 + 5 = 7) and write the 7 under the 5.

```
 42
+85
  7
```

Then have the child add then ten's digit (4 + 8 = 12) and write the 2 under the 8 and the 1 right next to it.

```
 42
+85
127
```

Thus: 42 + 85 = 127

Work a few problems like this with the child and then introduce problems where carrying is necessary and the result is more than one-hundred.

Example:

$$\begin{array}{r} 59 \\ \underline{+67} \end{array}$$

First have the child add the two one's digit (9 + 7 = 16.) Have the child place the 6 under the 7 and carry the 1.

$$\begin{array}{r} 1 \\ 59 \\ \underline{+67} \\ 6 \end{array}$$

Then have the child add the three numbers in the ten's column (1 + 5 + 6 = 12). Place the 2 under the 6 and place the 1 next to the 2.

$$\begin{array}{r} 1 \\ 59 \\ \underline{+67} \\ 126 \end{array}$$

Thus 59 + 67 = 126

Once the child has completed a few more problems like this, then create a worksheet from themathworksheetsite.com and check the "With Carrying" box.

The child should be able to complete the twenty problems in less than five minutes. After a few worksheets of this type have been completed by the child switch the type of worksheets to "Mixed."

Once the child has thoroughly mastered double digit addition with two addends, work with the child on triple digit and quadruple digit addition with two addends. Use the themathwork-sheetsite.com and on the Addition section, select, Multiple Digit. On this page select three for Number of Digits and two for Number of Addends.

At first begin the child on worksheets without carrying. This will create a worksheet of twenty problems. The child should be able to successfully complete this worksheet in less than ten minutes. Remember to treat this exercise as a fun challenge instead of a stressful chore for the child.

Once the child has mastered three digit addition without carrying, have the child work on worksheets that include carrying and mixed choices. Then once three digit addition with two addends are completely mastered by the child, use the website to teach the child four digit addition in the same manner.

Next, work on adding three single digit numbers with the child. The goal is to get the child to add the three numbers quickly without counting.

Example:

$$\begin{array}{r} 2 \\ 6 \\ \underline{+9} \end{array}$$

In this example have the child add the first two numbers and then take that sum and add it to the last number. Vocalize, "Two plus six equals eight. Eight plus nine equals seventeen."

Do a few more problems where the sum is less than twenty. After the child is comfortable adding three single digit numbers, work with the child adding three single digit numbers where the sum of two of the numbers is ten.

Example:

$$\begin{array}{r} 6 \\ 7 \\ \underline{+4} \end{array}$$

In this example ensure that the child recognizes that 6 + 4 = 10. Once the child recognizes this then vocalize, "Six plus four equals ten. Ten plus seven equals seventeen." Work a few problems such as this where the first and third numbers when added result in a sum of ten. Teach the child to add the first and third numbers to get ten and then the middle digit to get the final sum.

Next write down on a piece of paper five problems that are all addition of three single digit numbers. Have three of them that have two of the numbers with a sum of ten and two problems that do not.

Example:

$$\begin{array}{rrrrr} 7 & 8 & 2 & 4 & 4 \\ 4 & 6 & 4 & 5 & 3 \\ \underline{+3} & \underline{+3} & \underline{+8} & \underline{+9} & \underline{+6} \end{array}$$

In this case the first (7 + 3), the third (2 + 8), and the fifth (4 + 6) have a sum of ten. Just have the child point to the examples. The purpose of this exercise is to get the child to quickly recognize when ten can be used to add a set of single digit numbers.

Now occasionally have the child add five - three single digit number problems at a time. Sit with the child to ensure that the child verbalizes the addition of the numbers without counting. Five problems should take less than a minute to do. Doing this exercise twice a day, in addition to the other practices will instill competence and confidence in the child.

TEACHING ABOUT EVEN AND ODD NUMBERS

At this point the child should be very close to total mastery of addition. However, it is still necessary for continual daily practice. This practice should not take more than fifteen minutes a day. It is important for the child not to view this as a chore, but as a skill that needs to be improved by practice.

Before moving to subtraction, it is important to cover even and odd numbers. The goal is to get the child to identify whether a number is even or odd in less than one second. This mastery will help in understanding more advanced concepts at higher grade levels.

It is very simple. A number that has the one's digit of 0, 2, 4, 6, or 8 is even and a number that has a one's digit of 1, 3, 5, 7, or 9 is an odd number.

A simple way to demonstrate this is to use manipulatives. It is not necessary to purchase anything as pennies can be used to show the child the difference between even and odd numbers.

Take ten pennies and line them up in two columns of five rows.

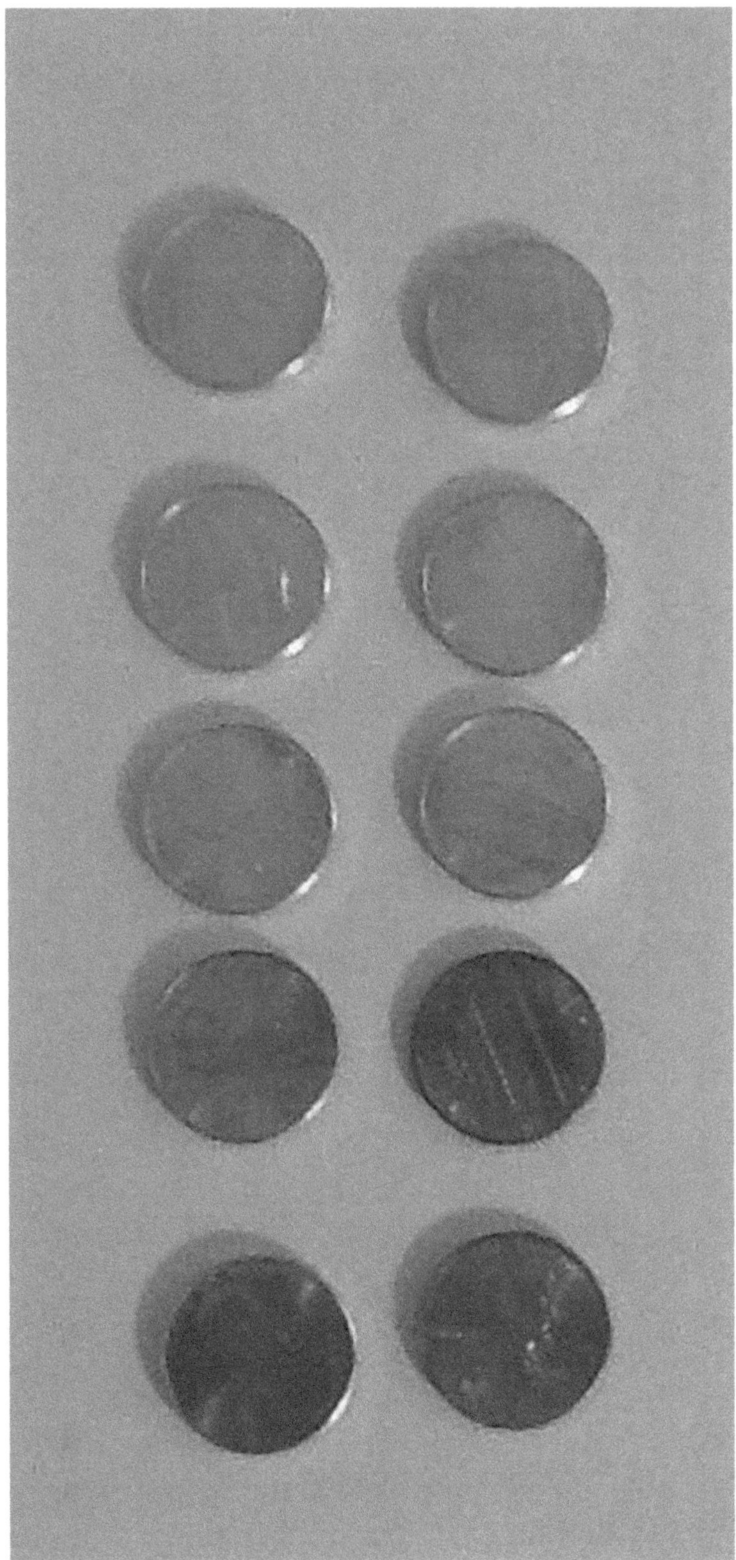

Point and count by twos, (2, 4, 6, 8, 10.) Explain that these are all even numbers.

Now remove the last penny so that nine are shown like this:

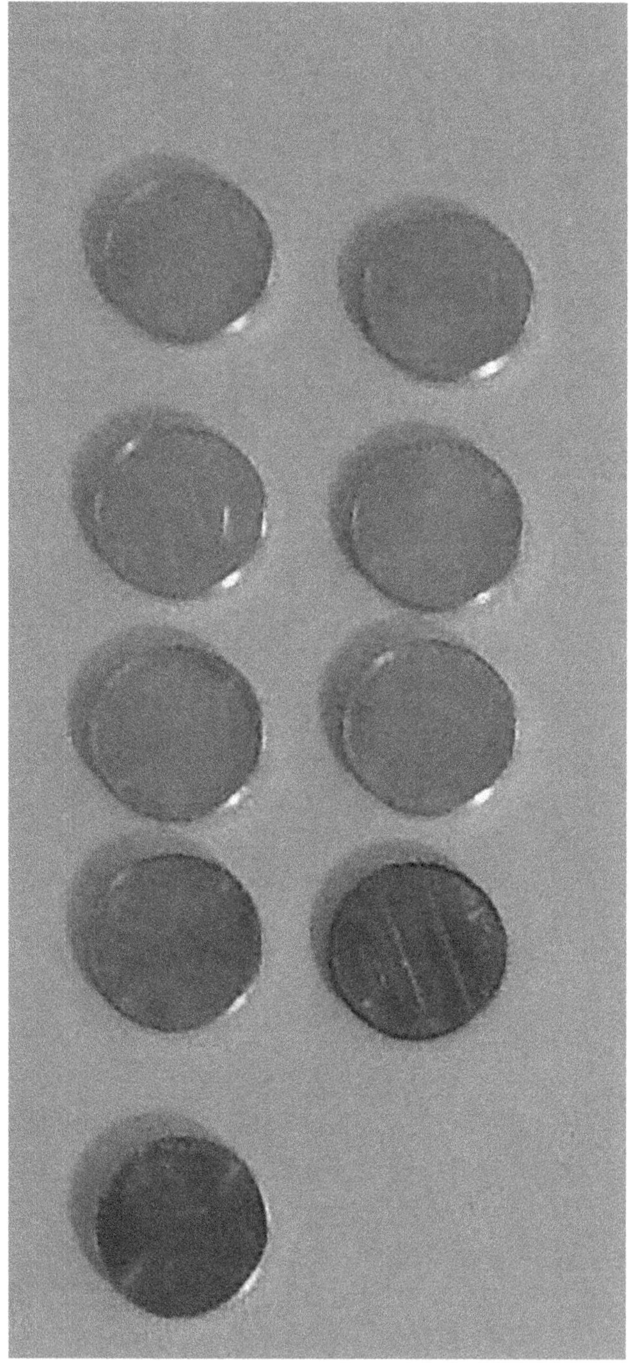

Explain that nine is an odd number and that odd numbers will have a space missing. Even numbers will have the space filled.

Try different numbers until you feel the child has a good understanding of even and odd numbers. Then take a deck of cards and remove the face cards. Turn the cards over and ask the child if the number is even or odd. Add this to the child's daily practice with the goal of the child recognizing whether a number is even or odd in less than one second.

To get the child to understand that it is the one's digit that determines if a number is even or odd, it is necessary for the child to see multiple digit numbers. Explain to the child that it is only necessary to look at the one's digit to determine whether a number is even or odd.

Example:

Take these numbers:

556 163 107 162

Explain to the child that the first number, 556, is even because the pone's digit (6) is even. The second number, 163, is odd because the one's digit (3) is odd. The number 107 is odd because the one's digit (7) is odd and the number 162 is even because the one's digit (2) is even.

To come up with several three digit numbers you can go to the themathworksheet.com website and under Addition, select Multiple Digit. For number of digits select 3 and for number of addends select 4. When the worksheet is created have the child state whether a number is even or odd, instead of having the child add the numbers.

Once you are convinced the child has total mastery of even and odd numbers explain these interesting facts about numbers:

When two even numbers are added together the sum is always an even number.

When two odd numbers are added together the sum is always an even number.

When an even number and an odd number are added together the sum is always an odd number.

Use themathworksheetsite.com to have the child practice determining if a sum is even or odd. Go to addition of multiple digits and select "2" for Number of Digits and "4" for Number of Addends. Create the worksheet.

Example:

$$\begin{array}{r} 23 \\ 32 \\ 18 \\ \underline{+14} \end{array}$$

Remember the purpose of this exercise is not to add the numbers but to quickly determine if the sum will be an even or odd number. The child needs only to concentrate on the one's digit (3, 2, 8, and 4). Verbalize with the child, "Odd plus even is odd. Odd plus even is odd. Odd plus even is odd so the answer will be an odd number."

The 3 and the 2 will have a sum that is an odd number. That odd number will be added to an even number (8) which will result in an odd number. That odd number will be added to an even number (4) which will make the sum of the four numbers an odd number. Practice four problems at a time. The child should be able to determine if the sum will be an even or odd number in less than five seconds.

Mastering the concept of even and odd numbers is very important for the child. In later years this mastery will make learning advanced mathematical concepts easier.

TEACHING SUBTRACTION

Once the child has mastered addition and the concept of even and odd numbers, it is time to teach the child subtraction. It is important to start with numbers five and smaller so that the child understands what is taking place when discussing subtraction.

Hold a hand to the child with all five fingers extended and ask the child, "How Many?"

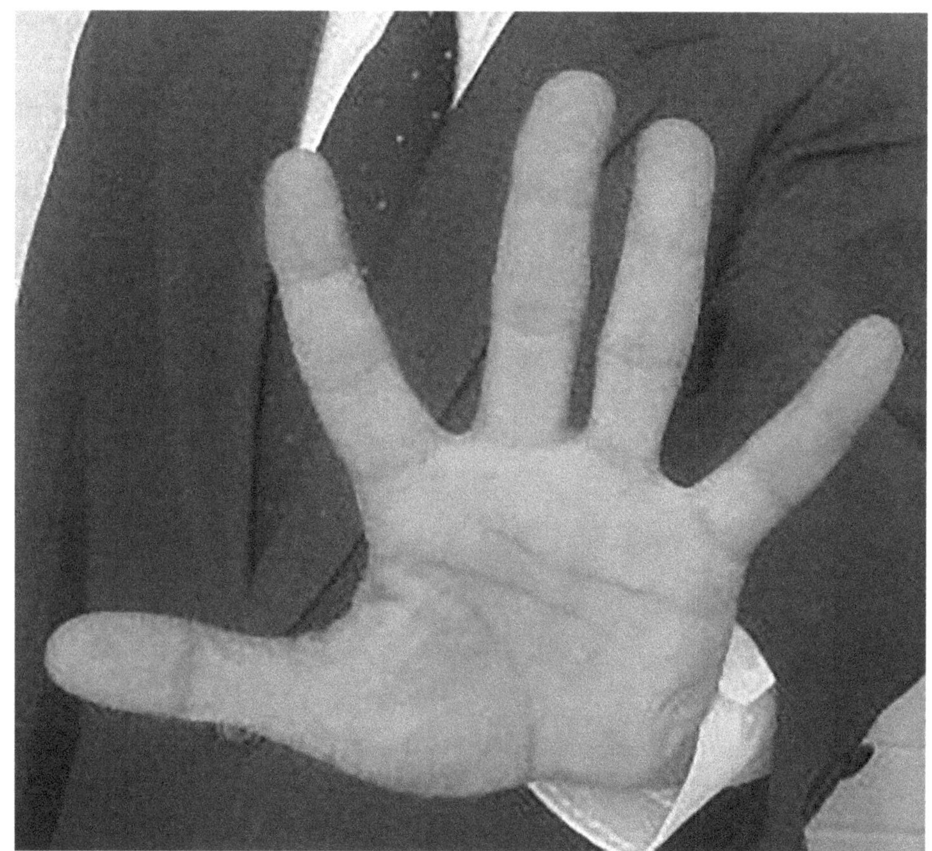

The child should answer, "Five."

Now bend down two fingers so that only three fingers are extended and once again ask the child, "How many?"

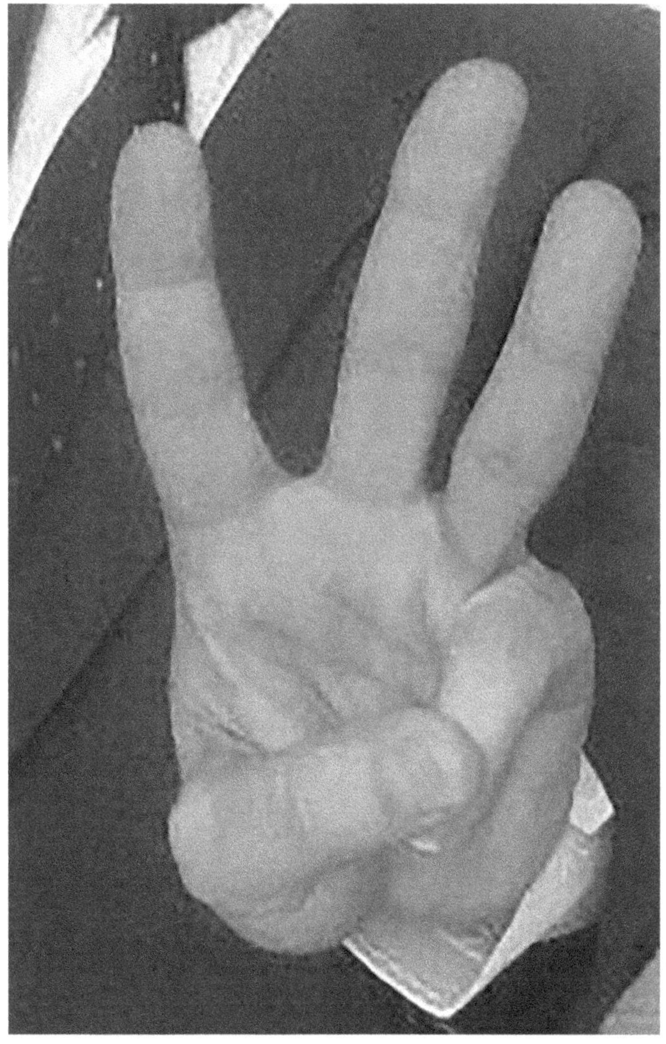

The child should answer, "Three."

Explain that you removed two fingers from five fingers to get three fingers, so five minus two equals three. This can also be expressed as five subtract to equals three, or five take away two equals three. When written it will look like this: 5 – 2 = 3.

Now work a few examples by using manipulatives such as pennies. Place five pennies in a row and cover some of them as you ask you child, "What is five minus four?"

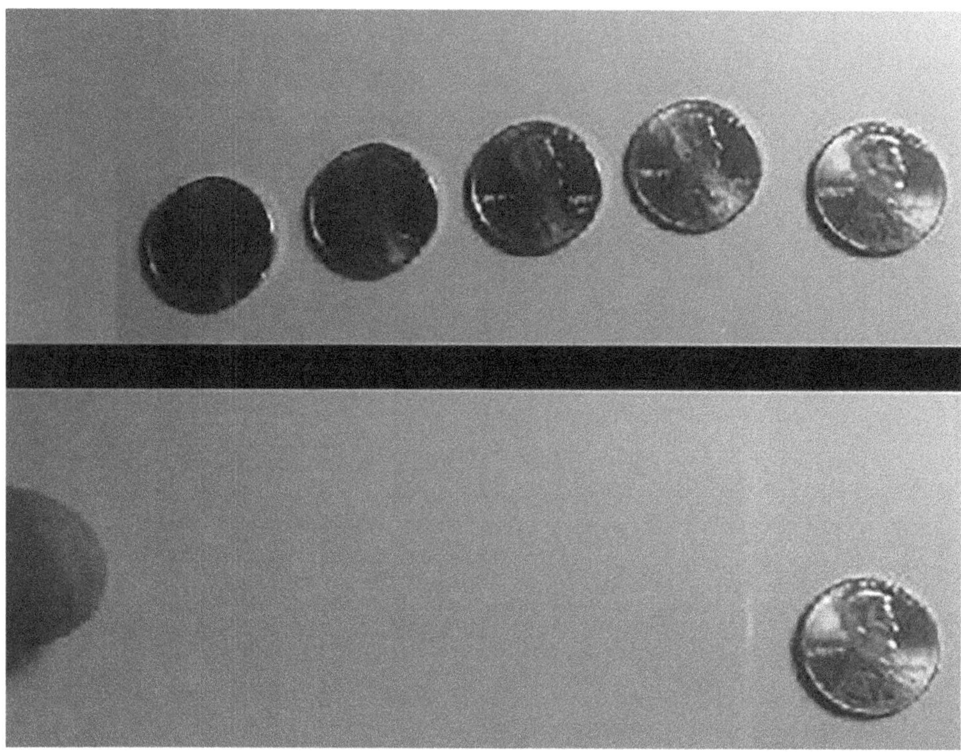

The child should answer, "One."

Do this several times with five pennies by covering one to four pennies. Then remove one penny so that there are four pennies remaining and ask, "What is four minus two?" and so on. Then do the same with three pennies and then with two pennies. (Two minus one equals one.) Treat this as a fun game that you are playing with the child.

Once the child understands the concept of subtraction, it is time to teach subtraction facts to mastery. Since the child has been exposed to the concept of "one less" begin with subtracting one from another number.

Teach the child the following:

10 − 1 = 9
9 − 1 = 8
8 − 1 = 7
7 − 1 = 6
6 − 1 = 5

5 − 1 = 4
4 − 1 = 3
3 − 1 = 2
2 − 1 = 1
1 − 1 = 0

Once again use the deck of cards to help the child practice subtraction. Take a black ace and place it on the table. The take the red cards and remove the king, queen and jack. Flip the red cards over so that they are to the left of the ace. This is important because the order that the numbers are subtracted matters.

The child should be able to answer each problem in one second. Practice this along with addition every night. It should not take long for the child to master subtracting one from a number.

Now have the child master subtracting ten from a number between twenty and ten. It should not take long for the child to master these subtraction facts.

20 − 10 = 10
19 − 10 = 9
18 − 10 = 8
17 − 10 = 7
16 − 10 = 6
15 − 10 = 5
14 − 10 = 4
13 − 10 = 3
12 − 10 = 2
11 − 10 = 1
10 − 10 = 0

Explain to the child when ten is subtracted from one of these numbers the answer is the ones digit.

Daily practice with these facts can be done very quickly. The back of envelopes that contain bills can be used before they are discarded. Simply write an expression such as "17 − 10" and then ask the child, "What is seventeen minus ten?" Three or four of these can be done on the back of an envelope or other paper before the paper is trashed.

Now the child has mastered subtracting one from a number and subtracting ten from a number.

Next, work with the child by teaching the child what numbers subtracted get an answer of ten. This concept should be easily mastered to the point where the child can say the answer in one second or less.

So the subtractions facts for this concept are:

19 − 9 = 10
18 − 8 = 10
17 − 7 = 10
16 − 6 = 10
15 − 5 = 10
14 − 4 = 10
13 − 3 = 10
12 − 2 = 10
11 − 1 = 10
10 − 0 = 10

If the one's digit is the same in both numbers (the minuend and subtrahend) and the first number (the minuend) has a ten's digit of one, then the answer (the difference) is ten.

You can practice these facts with the child the same way you subtracted by ten with the child.

Next, work on the subtraction of doubles. The child should have the doubles of addition mastered. So now teach the reverse when teaching the subtraction of doubles.

20 − 10 = 10
18 − 9 = 9
16 − 8 = 8
14 − 7 = 7
12 − 6 = 6
10 − 5 = 5
8 − 4 = 4
6 − 3 = 3
4 − 2 = 2
2 − 1 = 1

Some of these facts were previously learned but are included because they are also doubles. Point out to the child that all of the numbers in front (minuend) of the doubles is an even number.

Another way to reinforce this concept to mastery is to have the child tell you the addition of doubles and then the subtraction of doubles as part of the daily math practice. For instance have the child say, "Four plus four equals eight, so eight minus four equals four."

Have the child go through the doubles one plus one to ten plus ten nightly. This activity should take less than five minutes.

The next group of subtraction problems to master should be relatively easy for the child. This group consists of subtraction problems that will have a difference of one.

10 − 9 = 1
9 − 8 = 1
8 − 7 = 1
7 − 6 = 1
6 − 5 = 1
5 − 4 = 1
4 − 3 = 1
3 − 2 = 1
2 − 1 = 1

Explain to the child that these numbers are next to each other when counting.

Now it is time to discuss the concept of number families with the child. The concept is fairly simple. A number family consists of three numbers where the largest number is the sum of the other two numbers. For example the numbers 4, 6 and 10 are a number family because 4 + 6 = 10. These same three numbers are used in subtraction where the large number is the minuend.

10 − 6 = 4
10 − 4 = 6

Thus the family can consist of the following operations:

4 + 6 = 10
6 + 4 = 10
10 − 6 = 4
10 − 4 = 6

By now the child should have mastery when two numbers are added to obtain a sum of ten. Use the concept of number families to have the child master the following subtraction facts where the minuend is ten:

10 − 9 = 1
10 − 8 = 2
10 − 7 = 3
10 − 6 = 4
10 − 5 = 5
10 − 4 = 6
10 − 3 = 7
10 − 2 = 8
10 − 1 = 9

Now teach the child the families where the largest number is five and six respectively. The only new facts are as follows:

6 with 4 and 2
5 with 3 and 2

These are:

6 − 4 = 2
6 − 2 = 4
5 − 3 = 2
5 − 2 = 3

Add these four facts to the child's daily practice. Remember to verbalize, "Two plus four equals six, so six minus four equals two."

Next are the families where the largest number is seven, then eight and then nine. Practice each for a few days until they are mastered. Once all the families of these three numbers are mastered the child will have mastered all subtraction facts where the largest numbers is ten or lower.

First the sevens:

7 − 5 = 2
7 − 4 = 3
7 − 3 = 4
7 − 2 = 5

Remember to add these facts to the child's daily practice until they are mastered before learning the eights.

$$8 - 6 = 2$$
$$8 - 5 = 3$$
$$8 - 3 = 5$$
$$8 - 2 = 6$$

Remember, $8 - 4 = 4$ was previously memorized when the child mastered the doubles.

After a few days of practice it is time for the child to learn the nines.

$$9 - 7 = 2$$
$$9 - 6 = 3$$
$$9 - 5 = 4$$
$$9 - 4 = 5$$
$$9 - 3 = 6$$
$$9 - 2 = 7$$

Remember to emphasize the family aspect of these subtraction facts. Have the child say, "Three plus six equals nine, so nine minus six equals three and nine minus three equals six." Once this is done a few times the child should be able to answer the question, "What is nine minus six?" in a second without resorting to counting.

As you work your way with the child through the teen numbers, remember that some of these facts have been previously covered because they had ten subtracted from them, a number subtracted from them to get a difference of ten, or a double. Go through families where eleven, then twelve, thirteen, fourteen, fifteen, sixteen and finally seventeen is the largest number. The even numbers should have their respective doubles mastered. It is also important to practice other previously learned families and addition as the child goes through this learning process. Practice is very important.

Now teach the child the families of eleven:

$$11 - 9 = 2$$
$$11 - 8 = 3$$
$$11 - 7 = 4$$
$$11 - 6 = 5$$
$$11 - 5 = 6$$
$$11 - 4 = 7$$
$$11 - 3 = 8$$
$$11 - 2 = 9$$

As the child practices these families, remember to vocalize, "Nine plus two equals eleven so eleven minus nine equals two." Practice these with all of the elevens until the child can answer, "What is eleven minus six?" with all of the numbers until the child can answer them in two seconds without counting.

Next are the families of twelve:

12 − 9 = 3
12 − 8 = 4
12 − 7 = 5
12 − 6 = 6
12 − 5 = 7
12 − 4 = 8
12 − 3 = 9

Twelve minus six equals six is repeated from the doubles. Practice as before until the child can answer all the above subtraction facts in less than two seconds without counting.

Next are the families of thirteen.

13 − 9 = 4
13 − 8 = 5
13 − 7 = 6
13 − 6 = 7
13 − 5 = 8
13 − 4 = 9

There will be fewer facts to memorize as the child goes through the teen families. Be sure to praise the child and keep this a fun and stress free activity.

Next are the families of fourteen.

14 − 9 = 5
14 − 8 = 6
14 − 7 = 7
14 − 6 = 8
14 − 5 = 9

Remember that fourteen minus seven equals seven was previously covered when the child learned the doubles. The time that it takes to master these facts should decrease as the child goes up through the teen families. It is important to instill a sense of accomplishment in the child.

Next are the families of fifteen.

15 − 9 = 6
15 − 8 = 7
15 − 7 = 8
15 − 6 = 9

Notice that there are only two families. The child should master these quickly.

Next are the families of sixteen.

16 - 9 = 7
16 - 8 = 8
16 - 7 = 9

Now, sixteen minus eight equals eight is a double so it was previously mastered. The only new family that needs to be mastered is the family with sixteen, nine and seven.

Finally there is the family of seventeen.

17 - 9 = 8
17 - 8 = 9

There is only one family with two facts to learn so it should be mastered rather quickly.

Now the child could do daily five minute drills using worksheets from "themathworksheetsite.com"

Under the Subtraction heading selected, "5 minute drill." This creates a worksheet of one-hundred subtraction problems that have been previously mastered by the child. The child should be able to comfortably complete these problems in five minutes.

After a few days of this the child should be able to begin multiple digit subtraction. Start with problems that do not require borrowing, or as it might be called, renaming.

Go to themathworksheetsite.com and select "Multiple Digit," under the Subtraction heading. Under number of digits select "2" from the drop down box and then select the "Without Borrowing" button. This will create a worksheet of twenty problems that should be completed fairly quickly by the child.

Sample problem:

$$\begin{array}{r} 46 \\ \underline{-13} \end{array}$$

In multiple digit problems, always subtract the one's digit first. In this case the six and the three. Since six minus three equals three, place a three under the line under the three.

$$\begin{array}{r} 46 \\ \underline{-13} \\ 3 \end{array}$$

Then subtract the ten's digit, in this case four minus one. Since four minus one equals three, write a three under the line under the one.

$$\begin{array}{r} 46 \\ \underline{-13} \\ 33 \end{array}$$

The problem is finished. Each problem should take less than five seconds to complete. It is very important that the child into the habit of subtracting right to left, that is from the one's digit to the ten's digit.

After the child does a few of these assignments, begin doing subtraction problems with three digits.

Go to themathworksheetsite.com page and select "Multiple Digit," under the Subtraction heading. Under number of digits, select "3" from the drop down box and the bullet "Without Borrowing" and then create the worksheet. You will get a worksheet of twenty subtraction problems.

Sample problem:

$$\begin{array}{r} 837 \\ \underline{-313} \end{array}$$

First subtract the one's digits. Seven minus three equals four.

$$\begin{array}{r} 837 \\ \underline{-313} \\ 4 \end{array}$$

Then subtract the ten's digits. Three minus one equals two.

$$\begin{array}{r} 837 \\ \underline{-313} \\ 24 \end{array}$$

Finally subtract the hundred's digits. Eight minus three equals five.

$$\begin{array}{r} 837 \\ \underline{-313} \\ 524 \end{array}$$

The problem is finished. The child should be able to do each problem in less than ten seconds. Thus all problems should be completed in less than four minutes.

Once the child has done a few of these, then create worksheets that consist of four digit numbers to be subtracted. These will not have problems with borrowing. The worksheets will consist of twenty problems that the child should be able to solve within ten minutes. When the child achieves complete mastery solving these types of problems then it will be time to teach the child how to subtract with borrowing.

Borrowing is necessary in subtraction when the same digit in the minuend (top number) is smaller than the subtrahend (bottom number). When this occurs the problem is changed by borrowing to get a temporary subtraction problem where the top number becomes a double digit number in the teens that will have the single digit subtrahend subtracted from it. This is something that has been previously mastered by the child.

Example:

$$\begin{array}{r} 84 \\ \underline{-27} \end{array}$$

Since four is less than seven borrowing is necessary in order to solve this problem. First cross out the eight in the minuend and make it a seven.

$$\begin{array}{r} {}^{7}\cancel{8}4 \\ -27 \\ \hline \end{array}$$

The eight actually represents eighty in the problem. When the eight is crossed out the extra ten is added to the four to make fourteen.

$$\begin{array}{r} {}^{7}\cancel{8}{}^{1}4 \\ -27 \\ \hline \end{array}$$

Now subtract the one's digit. (Fourteen minus seven equals seven.)

$$\begin{array}{r} {}^{7}\cancel{8}{}^{1}4 \\ -27 \\ \hline 7 \end{array}$$

Now subtract the ten's digit. (Seven minus two equals five.)

$$\begin{array}{r} {}^{7}\cancel{8}{}^{1}4 \\ -27 \\ \hline 57 \end{array}$$

So the answer is fifty-seven.

Now create a worksheet for the child. Go to the website themathworksheetsite.com and under the "Subtraction" heading select "Multiple Digit." For "Number of Digits," select "2". Under "Borrowing" select "With Borrowing" and finally select, "Do not include borrowing across zeros." Hit the "Create Worksheet" button and the website will create a worksheet of twenty problems for the child to complete.

Practice subtracting with borrowing until mastery is achieved. This may take some time for the child so patience is necessary. It this concept is too challenging for the child do one row of problems a day while reinforcing the addition and subtraction skills previously mastered so the child never loses confidence in previously learned mathematical skills.

It is important that the child does not feel overwhelmed, so do only one row a night until the child gets comfortable doing subtraction problems with borrowing. The goal is to get the child to do twenty problems successfully in ten minutes.

Once the child has mastered two digit subtraction with borrowing, have the child practice with worksheets that include problems with and without borrowing. In this case select the "Mixed" button under "Borrowing" and select "Do no include borrowing across zeros." Click the "Create It," button.

Before having the child actually solve the problems, have the child tell you whether or not borrowing is required. Point to a problem and ask, "Do you need to borrow?" The child should answer, "Yes," or "no."

For example:

$$\begin{array}{r} 89 \\ \underline{-64} \end{array}$$

The child should answer, "No," because in the minuend (top number) the one's digit (9) is larger than the one's digit in the subtrahend (bottom number) (4).

However the problem:

$$\begin{array}{r} 82 \\ \underline{-39} \end{array}$$

The child should answer "Yes," because two is larger than nine. The goal is to have the child correctly determine if borrowing is needed in twenty problems in less than one minute.

Once the child can quickly determine whether or not borrowing is necessary for a subtraction problem then it is time for the child to start doing worksheets that contain two digit subtraction problems that both require and do not require borrowing. A goal is to have the child correctly complete twenty problems in ten minutes or less.

Once the child masters subtraction of two digit numbers with borrowing it is time to teach three digit subtraction with borrowing. Some problems will require borrowing with only the one's digit, some problems will require borrowing with just the ten's digit and some problems will require borrowing with both the ten's and one's digit.

For instance the problem:

$$\begin{array}{r} 792 \\ \underline{-536} \end{array}$$

requires borrowing on only the one's digit since the "2" in the top number (minuend) is smaller than the "6" in the bottom number (subtrahend). The ten's digit does not require borrowing because the "9" (which will become 8) is larger than the "3".

The problem:

$$\begin{array}{r} 936 \\ \underline{-284} \end{array}$$

only requires borrowing in the ten's digit.

The problem:

$$\begin{array}{r} 731 \\ \underline{-564} \end{array}$$

will require borrowing in both the one's and ten's digit.

To solve the first problem:

```
 792
-536
----
```

Remember to always begin subtraction problems from the right. Since the "2" is smaller than the "6" it is necessary to borrow from the "9" and make the "2" a "12".

```
  8
 7 9 12
-5 3 6
------
```

Now subtract the one's digit (12 – 6 = 6) and write a "6" under the "6".

```
  8
 7 9 12
-5 3 6
------
     6
```

Then subtract the ten's digit (8 – 3 = 5 and write a "5" under the "3".

```
  8
 7 9 12
-5 3 6
------
   5 6
```

Finally subtract the hundred's digits (7 – 5 = 2) and write a "2" under the "5".

```
  8
 7 9 12
-5 3 6
------
 2 5 6
```

The answer is 256.
To solve the second problem:

```
 936
-284
----
```

When subtracting the one's digit no borrowing is necessary, (6 – 4 = 2) so write "2" under the "4".

```
 936
-284
----
   2
```

In order to subtract the ten's digit borrowing is necessary because the "3" is less than the "8". Borrow from the hundred's place "9" and make it an "8", while changing the "3" in the ten's place to "13".

```
8
 9̸¹36
-284
----
   2
```

Now subtract the ten's digit (13 – 8 = 5) and write "5" under the "8".

```
8
 9̸¹36
-284
----
  52
```

Finally subtract the hundred's digit (8 – 2 = 6) and write "6" under the "2".

```
8
 9̸¹36
-284
----
 652
```

The answer is 652.
To solve the final problem:

```
 731
-564
----
```

Have the child begin with the one's digit. Since the "1" is less than the "4", borrowing is required. Borrow from the "3" in the ten's place and make the "1" an "11".

```
  2
 73̸¹1
-564
----
```

Now subtract the one's digit (11 – 4 = 7), and write a "7" under the "4".

```
   2
 7 3 11
-5 6 4
     7
```

It is also necessary to borrow in the ten's place because the "2" is less than the "6". Borrow from the "7" in the hundred's place and make the "2" a "12".

```
 6 12
 7 3 11
-5 6 4
     7
```

Now subtract the ten's digit (12 – 6 = 6) and write a "6" under the "6".

```
 6 12
 7 3 11
-5 6 4
   6 7
```

Now all that is left is to subtract the hundred's digit (6 – 5 = 1). Write a "1" under the "5".

```
 6 12
 7 3 11
-5 6 4
 1 6 7
```

The answer is 167.

Now create some worksheets for the child. Go to the mathworksheetsite.com and select "Multiple Digit" under the "Subtraction" heading. Select "3" from the "Number of Digits" dropdown box, choose "With Borrowing" and then "Do not include problems with borrowing across zeros." (This will be discussed next.)

A twenty problem worksheet will be created. The child should be able to complete all twenty problems in ten minutes. Once the child can do this consistently, change the worksheet to "mixed". Once the child can consistently do all twenty correctly in ten minutes it is time to work on four digit problems.

Select "4" from the dropdown box. This will create a worksheet with twenty problems. Again, the child should be able to complete twenty problems correctly in ten minutes in order to demonstrate mastery. Once this is achieved it will be time to teach the concept of borrowing across zeros.

When teaching borrowing across zeros, the concept is to make a zero a ten and then borrow from that ten to make nine.

Example:

```
  903
 -625
 ----
```

Start with the one's place. Since the "3" is less than the "5", borrowing is necessary. However, since the ten's digit is a "0" it is necessary to borrow from the hundred's digit. Borrow from the "9" and change it to "8" and make the "0" a "10".

```
  8
  9¹03
 -625
 ----
```

Now it is possible to borrow from the ten's digit. Change the "10" to "9" and then make the "3" a "13".

```
  8 9
  9¹0¹3
 -625
 ----
```

Now work from the one's place to the hundred's place. For the one's place (13 – 5 = 8), so write an "8" under the "5".

```
  8 9
  9¹0¹3
 -625
 ----
    8
```

Next subtract the ten's digit (9 – 2 = 7) and write a "7" under the "2".

```
  8 9
  9¹0¹3
 -625
 ----
   78
```

Finally subtract the hundred's digit (8 – 6 = 2) and write a "2" under the "6".

```
  8 9
  9¹0¹3
 -625
 ----
  278
```

The answer is 278.

Now go to themathworksheetsite.com and create a worksheet for the child. Under the "Subtraction" heading select "Multiple Digit"." Select "3" for "Number of Digits", select "With Borrowing" and "Allow problems with borrowing across zeros."

Once you hit the "Create it" button a worksheet with twenty problems will be created. Now every problem will require borrowing across zeros, but there will be enough so that the child can practice to mastery. The goal is for the child to correctly complete twenty problems in ten minutes.

Four digit sample problem:

```
 9000
-4638
```

Start with the one's digit and recognize that "0" is less than "8" so borrowing is required. However both the ten's digit and the hundred's digit are both "0" so it is necessary to borrow from the thousand's digit, which is "9". Borrow from the "9" and make it an "8" and change the "0" in the hundred's digit to "10".

```
 8
 9000
-4638
```

Now borrow from the "10" in the hundred's place by changing it to a "9" and make the "0" in the ten's place a "10".

```
 89
 9000
-4638
```

Now borrow from the "10" in the ten's place by changing it to a "9" and make the "0" in the one's place a "10".

```
 899
 9000
-4638
```

Finally subtract from back to front. Starting with the one's place (10 – 8 = 2) and write a "2" under the "8".

```
 899
 9000
-4638
    2
```

Subtract the ten's place (9 – 3 = 6) and write a "6" under the "3".

```
 8 9 9
 9 0 0 10
-4 6 3 8
--------
     6 2
```

Subtract the hundred's place (9 – 6 = 3) and write a "3" under the "6".

```
 8 9 9
 9 0 0 10
-4 6 3 8
--------
   3 6 2
```

Finally subtract the thousand's digit (8 – 4 = 4 and write a "4" under the "4".

```
 8 9 9
 9 0 0 10
-4 6 3 8
--------
 4 3 6 2
```

The answer is 4362.

Now go to themathworksheetsite.com and create a worksheet for the child. Under the "Subtraction" heading select "Multiple Digit"." Select "4" for "Number of Digits", select "With Borrowing" and "Allow problems with borrowing across zeros."

Once you hit the "Create it" button a worksheet with twenty problems will be created. The goal is for the child to correctly complete twenty problems in ten minutes.

Now the child should have mastery in both addition and subtraction. It is still necessary for the child to practice daily. It is important to vary the routine. Have the child work on an addition worksheet one day, then a subtraction worksheet the next day and then ten minutes with a deck of cards the following day. Practice should take no more than ten to fifteen minutes each day. The child should look at these activities as enjoyable challenges and not as punishment.

It is important not to underestimate the impact on the child's confidence by having mastery over simple addition and subtraction. By continually improving the child's skills the child will have a strong foundation in mathematics, which will be important when learning more advanced concepts.

TEACHING MULTIPLICATION

Learning multiplication is an extremely important skill for a child. Mastery of this skill can make a huge difference as the child progresses through elementary and secondary education. In algebra, for instance, when a child has not mastered multiplication problems involving factoring become confusing, frustrating, and time consuming. However, if a child has total mastery of multiplication these same problems become so easy that they can be solved correctly in less than five seconds.

To begin teaching the concept of multiplication it is necessary to explain what multiplication means. A good way to explain this is to use grouping. Have several groups of items where the same number of items is in each group.

For example take twelve pennies and arrange them into four groups of three

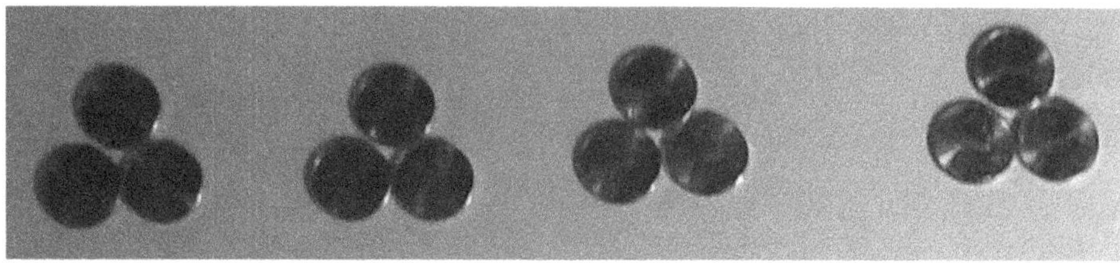

Point to each group and count, "One two, three four," after that count by threes, "Three, six, nine, twelve, so four times three equals twelve."

Since multiplication is the same as grouping, start by explaining to the child that it is like adding the same number a certain number of times. For instance if four times three equals twelve it is the same as adding three four times.

$$3 + 3 + 3 + 3 = 12$$

Also explain that there is a commutative property of multiplication. This means that it does not matter the order the two numbers (called factors) are multiplied, the answer (called the product) will be the same.

For instance:

$$4 \times 3 = 12$$
$$3 + 3 + 3 + 3 = 12$$

and

$$3 \times 4 = 12$$
$$4 + 4 + 4 = 12$$

Now it is time to begin learning the multiplication tables or multiplications facts. The first group will be numbers multiplied by one.

1 x 1 = 1
1 x 2 = 2
1 x 3 = 3
1 x 4 = 4
1 x 5 = 5
1 x 6 = 6
1 x 7 = 7
1 x 8 = 8
1 x 9 = 9
1 x 10 = 10

So when explaining 1 x 5 = 5, tell the child that it is one group of five. Any number multiplied by one will stay the same.

The child should know the doubles when the child learned addition. Multiplication by two is the same as adding the same number by itself.

2 x 1 = 2
2 x 2 = 4
2 x 3 = 6
2 x 4 = 8
2 x 5 = 10
2 x 6 = 12
2 x 7 = 14
2 x 8 = 16
2 x 9 = 18
2 x 10 = 20

For the child to learn multiplication, have the child repeat this three times a day. Type these facts on a piece of paper, or write them on the back of an envelope and have the child say out loud, "Two times one equals two," and so on until "Two times ten equals twenty."

After a few days rewrite the multiplication facts without the answers and see if the child can recite them correctly. After a few days of the child being able recite the facts in order without error, work with a deck of playing cards to get the child to obtain mastery of multiplying a number by two.

Mastery of multiplication by two occurs when the child can successfully multiply these facts in random order. Take the deck of playing cards and remove the face cards and then separate the remaining cards into two stacks, one of black cards and one of red cards. Shuffle the stack of red cards and remove a two from the stack of black cards. Now turn over the red cards one at a time and ask the child to multiply the two numbers.

The child should be able to correctly answer each multiplication problem in less than four seconds to achieve mastery in multiplying a number by two. Once this is accomplished the child should begin completing worksheets. Go to themathworksheetsite.com and under the "Multiplication" heading select, "Single Digit, Horizontal."

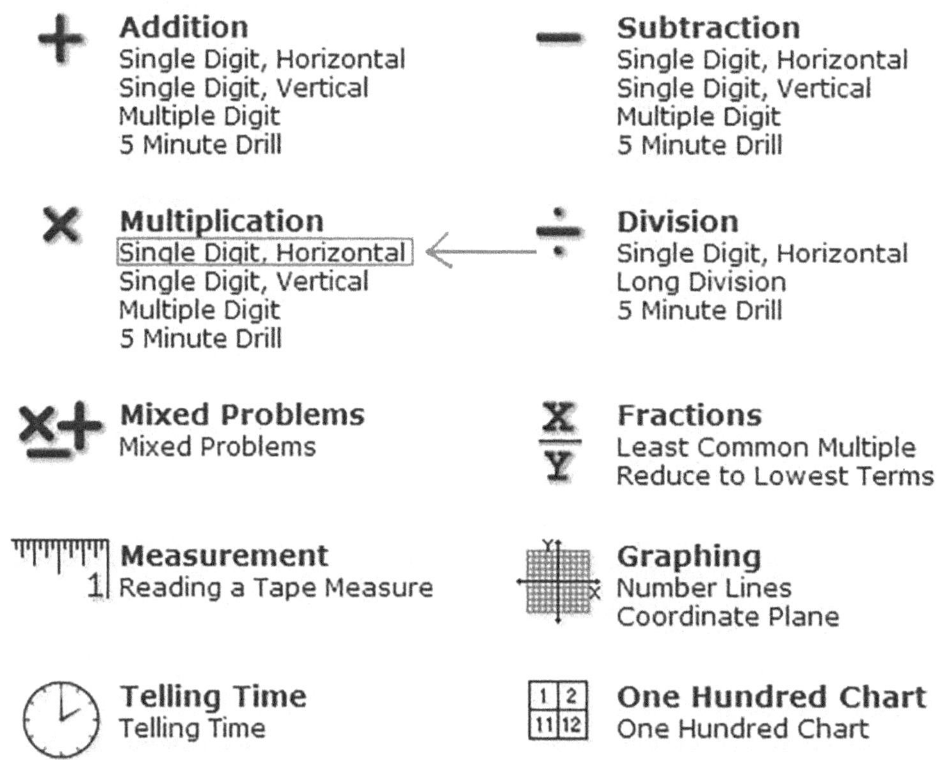

Select "20 problems" and select "1 and 2" under "Multiply These Numbers…" and deselect the "0" under "By These Numbers."

Multiplication: Single Digit Horizontal

Each problem will have one factor from the selections on the left and one factor from the selections on the right. If there are no factors selected in one of the lists, the numbers 0 through 9 will be used.

Number of problems

- 10 problems
- 16 problems
- 20 problems (selected)

Multiply These Numbers...

Checked: 1, 2. Unchecked: 0, 3, 4, 5, 6, 7, 8, 9, 10, 11, 12

All 0-9 Clear

By These Numbers.

Checked: 1, 2, 3, 4, 5, 6, 7, 8, 9. Unchecked: 0, 10, 11, 12

All 0-9 Clear

Include Answer Key (checked)

Create It

This will create a worksheet for the child for daily practice. The goal is for the child to consistently complete the worksheet successfully in less than two minutes.

Now that the child has mastered multiplying by one and two, the next step is to have the child master multiplying numbers by ten. Begin this by having the child counting to one-hundred by tens. Say with the child, "ten, twenty, thirty, forty, fifty, sixty, seventy, eighty, ninety, one-hundred." This should take less than five seconds.

Once the child is able to do this with ease, show how to multiply by ten.

10 x 1 = 10
10 x 2 = 20
10 x 3 = 30
10 x 4 = 40
10 x 5 = 50

10 x 6 = 60
10 x 7 = 70
10 x 8 = 80
10 x 9 = 90
10 x 10 = 100

Explain to the child that when a number is multiplied by ten the answer is that number with a zero after it. For instance when ten is multiplied by five the answer is fifty (a five with a zero after it).

Work with the child using the deck of cards. Take a black ten and a deck of red numbered cards. Practice multiplying numbers by ten with the child the same way as multiplication by two was practiced.

The child should be able to master this fairly quickly. Go to themathworksheetsite.com and create some worksheets the uses ten as a factor (number to be multiplied) for the child to practice.

Now the child should have mastery when multiplying by one, two and ten. The next number for the child to master is five.

As with ten have the child count by five to fifty. Say with the child, "five, ten, fifteen, twenty, twenty-five, thirty, thirty-five, forty, forty-five, fifty." Once again this should take less than five seconds.

Once the child is able to do this show the multiples of five.

5 x 1 = 5
5 x 2 = 10
5 x 3 = 15
5 x 4 = 20
5 x 5 = 25
5 x 6 = 30
5 x 7 = 35
5 x 8 = 40
5 x 9 = 45
5 x 10 = 50

Show the child that when five is multiplied by an even number the product (answer to a multiplication problem) always ends in a zero. Likewise when five is multiplied by an odd number the product will always end in five.

Show the child that when five is multiplied by an even number that the tens digit will always be one half of what the factor that is multiplied by five.

5 x 2 = 10
5 x 4 = 20
5 x 6 = 30
5 x 8 = 40
5 x 10 = 50

For example: the multiplication fact 5 x 6 = 30; the tens digit of the product (3) is half of the factor (6) that is multiplied by five.

Practice multiplying five by an even number by using a deck of cards. Take a black five and make a small deck of the red even numbered cards. Turn over the red card one at a time. The goal is to have the child consistently answer correctly the problems in less than four seconds.

Once the child has mastered multiplying five by an even number, start working with the odd numbers by teaching five times five is twenty-five. Do this by using five nickels and one quarter.

Explain that each nickel is five cents and one quarter is twenty-five cents. Count the nickels by five (five, ten, fifteen, twenty, twenty-five) and then tell the child five times five equals twenty-five.

The child should now have memorized and mastered the following two problems where five is multiplied by an odd number:

$$5 \times 1 = 5$$
$$5 \times 5 = 25$$

Explain to the child that since three is between one and five, so $5 \times 3 = 15$ since fifteen is between five and twenty-five.

Now all that is left to complete the multiplication by five facts are seven and nine. Since both of these numbers are greater than five, the products when these numbers are multiplied by five will be greater than twenty-five. Also since these two numbers are less than ten, the products of these numbers will be less than fifty.

$$5 \times 7 = 35$$

$$5 \times 9 = 45$$

Now once the child has mastered the multiplication facts where the factors are five and an odd number, work with the cards and create worksheets so that the child can practice daily multiplying by five. The goal with the cards is the have the child consistently answer correctly within four seconds and the goal with the worksheet is to consistently answer twenty problems correctly in less than two minutes.

Now it is time to work with the child on multiplying numbers by three. To begin, count to ten but pause after every three numbers. Say, "one, two, three," pause for a moment, "four, five, six," pause, "seven, eight, nine," and pause and say, "ten."

Once the child does this a few times, work with the first group of multiplication facts.

$$3 \times 1 = 3$$
$$3 \times 2 = 6$$
$$3 \times 3 = 9$$

A good visual aid is to get a series of cards showing the three, six and nine.

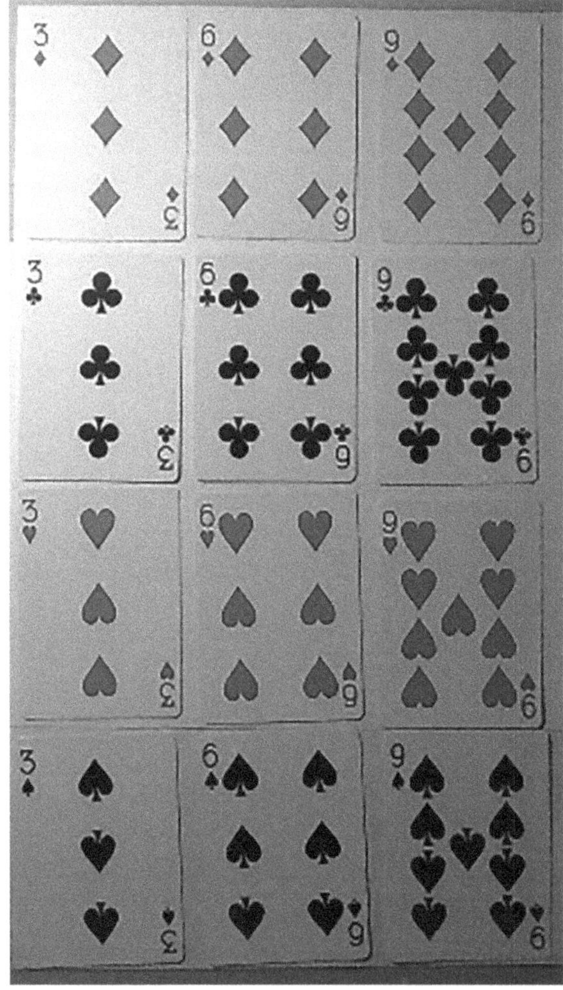

Explain to the child that the first three multiples of three are all single digit numbers.

So after the child has worked with and mastered the first three multiplication facts it is time to work with the next three.

3 x 4 = 12
3 x 5 = 15
3 x 6 = 18

Explain to the child that this next group of three all have a one in the ten's place. Also show the child when the two digits are added the sum will be three, six and nine.

3 x 4 = 12 and 1 + 2 = 3
3 x 5 = 15 and 1 + 5 = 6
3 x 6 = 18 and 1 + 8 = 9

Now work with the child until these next three multiplication facts are mastered. Use the cards by taking a black three out and the first six numbered red cards.

After the child has mastered the first six multiplication facts with a factor of three, it is time to work on the next group of three. These next three products will be in the twenties.

3 x 7 = 21
3 x 8 = 24
3 x 9 = 27

Once again the three products will make a sum of three, six and nine respectively.

3 x 7 = 21 and 2 + 1 = 3
3 x 8 = 24 and 2 + 4 = 6
3 x 9 = 27 and 2 + 7 = 9

Work with the child on these three facts until mastery. Once mastery is achieved review the fact that the multiples of three can be grouped into three groups of three multiples each.

3 x 1 = 3	3 x 4 = 12	3 x 7 = 21
3 x 2 = 6	3 x 5 = 15	3 x 8 = 24
3 x 3 = 9	3 x 6 = 18	3 x 9 = 27

The final fact is 3 x 10 = 30. This should be easy to remember because the child previously achieved mastery multiplying a number by ten, just add a zero after the three.

The final step is to use the deck of cards and the worksheet. The goal with the cards is to consistently answer correctly the problem in less than four seconds. The goal for the worksheet is to consistently answer correctly twenty problems in two minutes.

The next number for the child to master is four. Start the child with these four facts:

4 x 1 = 4
4 x 2 = 8
4 x 5 = 20
4 x 10 = 40

These should have been previously mastered by the child. The two products when four is multiplied by five and ten will end in zero. These are the only two that will end in zero. Also explain that the one's digit will always follow the following sequence:

4, 8, 2, 6, 0

Look at the first five multiplication facts.

4 x 1 = 4
4 x 2 = 8
4 x 3 = 12
4 x 4 = 16
4 x 5 = 20

Notice the pattern of the one's digit. Since the child has previously mastered four of the five facts listed above, the only new fact is 4 x 4 = 16, so use the deck of cards with a black four and the ten red cards numbered one through five for the child to practice. It should not take long for the child to master these five facts, which will occur when the child can consistently answer the problems correctly in less than four seconds.

Next show the child the next five facts

4 x 6 = 24
4 x 7 = 28
4 x 8 = 32
4 x 9 = 36
4 x 10 = 40

Notice again the pattern of the one's digit (4, 8, 2, 6, 0). Explain that the numbers six, seven, eight and nine are between five and ten, so the products of these numbers when multiplied by four are going to be between twenty and forty. The first two numbers, six and seven, will make the product in the twenties, and the next two, eight and nine will make a product in the thirties. Show the child two in the twenties and two in the thirties.

Now have the child practice all of the numbers with the deck of cards by having a black four and the red numbered cards. Once again to goal is to have the child consistently answer correctly in less than four seconds. Once the child achieves mastery, then create worksheets with the goal of the child answering twenty problems correctly in less than two minutes.

Before continuing with the other single digit numbers, have the child practice with worksheets with the numbers previously mastered. Create a worksheet that has three, four and five multiplied by the other single digit numbers. Let the child practice with these worksheets for a few days until the child has total mastery of all the multiplication facts previously learned.

Now it is time to work on multiplication by nine. This can actually be fun for the child when it is taught because of a rule with nine. Start by having the child write down the numbers zero through nine on a piece of paper. The paper could be the back of an envelope. It is important to write the numbers down instead of across. It is also important to write the zero.

0
1
2
3
4
5
6
7
8
9

Once this is done have the child write backwards nine through zero next to the previously written numbers.

09
18
27
36
45
54
63
72
81
90

It is very easy for a child to remember this exercise. The purpose of having the child do this is to show the multiples of nine.

9 x 1 = 09
9 x 2 = 18
9 x 3 = 27
9 x 4 = 36
9 x 5 = 45
9 x 6 = 54
9 x 7 = 63
9 x 8 = 72
9 x 9 = 81
9 x 10 = 90

Also show the child that when the digits in the product are added the sum is always nine.

9 x 1 = 09	0 + 9 = 9
9 x 2 = 18	1 + 8 = 9
9 x 3 = 27	2 + 7 = 9
9 x 4 = 36	3 + 6 = 9
9 x 5 = 45	4 + 5 = 9
9 x 6 = 54	5 + 4 = 9
9 x 7 = 63	6 + 3 = 9
9 x 8 = 72	7 + 2 = 9
9 x 9 = 81	8 + 1 = 9
9 x 10 = 90	9 + 0 = 9

Point out to the child that a number multiplied by nine will result in a product less than the number multiplied by ten. For instance 10 x 6 = 60, so 9 x 6 will be less than sixty. In fact the product will have five as the ten's digit. Since five plus four is nine, the answer is fifty-four.

The child should have perfect mastery of numbers that produce a sum of nine. Therefore all the child has to do is to take the number that is one less than the factor when multiplied by ten and put that number in the ten's place and place the number that produces a sum of nine in the one's place.

Now have the child practice with a deck of cards (black nine and red numbered cards) and then a worksheet. The goals are the same with four seconds with the cards and twenty problems in two minutes with the worksheet.

The next number to work with the child will be six. This will be taught in two stages. The first stage is where the factor multiplied by six is even and the second stage is where the factor is odd. An interesting occurrence happens when six is multiplied by an even number; the one's digit of the product will be that even number.

6 x 2 = 12
6 x 4 = 24
6 x 6 = 36
6 x 8 = 48
6 x 10 = 60

Now the child should have previously mastered 6 x 2 and 6 x 10, so work with the middle three multiplication facts. Point out to the child that they rhyme. Say, "six times four is twenty-four," then say, "six time six is thirty-six," and finally say, "six times eight is forty-eight." Each of these facts can be memorized as a line in a poem.

Practice with the child by using the deck of cards. Take a black six and all of the even numbered red cards. The child should quickly master multiplying six by an even number as demonstrated by consistently answering the problem correctly in less than four seconds.

Once multiplying six by an even number is mastered it is time to master multiplying six by an odd number.

6 x 1 = 6
6 x 3 = 18
6 x 5 = 30
6 x 7 = 42
6 x 9 = 54

Notice that four of the five multiplication facts have previously been mastered by the child. Use the fact that multiplication is commutative, that is it does not matter the order in which two factors are multiplied the product will be the same (i.e. 6 x 3 = 18 and 3 x 6 = 18). Therefore the only new fact to be memorized is 6 x 7 = 42.

Now finish off mastery of multiplication by six by working with the cards and creating worksheets for practice. Once mastery is achieved teach multiplication by eight.

To begin teaching multiplication by eight, start with these four multiplication facts that the child should have previously mastered.

8 x 1 = 8
8 x 2 = 16
8 x 5 = 40
8 x 10 = 80

These four should be rapidly mastered and then go to the next four multiplication facts that were previously mastered and use the commutative property of multiplication to teach these to the child.

8 x 3 = 24
8 x 4 = 32
8 x 6 = 48
8 x 9 = 72

Once that is accomplished, there are only two more facts to learn.

8 x 7 = 56
8 x 8 = 64

While 8 x 8 = 64 must be memorized, there is an interesting trick that can be used to teach eight times seven. Write the following on a piece of paper:

5 6 7 8

Your child knows this sequence of numbers, so all that is necessary is to place an equal sign between the six and the seven and then a multiplication sign between the seven and the eight.

56 = 7 x 8

Now work with the child with the cards and the worksheet until mastery with multiplication by eight is achieved. Once that is accomplished it is time to teach the child multiplication by seven.

The list of multiples of seven is as follows:

7 x 1 = 7
7 x 2 = 14
7 x 3 = 21
7 x 4 = 28
7 x 5 = 35
7 x 6 = 42
7 x 7 = 49
7 x 8 = 56
7 x 9 = 63
7 x 10 = 70

Even though the child has previously mastered all but one of these multiplication facts (7 x 7 = 49 being the exception), there are certain things that should be pointed out to the child. The first is that all of the products of seven and a number that is ten or less will have a different one's digit. (i.e. 7 x 1 = 7 so no other multiple of seven on the list above will have a seven in the one's place.) Also explain that if seven is multiplied by an odd number then the one's digit will be an odd number and if seven is multiplied by an even number then the one's digit will be an even number. First show the odd numbers:

7 x 1 = 7
7 x 3 = 21
7 x 5 = 35
7 x 7 = 49
7 x 9 = 63

Now show the even numbers:

7 x 2 = 14
7 x 4 = 28
7 x 6 = 42
7 x 8 = 56
7 x 10 = 70

This phenomenon holds true for all natural numbers. When an odd number is multiplied by an odd number the product will always be an odd number. However any time an even number is multiplied by another number, regardless if it is odd or even the product will always be an even number.

Now practice with the deck of cards and the work sheets until the child achieves mastery with multiplication by seven. Once this is achieved work on multiplication with all single digit numbers and ten.

Now take the deck of cards and separate them into two small decks, one of black numbered cards and another of red numbered cards. Turn over the cards one at a time and have the child multiply the two cards.

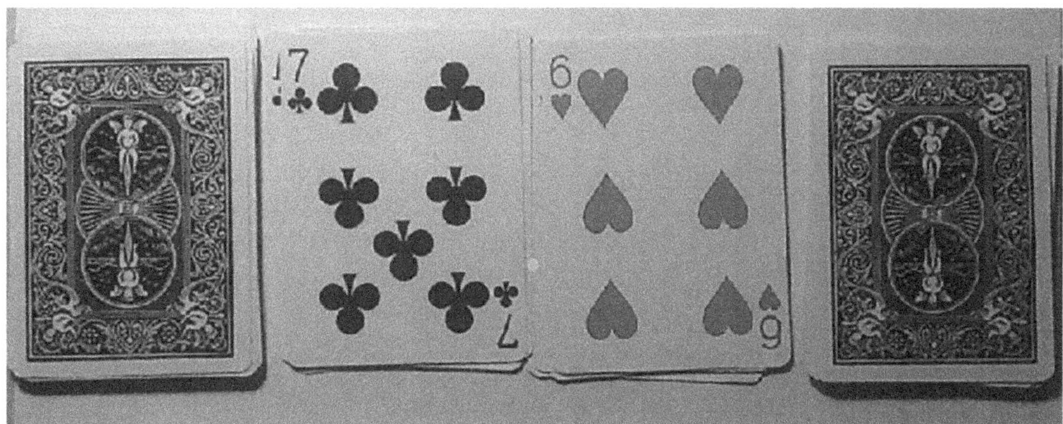

Once the child is comfortable with this exercise teach the child multiplication with zero, which is the easiest thing to do in math. When a number, any number, is multiplied by zero the product is always zero.

1 x 0 = 0
18 x 0 = 0
356 x 0 = 0

Once this is explained to the child it is now time for the child to practice five minute drill worksheets.

Go to themathworksheetsite.com and under the "Multiplication" heading select "5 minute drill."

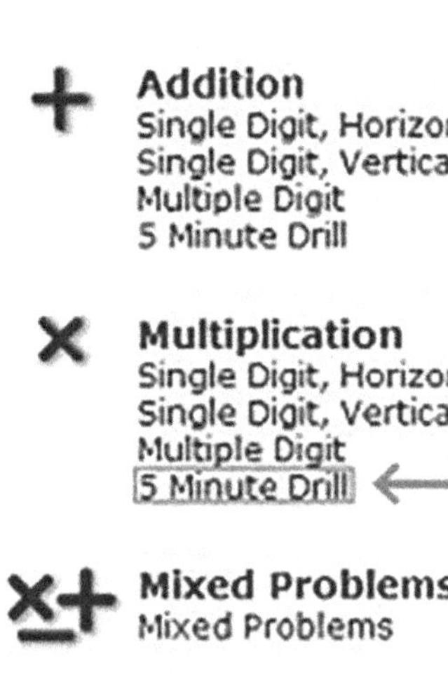

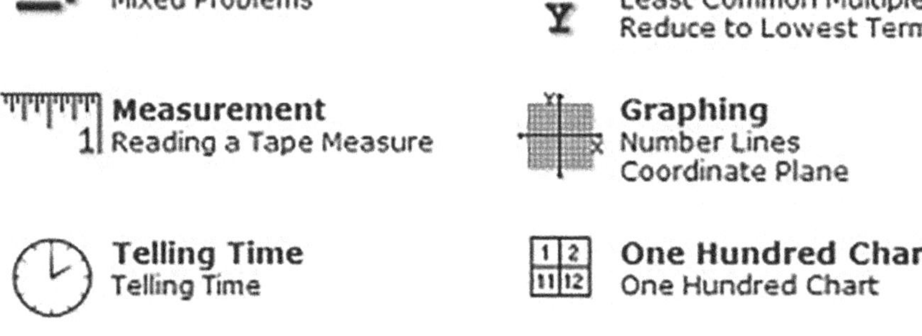

This will create a worksheet of one-hundred problems that the child should be able to answer correctly in five minutes. When the child can successfully complete the worksheet, have the child do a worksheet once a week to improve multiplication skills.

Before teaching the child multiple digit multiplication, take a moment to teach the child multiplication be eleven. Multiplication by eleven has some fascinating aspects about it that the child could find intriguing. First show the numbers one through nine.

11 x 1 = 11
11 x 2 = 22
11 x 3 = 33
11 x 4 = 44
11 x 5 = 55

11 x 6 = 66
11 x 7 = 77
11 x 8 = 88
11 x 9 = 99

This should be mastered rather quickly by the child. However, the real eye opener is when eleven is multiplied by numbers ten through eighteen.

11 x 10 = 110
11 x 11 = 121
11 x 12 = 132
11 x 13 = 143
11 x 14 = 154
11 x 15 = 165
11 x 16 = 176
11 x 17 = 187
11 x 18 = 198

When multiplying eleven by a two digit number, take that two digit number and add them together and the sum will go in between those two digits to obtain the product.

Example:

11 x 14
1 + 4 = 5

Write the one and the four with a space in between them.

1 4

Place the five in between them.

154

Therefore 11 x 14 = 154

The purpose of showing the child this phenomenon that happens when eleven is a factor is to instill in the child a sense on wonderment and exploration with a natural curiosity when it comes to studying mathematics. Far too often many children look upon the study of mathematics with fear. Change the mindset of your child so that mathematics is something to explore and not something to fear. Once the child experiences this change in mindset, competence and confidence in mathematics will soar.

Now it is time to teach the child multiple digit multiplication. Start where on factor is a two-digit number and the other factor is a one-digit number.

Example:

$$\begin{array}{r} 63 \\ \underline{\times\ 8} \end{array}$$

When doing such a multiplication problem it is important to teach the child to work from back to front. Also teach the key number is the number at the bottom, in this case the eight. Multiply the eight by the three to obtain a product of twenty-four. Now it is important just to place the four (one's digit) under the eight.

$$\begin{array}{r} 63 \\ \underline{\times\ 8} \\ 4 \end{array}$$

The two that represents twenty (ten's digit) will be placed above the six to be carried.

$$\begin{array}{r} 2 \\ 63 \\ \underline{\times\ 8} \\ 4 \end{array}$$

Now multiply the eight by the six to obtain a product of forty-eight. Take the forty-eight and add the two that was to be carried to get a sum of fifty. Place the zero of the fifty under the six next to the four.

```
  2
 63
 x 8
 04
```

Finally place the five from the fifty next to the zero.

```
  2
 63
 x 8
504
```

Thus, the answer is 504.

Also note that not every problem requires carrying. If that is the case just multiply the bottom number twice, back to front.

Example:

```
 63
 x 3
```

Take the bottom number, which is a three, and multiply that by the back number on the top, which is also a three, to get a product of nine. Write the nine under the three on the line.

```
 63
 x 3
  9
```

Now multiply the three on the bottom by the six on the top to get a product of eighteen. Write the eighteen next to the nine.

```
 63
 x 3
189
```

Thus, the answer is 189.

Now it is time to create a worksheet and have the child practice these types of multiplication problems. On themathworksheetsite.com select "Multiple Digit".

Addition
Single Digit, Horizontal
Single Digit, Vertical
Multiple Digit
5 Minute Drill

Subtraction
Single Digit, Horizontal
Single Digit, Vertical
Multiple Digit
5 Minute Drill

Multiplication
Single Digit, Horizontal
Single Digit, Vertical
Multiple Digit
5 Minute Drill

Division
Single Digit, Horizontal
Long Division
5 Minute Drill

Mixed Problems
Mixed Problems

Fractions
Least Common Multiple
Reduce to Lowest Terms

Measurement
Reading a Tape Measure

Graphing
Number Lines
Coordinate Plane

Telling Time
Telling Time

One Hundred Chart
One Hundred Chart

There will be two drop down boxes, one that says, "Number of Digits in Multiplicand" (top factor), and the other that says, "Number of Digits in Multiplier" (bottom factor). Choose "2" for the top factor and "1" for the bottom factor and hit the "Create" button.

The Math Worksheet Site.com
On-line Math Worksheet Generator

Multiplication: Multiple Digit

Number of Digits in Multiplicand

XX
× X

Number of Digits in Multiplier

Include Answer Key

Create It

This will create a worksheet of twenty problems for the child to practice. The goal is to do all twenty problems correctly in less than five minutes to demonstrate mastery.

Next work on multiplication problems where one factor has three digits, and the other factor has one digit. This will be very similar to the previous types of problems that the child has master, so the child should not have too much difficulty solving these problems.

Example:

$$\begin{array}{r} 296 \\ \underline{\times\ 8} \end{array}$$

First multiply the eight by six to get a product of forty-eight. Write an eight below the eight and carry the four by writing it above the nine.

$$\begin{array}{r} 4\ \ \\ 296 \\ \underline{\times\ 8} \\ 8 \end{array}$$

Now multiply the eight by nine to get a product of seventy-two. Add then four that was carried to seventy-two to get a sum of seventy-six. Write the six in front of the eight under the line and write a seven above the two.

$$\begin{array}{r} 74\ \ \\ 296 \\ \underline{\times\ 8} \\ 68 \end{array}$$

The last step is to multiply the eight by the two to get a product of sixteen. Add seven to sixteen to get a sum of twenty-three. Write the three from twenty-three in front of the six and then write the two in front of the three.

$$\begin{array}{r} 74\ \ \\ 296 \\ \underline{\times\ 8} \\ 2368 \end{array}$$

The answer is 2368.

Have the child practice by making worksheets where a three-digit factor is multiplied by a one-digit factor. This will create a worksheet with twenty problems that the child should be able to consistently complete correctly in less than five minutes to achieve mastery.

Next teach the child multiplication with a four-digit factor and a one-digit factor. Since the child now has mastery of multiplying a single digit factor with a double-digit factor and a triple digit factor, this concept should be quickly and easily mastered by the child.

Example:

```
 8395
x   3
```

Remember to work back to front in multiplying three by the four-digit factor. Start by multiplying three by five to get a product of fifteen. Write a five below the three and carry the one by writing it above the nine.

```
   1
 8395
x   3
    5
```

Next multiply the three by the nine to get a product of twenty-seven. Add the one that was carried to get a sum of twenty-eight. Write the eight in front of the five and carry the two by writing it above the three.

```
  21
 8395
x   3
   85
```

Now multiply three by three to get a product of nine. Add the carried two to the nine to get a sum of eleven. Write a one in front of the eight and write the carried one above the eight.

```
 121
 8395
x   3
  185
```

Finally multiply the three by the eight to get a product of twenty-four. Add the carried one to get a sum of twenty-five. Write the five in front of the one and then the two in front of the five.

```
 121
 8395
x   3
25185
```

The answer is 25,185.

Have the child practice by making worksheets where a four-digit factor is multiplied by a one-digit factor. This will create a worksheet with twenty problems that the child should be able to consistently complete correctly in less than five minutes to achieve mastery.

Now it is time to teach the child multiplication that involves two-digit factors. This could be a bit more challenging for the child master because it is a little more complex than multiplication where at least one of the factors is a single digit number.

Explain to the child that the process of multiplication with a two-digit factor will consist of three steps. These are:

1. Multiplication by the one's digit of the bottom number.
2. Multiplication by the ten's digit of the bottom number.
3. Addition to get the final product.
   Example:

```
 38
x94
```

To begin have the child multiply the top number by four and then the top number by nine. Since four times eight equals thirty-two write a two-under the four and carry the three by writing it above the three.

```
 3
 38
x94
  2
```

Now multiply the four by the three to get a product of twelve. Add the carried three to the twelve to get a sum of fifteen. Write the fifteen in front of the two.

```
 3
 38
x94
152
```

Now the first step is complete. The second step is to multiply the nine by the top number. However, before that, place and X under the two and cross out the carried three.

```
 3̸
 38
x94
152
  X
```

The reason to cross out the carried three is that when the nine is multiplied carrying will be required. The new carried number could be confused with the old carried number. The reason to place the X under the two is the top number is actually being multiplied by ninety. Therefore, the result must be shifted over to the ten's place.

Now multiply the nine by the eight to get a product of seventy-two. Write a two under the five and carry the seven by writing it above the crossed-out three.

```
  7
  3̸
  38
 X94
 152
  2X
```

Now multiply the nine by the three to get a product of twenty-seven. Add the carried seven to get a sum of thirty-four. Write the thirty-four next to the two.

```
  7
  3̸
  38
 X94
 152
342X
```

Now the second step in complete. The final step is to add the two products to get a final product, so have the child draw a line under the bottom product.

```
  7
  3̸
  38
 X94
 152
342X
----
```

Now add the two numbers to get the final product.

```
  7
  3̸
  38
 X94
 152
342X
3572
```

The answer is 3,572.

Now go to themathworksheetsite.com and create a worksheet for the child for daily practice. Select "2" and "2" when creating the worksheet. Also check the "Include Answer Key" box. This will show how the problems are solved by addition. This will create a worksheet of sixteen problems. The child should comfortably answer these correctly in ten minutes to achieve mastery. After daily practice it is time for the child to work on multiplication with two digit and three-digit factors.

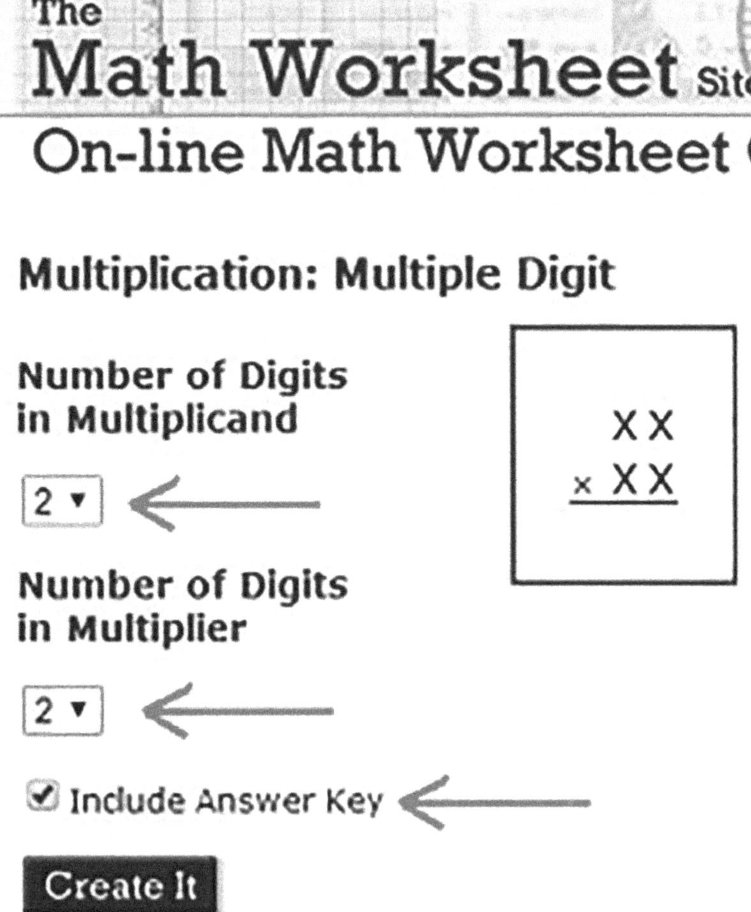

Teaching the child how to multiply a two-digit number by a three-digit number will be fairly easy once the child has mastered two digit by two-digit multiplication. The concept is the same, the child will do the same three steps, it is just that the two multiplication steps will be with a three-digit number.

Example:

$$\begin{array}{r} 285 \\ \underline{\text{x } 43} \end{array}$$

Once again, the child will multiply the top number twice, first by three and then by four. Since three times five is fifteen, write a five under the three and carry the one by writing it above the eight.

$$\begin{array}{r} 1 \\ 285 \\ \underline{\text{x } 43} \\ 5 \end{array}$$

Next multiply the eight by the three to get a product of twenty-four. Add the carried one to get a sum of twenty-five. Write a five under the four and write the carried two above the two in the top factor.

```
 21
285
x43
 55
```

To finish off the first step multiply three by two to get a product of six. Add the carried two to six to get a sum of eight and write the eight down in front of the five.

```
 21
285
x43
855
```

Now the first step is complete. Before beginning the second step, write an X below the five in the one's place and cross out the carried two and one.

```
  2̶1̶
  285
X  43
-----
  855
    X
```

Now multiply the four by five to get a product of twenty. Write a zero next to the X and write a two above the crossed out one.

```
    2
  2̶1̶
  285
X  43
-----
  855
   0X
```

Next multiply the four by eight to get a product of thirty-two. Add the carried two to thirty-two to get a sum of thirty-four. Write the four next to the zero and write the carried three above the crossed out two.

```
   32
   21
  285
X  43
-----
  855
  40X
```

To complete the second step, multiply the four by two to get a product of eight. Add the carried three to the eight to get a sum of eleven. Write the eleven in front of the four.

```
   32
   21
  285
X  43
-----
  855
1140X
```

To complete the problem, draw a line under the second product and add the two numbers. (8 + 4 = 12, so the one must be carried.)

```
   32
   21
  285
X  43
-----
  855
1140X
-----
12255
```

The answer is 12,255.

Now go to themathworksheetsite.com and create a worksheet for the child for daily practice. Select "3" and "2" when creating the worksheet. Also check the "Include Answer Key" box. This will show how the problems are solved by addition. This will create a worksheet of sixteen problems. The child should comfortably answer these correctly in ten minutes to achieve mastery, after that have the child do worksheets where a four-digit number is multiplied by a two-digit number. Create a worksheet of sixteen problems that contain these types of problems. Once mastery is achieved have the child work on multiplication where both factors have three digits.

When teaching the child multiplication with two triple digit factors, four steps will be required.

1. Multiply the top factor by the one's digit of the bottom factor.
2. Multiply the top factor by the ten's digit of the bottom factor.

3. Multiply the top factor by the hundred's digit of the bottom factor.
4. Add the three products to get the final answer.

It is important to note that when the top factor is multiplied by the hundred's digit in the bottom factor two X's must be placed on the line of the third product. This is because when multiplying the top factor by the hundred's digit, the top factor is really multiplied by one-hundred times the value of hundred's digit.

Example:

```
  697
x 573
```

The first step involves multiplying three by the top factor. Have the child multiply three by seven to get a product of twenty-one. Write a one below the three and carry the two by writing it above the nine.

```
   2
  697
x 573
    1
```

Next multiply the three by the nine to get a product of twenty-seven. Add the carried two to get a sum of twenty-nine. Write a nine below the seven and carry the two by writing it above the six.

```
  22
  697
x 573
   91
```

To complete the first step, multiply the three by six to get a product of eighteen. Add the carried two to get a sum of twenty. Write the twenty in front of the nine.

```
  22
  697
x 573
 2091
```

Now the first step is complete. Cross out the two carried twos and write an X below the one before continuing to the second step.

```
   22   (crossed out)
   697
X  573
  2091
     X
```

To start the second step, multiply the seven by seven to obtain a product of forty-nine. Write a nine in front of the X. Carry the four by writing it above the crossed out two.

```
    4
   22
   697
 X 573
  2091
    9X
```

The next step is to multiply the seven by the nine to get a product of sixty-three. Add the carried four to get a sum of sixty-seven. Write the seven under the zero and carry the six by writing it above the crossed-out two.

```
   64
   22
   697
 X 573
  2091
   79X
```

To complete the second step, multiply the seven by the six to get a product of forty-two. Add the carried six to the forty-two to obtain a sum of forty-eight. Write the forty-eight in front of the seven.

```
   64
   22
   697
 X 573
  2091
 4879X
```

Before beginning the step of multiplying the top factor by the hundred's digit, cross-out the carried six and the four and write two X's on the third line to be added.

~~64~~
~~22~~
697
X 573
2091
4879X
XX

To begin the third step, multiply the five by the seven to obtain a product of thirty-five. Write the five in front of the X and write the carried three above the crossed-out four.

3
~~64~~
~~22~~
697
X 573
2091
4879X
5XX

Next multiply the five by the nine to obtain a product of forty-five. Add the carried three to get a sum of forty-eight. Write the eight in front of the five and write the carried four above the crossed-out six.

43
~~64~~
~~22~~
697
X 573
2091
4879X
85XX

To complete the third step, multiply the five by the six to get a product of thirty. Add the carried four to obtain a sum of thirty-four. Write the thirty-four in front of the eight.

```
    43
    64
    22
   697
 X 573
  2091
 4879X
3485XX
```

Finally, to complete the problem, underline and add, (carrying will be necessary).

```
    43
    64
    22
   697
 X 573
------
  2091
 4879X
3485XX
------
399381
```

The answer is 399,381.

Now go to themathworksheetsite.com and create a worksheet for the child for daily practice. Select "3" and "3" when creating the worksheet. Also check the "Include Answer Key" box. This will show how the problems are solved by addition. This will create a worksheet of twelve problems. The child should comfortably answer these correctly in ten minutes to achieve mastery, after that have the child do worksheets where a four-digit number is multiplied by a three-digit number. Create a worksheet of twelve problems that contain these types of problems.

Once mastery is achieved with these concepts, the child will have mastery in multiplication. This mastery will be a great advantage to the child as more advanced mathematical concepts are introduced.

Daily practice with the deck of cards, five-minute drill worksheets, and multiple digit multiplication worksheets should continue. This practice does not need to take more than ten to fifteen minutes from the child's daily schedule.

TEACHING NUMBER RECOGNITION TO ONE MILLION

As the child advances in mathematics, large numbers will be encountered and used. It is important for the child to be comfortable understanding and working with large numbers. Therefore, it is necessary for the child to properly understand and describe these large numbers.

Start with the number:

28

This is verbalized as twenty-eight.

Now look at this number:

400

This is verbalized as four hundred.

When combined the number is:

428

This is verbalized as four-hundred twenty-eight. Note that it is incorrect to state four-hundred *and* twenty-eight. The word 'and' implies a decimal.

Now look at the following number:

1,000

This is verbalized as one thousand. The comma is included for grouping purposes.

Numbers are grouped by three digits. The first group of three digits knows as the 'hundreds' and the second group of three digits is known as the 'thousands.'

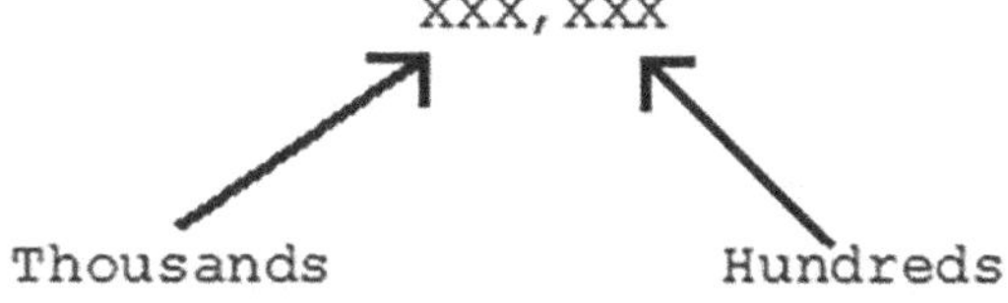

For example:

428,000

This number is verbalized as four-hundred twenty-eight thousand. When a comma is reached the naming of the number starts over.

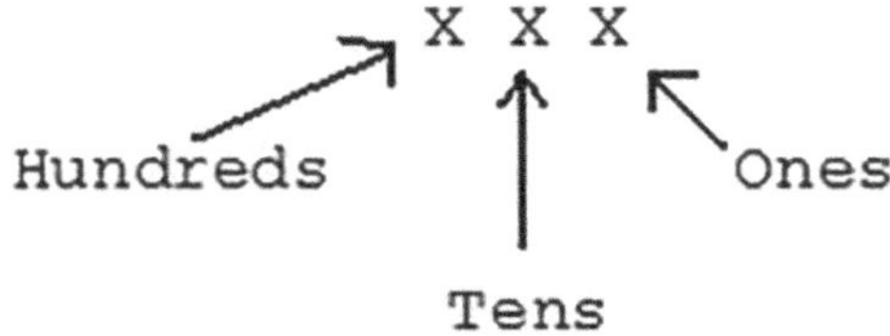

Consider the numbers:

428 and 428,000

Both of these numbers will have four-hundred twenty-eight when they are verbalized. The second number will have the word 'thousand' included in the vocalization.

Now keep the four, two and eight in the same order but write the number like this:

42,800

This number is vocalized as forty-two thousand eight hundred. Notice how the comma separator acts in the verbalization. The two digits in front of the comma (forty-eight) are spoken as a separate sub-unit, and the three digits after the comma (eight hundred) are spoken as a separate subunit.

Remove a zero (in effect dividing by ten) and this is the number:

4,280

This number is verbalized as four-thousand two-hundred eighty. Once again notice the digit in front of the comma (four thousand) is spoken as a subunit, and the three digits after the comma (two-hundred eighty) are spoken as a separate subunit.

What this means that if the child can recognize and vocalize any number less than one thousand, then the child can easily be taught to recognize and vocalize any number less than one million. Explain to the child that the digits in front of the comma will be spoken as a number with the word thousand and the numbers after the comma will then be spoken.

Example:

428,657

This number is verbalized as four-hundred twenty-eight thousand six-hundred fifty-seven.

For practice write a few six-digit numbers on the back of an envelope and have the child say the numbers. This can be done every few days to go along with daily practice.

To get to one million show the child this number:

999,999

This number is nine-hundred ninety-nine thousand nine-hundred ninety-nine. If one is added to this number, the result is:

1,000,000

That number is one million.

Now the child should be able recognize, understand and verbalize all numbers up to and including one million.

TEACHING MEASUREMENTS

There are several measurements that the child needs to learn while the child is in early elementary school. These are common measurements that are a part of everyday life and are used in mathematical problems at all levels. The child is expected to know these measurements.

The metric system will be covered later. The measurements in question cover the three aspects of length, volume and weight. For length discuss inches, feet, yards and miles. For volume discuss ounces, cups, pints, quarts and gallons. For weight discuss ounces, pounds and tons.

When teaching the child about linear measurements it is helpful to show the child a standard ruler.

Explain to the child that the numbers on the ruler are inches and that there are twelve inches in a foot. Then, for a fun activity, have the child measure various things that are less than a foot in length. Examples include utensils, toilet paper roles, books, bottles, toothbrushes, bars of soap, game controls, pictures, cups, and glasses. Take a piece of paper and five items. Make a list of the five items on the piece of paper and then have the child measure the items. After that have the child write down the length in inches by the name of the item on the paper.

If the parent has a tape measure, things that are longer than a foot can be measured. A good example is the length across on a large screen television. Once the child has achieved mastery in division, then the child will be able to convert a measurement in inches to a measurement of feet and inches.

After a few days of such activities the child should always know that there are twelve inches in a foot.

The next linear measurement to teach the child is the yard. The yard is the same distance as three feet. Almost all classrooms have at least one yardstick, so ask the child where the yardstick is kept in the classroom.

If the family enjoys watching football that is played in the United States, it will be very easy to expose the child to the concept of the yard. The football field is measured in yards and several accomplishments by players are measured in yards. For example a football field is one-hundred yards long (discounting the area in the end zone), therefore explain to the child that since one yard is the same as three feet a football field is three-hundred feet long.

So far the child has learned that there are twelve inches in a foot and three feet in a yard. Now have the child do a simple multiplication problem to determine the number of inches in a yard.

$$\begin{array}{r} 12 \\ \underline{\times\ 3} \end{array}$$

Write this on the back of an envelope. Ask the child, "Since there are twelve inches in a foot and three feet in a yard, how many inches are in a yard?"

Have the child multiply to get the answer.

$$\begin{array}{r} 12 \\ \underline{\times\ 3} \\ 36 \end{array}$$

Answer: there are thirty-six inches in a yard.

Next it is time to explain miles to the child. Many children have difficulty learning the concept of miles because they cannot visualize the distance the same way they can visualize inches, feet and yards. There are a few ways to help the child understand the concept of a mile.

If the parent or grandparent has a vehicle they could drive a mile from the home and make a note by using an odometer of the vehicle. When a mile is reached look for a landmark or specific house, it does not have to be exact. Later either walk or ride a bike with the child from the house to the spot and explain that how far that you have traveled from the house to that point is one mile.

The important relationship that the child needs to know when it comes to the mile is this:

1 mile = 5,280 feet

While this could be memorized, there is a fun way to have the child figure out this number. Use the fact that a typical track in the United States (before being converted to the metric system to conform to international standards) is a distance of 440 yards.

Tell the child that four laps is equal to one mile. Therefore if the child multiplies four-hundred forty by four, the number of yards in a mile can be determined.

$$\begin{array}{r} 440 \\ \underline{x\ 4} \\ 1760 \end{array}$$

That means:

1 mile = 1,760 yards

Now multiply that number by three to figure out the number of feet in a mile.

$$\begin{array}{r} 1760 \\ \underline{x\ 3} \\ 5280 \end{array}$$

So that is a fun way for the child to figure out the number of feet in a mile.

Next teach the child volume measurements. For the purpose of this lesson, only liquid volume measurements will be considered. The first measurement to teach the child will be the ounce.

Try to find a measuring cup such as this one:

Show the child one ounce and then pour an ounce of water in the cup, and transfer that to a clear drinking glass, so that the child could see what an ounce looks like. Also show the child the bottom of a soda can that displays the volume.

Now pour eight ounces to make a cup. Show the child on the measuring cup that eight ounces equals a cup. Pour a cup of water into the measuring cup and then transfer that water into a clear drinking glass. Compare two similar glasses, one with one ounce of water and the other with a cup of water. Show the child the difference. The important relationship for the child to remember is this:

1 cup = 8 ounces

Once the child masters and understands this relationship, the rest is easy.

1 pint = 2 cups
1 quart = 2 pints
1 gallon = 4 quarts

The child should be familiar with this addition fact:

$$2 + 2 = 4$$

So tell the child, "Two cups equal one pint, two pints equals one quart, and four quarts equals one gallon.

It is easy to show the child one quart because a quart of milk can be easily purchased at a grocery store.

Likewise it is easy to show a gallon because a gallon of milk is likewise easy to purchase at any grocery store.

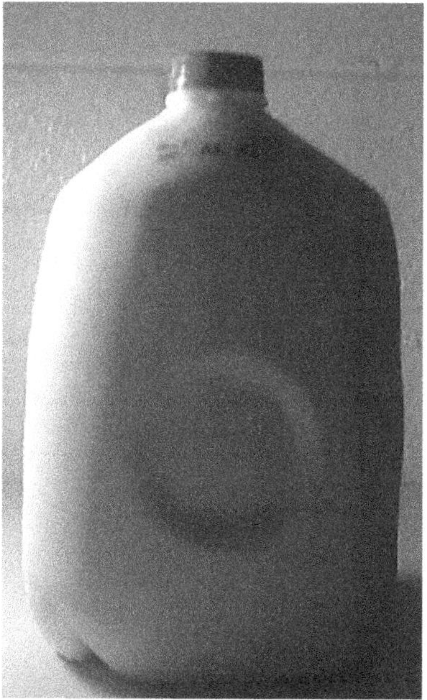

Then show the child that four quarts is equal to one gallon.

Once the child has mastered liquid volume it is time to teach the child measurements of weight.

Teaching measurement in weight is fairly easy as there are only two relationships for the child to remember. These relationships are:

1 pound = 16 ounces
1 ton = 2,000 pounds

The concept of pounds is the measurement of weight that the child will be most familiar with in early elementary school. If the parent has a scale it is easy to have the child stand on the scale and see the child's weight in pounds.

A fun activity for the child learning about weight is to weigh the child, write down the weight and then weigh the child holding something and then write down that weight. The difference between these two numbers will be the weight of the thing that the child held in pounds.

Example:

Suppose a child stepped on the scale and weighed sixty-eight pounds and then the child holds a cat and steps on the scale again. Suppose the new weight of the child and the cat is seventy-three pounds. What is the weight of the cat?

Solution:

Take the larger number (73), which represents the weight of the child and the cat, and subtract the smaller number (68), which represents the weight of the just the child.

$$\begin{array}{r} 73 \\ \underline{-68} \end{array} \qquad \begin{array}{r} \text{cat + child} \\ \underline{-\quad\quad \text{child}} \end{array}$$

Now subtract the two numbers.

$$\begin{array}{r} {}^{6} \\ \not{7}{}^{1}3 \\ \underline{-68} \\ 5 \end{array} \qquad \begin{array}{r} \text{cat + } \not{\text{child}} \\ \underline{- \quad\quad \not{\text{child}}} \\ \text{cat} \end{array}$$

Thus the cat weighs five pounds.

The fact that ounces are used in both volume and weight can be confusing to the child. Show the child a package, can or container of food that has a weight in ounces.

Explain to the child that if a container expresses the ounces as fluid ounces (often abbreviated as FL OZ) then it is a volume measure. If it is expressed as net weight (often abbreviated as NET WT), then it is a weight measure.

The fact that one ton is equal to two-thousand pounds is something that must be memorized by the child. A fun activity can be to look up the weight of the family vehicle online. Since this weight is express in pounds, have the child figure out the weight in pounds by subtracting two-thousand from the weight until a final answer of less than two-thousand is obtained.

Example:

A family went online and found that the weight of their vehicle was 4,563 pounds (this may be abbreviated as lbs.). What is the weight in tons and pounds.

Solution:

Since there are two-thousand pounds per ton, every time the child subtracts 2,000 from the original weight will represent one ton.

$$\begin{array}{r} 4563 \\ \underline{-2000} \\ 2563 \end{array}$$

That counts as one ton. Now take the difference and subtract 2,000 from that number.

$$\begin{array}{r} 2563 \\ \underline{-2000} \\ 563 \end{array}$$

That counts as two tons. Since 563 is less than 2,000 then the weight of the car is:

2 tons, 563 pounds

As the child progresses through mathematics all of the relationships pertaining to measurement previously discussed are expected to be known. Many problems on end of year tests will expect the child to know these relationships.

TEACHING ROUNDING

A key skill for children to master in mid elementary school is the concept of rounding. The next several pages will concentrate on rounding to the nearest ten, hundred and thousand.

The key number when it comes to rounding is five. If the determining number is less than five then the rounded number will stay the same. If the determining number is five or more than one will be added to the rounded number.

The determining digit will be to the immediate right of the rounded digit. For example, if a number is to be rounded to the nearest ten, then the ten's digit is the rounded digit and the one's digit is the determining digit. If the one's digit is less than five (0, 1, 2, 3, or 4) then the ten's digit will remain the same. However, if the one's digit is five or more (5, 6, 7, 8, or 9) then one will be added to the ten's digit.

To show the child the concept of rounding chose two numbers that are multiples of ten and less than one hundred. Then write those two numbers and the numbers in between in descending order. For example, if the numbers chosen are thirty and forty, write them down like this.

40
39
38
37
36
35

34
33
32
31
30

The next step is to draw a line between the numbers 35 and 34.

40
39
38
37
36
35

34
33
32
31
30

Now draw two arrows similar to these:

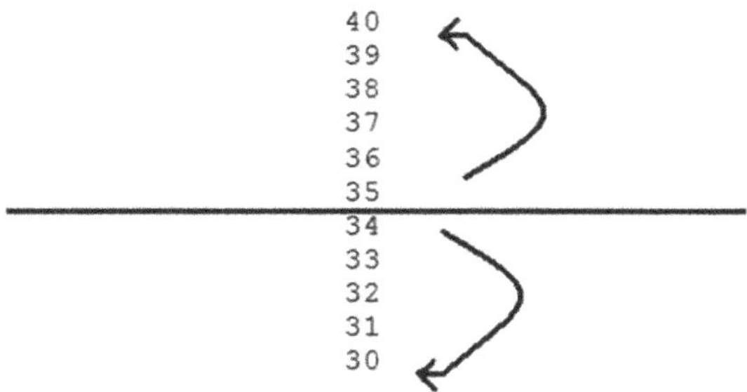

Finally add the words, "Closer to 40," and "Closer to 30."

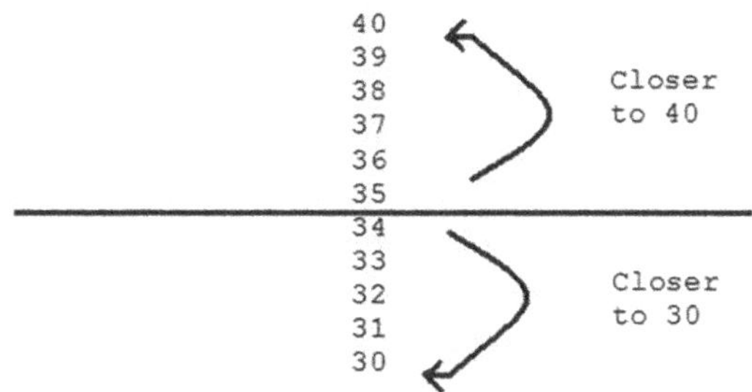

So let's look at an example:

Round 53 to the nearest ten.

Solution:

Since the rounded digit is five (ten's digit), that means that the rounded number will be either 50 or 60. To determine the answer, look at the determining digit (one's digit). Since that digit is three that means the rounded digit stays the same, so the answer is 50.

Now let's look at a very similar problem:

Round 57 to the nearest ten.

Solution:

In this case the determining digit is seven. That means one will be added to the rounding digit. One more than five is six so the answer is 60.

It is also important to work with the child one numbers greater than one-hundred.

For example:

Round 325 to the nearest ten.

Solution:

It is important to realize that rounded number is two. That means the three in the hundred's place is ignored because the answer will either be 320 or 330 depending on the determining digit. Since the determining digit is five that means one has to be added to the rounding digit, so the answer is 330.

When the rounded digit is nine the number to the left to the rounded digit has the potential to be increased by one based on the determining digit.

Example:

Round 395 to the nearest ten.

To help answer this problem make a chart like this and draw a line between 395 and 394.

```
      400
      399
      398
      397
      396
      395
-------------------
      394
      393
      392
      391
      390
```

Note that 395 is closer to 400 than to 390, so the answer is 400.

However, it is not feasible to draw a chart every time nine is a rounded number. Just remember to increase the digit to the left of the rounded digit by one and change the rounded digit to zero.

For practice write a few two digit numbers on the back of an envelope (or any other piece of paper) and ask the child to round these numbers to the nearest ten. This exercise should take less than a minute. Five problems in a minute should easily be mastered in less than a week.

Once the child has mastered rounding to the nearest ten, teach the child rounding to the nearest hundred. This will be very similar to rounding to the nearest ten. The difference will be that the hundreds digit is the rounded number and the ten's digit is the determining number.

Example:

Round 673 to the nearest hundred.

Solution:

Since the rounded digit is six (the hundred's digit) that means that the rounded number will be either 600 or 700. To determine the answer look at the determining digit (ten's digit). Since that digit is seven, one will be added to the rounded digit. So the answer is 700.

It is important to explain to the child that the one's digit (3) has nothing to do with the answer. It is ignored.

The same rule applies for rounding to the nearest hundred if the rounded digit is nine, as it was if the rounded digit was ten.

Example:

Round 3,981 to the nearest hundred.

Solution:

In this case the rounded digit is nine. That means that the hundred's digit will either be a nine or a zero when the problem is complete. If the answer has a zero in the rounded digit's place, then the digit to the immediate left of the rounded digit (in this case the thousand's digit) must be increase by one.

Since the determining digit is eight, the rounded digit must be increased by one. Now since the rounded digit is nine, the rounded digit is changed to zero and the digit to the immediate left of the rounded digit is increased by one, making it a four. Therefore the answer is 4,000.

Daily practice on rounding to the nearest hundred can be done the same way he child practiced rounding to the nearest ten. It is important to make this practice quick and easy. Nothing about rounding exercises should be stressful to the child.

These same concepts can be used when rounding to the nearest thousand. The thousand's digit is the rounded digit and the hundred's digit is the determining digit.

Example:

Round 42,387 to the nearest thousand.

Since the rounded digit is a two, the answer will either be 42,000 or 43,000. Now the determining digit is three, therefore the rounded digit will stay the same, so the answer is 42,000.

Once the child achieves mastery in rounding whole numbers, a few minutes of practice a week should be all that is necessary to maintain rounding skills. Once the child learns about decimals, rounding with decimals will be a bit more challenging. However, the overall concept is the same and the key number for the determining digit will always be five.

TEACHING DIVISION

Division relates to multiplication the same way subtraction relates to addition. Once multiplication facts are mastered and memorized the child should be able to master division facts in a few week's time, if not sooner.

The concept of families can be used in multiplication and division just as it was used in addition and subtraction. However, the use of groups is a good way to introduce the concept of division to the child.

A good start is to take twenty pennies and arrange them in five rows of four on a piece of paper.

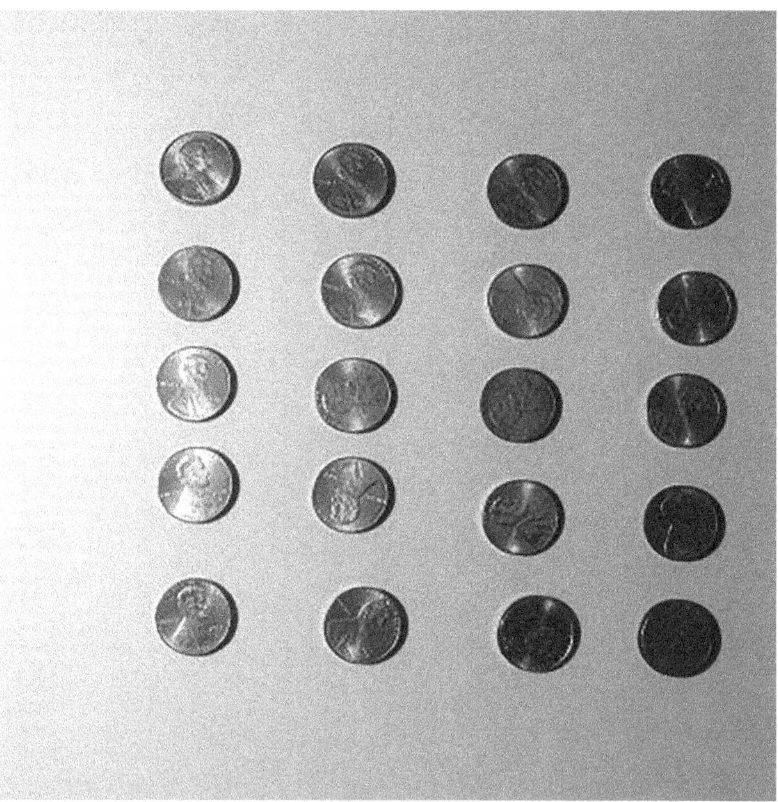

Take a pen, marker or crayon and draw an oval around each group of five.

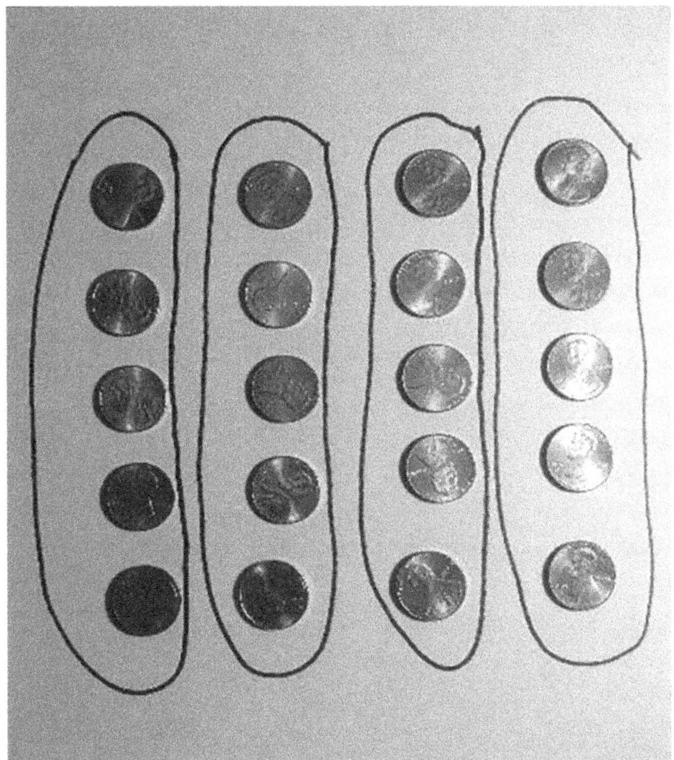

Since the twenty pennies are divided into four groups of five pennies each, verbalize to the child, "Twenty divided by four equals five." This will be written as:

$$20 \div 4 = 5$$

Next replace the paper under the twenty pennies. Now draw ovals sideways so that there are five groups of four.

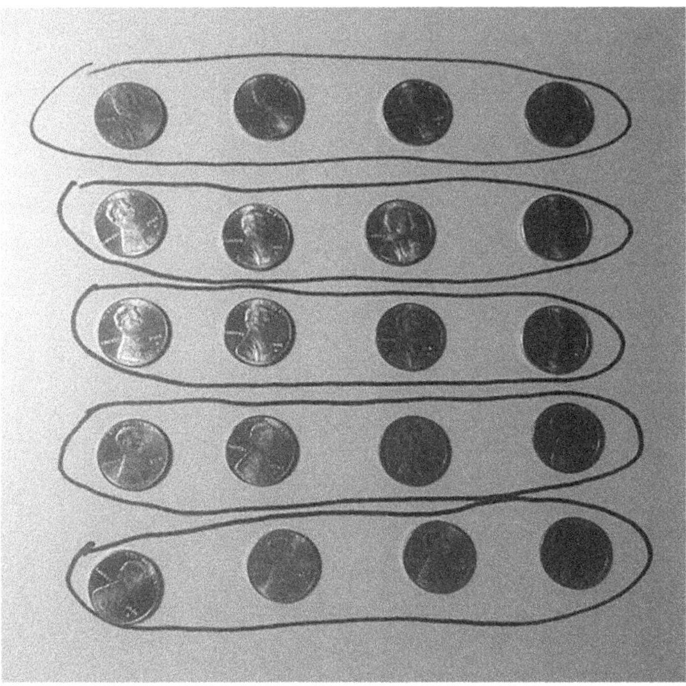

Now the twenty pennies are divided into five groups of four. Verbalize to the child, "Twenty divided by five equals four." This will be written as:

$$20 \div 5 = 4$$

Explain to the child that these three numbers make a family. The largest number will be the product of the other two numbers. In this example the numbers in the family are 4, 5, and 20 because 4 x 5 = 20. Thus the family consists of the following operations:

$$4 \times 5 = 20$$
$$5 \times 4 = 20$$
$$20 \div 4 = 5$$
$$20 \div 5 = 4$$

Once this is explained to the child and the child understands, it is time to begin teaching division facts to the child.

Begin with the idea that any number divided by itself will always be one.

If $10 \times 1 = 10$
Then $10 \div 10 = 1$

Thus the child should easily master the following:

$$9 \div 9 = 1$$
$$8 \div 8 = 1$$
$$7 \div 7 = 1$$
$$6 \div 6 = 1$$
$$5 \div 5 = 1$$
$$4 \div 4 = 1$$
$$3 \div 3 = 1$$
$$2 \div 2 = 1$$
$$1 \div 1 = 1$$

The next groups of facts are really easy. If a number is divided by one then it will not change.

$$9 \div 1 = 9$$
$$8 \div 1 = 8$$
$$7 \div 1 = 7$$
$$6 \div 1 = 6$$
$$5 \div 1 = 5$$
$$4 \div 1 = 4$$
$$3 \div 1 = 3$$
$$2 \div 1 = 2$$
$$1 \div 1 = 1$$

Now show the child the facts when a number is divided by two. These are the doubles that were learned in both addition and multiplication.

$$\begin{aligned} 20 \div 2 &= 10 \\ 18 \div 2 &= 9 \\ 16 \div 2 &= 8 \\ 14 \div 2 &= 7 \\ 12 \div 2 &= 6 \\ 10 \div 2 &= 5 \\ 8 \div 2 &= 4 \\ 6 \div 2 &= 3 \\ 4 \div 2 &= 2 \\ 2 \div 2 &= 1 \end{aligned}$$

Notice when division facts of the same divisor (in this case 2) are listed in order it is the quotient (the answer to a division problem) that will proceed in numerical order.

The next group will be those where the divisor is five. This might take a bit longer for the child to master.

$$\begin{aligned} 50 \div 5 &= 10 \\ 45 \div 5 &= 9 \\ 40 \div 5 &= 8 \\ 35 \div 5 &= 7 \\ 30 \div 5 &= 6 \\ 25 \div 5 &= 5 \\ 20 \div 5 &= 4 \\ 15 \div 5 &= 3 \\ 10 \div 5 &= 2 \\ 5 \div 5 &= 1 \end{aligned}$$

Now as the child is working to master these facts, use the knowledge that the child has when multiplying by five was mastered.

Example:

$$30 \div 5 = ?$$

If child hesitates asks the child, "What times five equals thirty?" This should help the child achieve mastery in division.

At this point go online to themathworksheetsite.com and under the "Division" heading select "5 Minute Drill."

Addition
Single Digit, Horizontal
Single Digit, Vertical
Multiple Digit
5 Minute Drill

Subtraction
Single Digit, Horizontal
Single Digit, Vertical
Multiple Digit
5 Minute Drill

Multiplication
Single Digit, Horizontal
Single Digit, Vertical
Multiple Digit
5 Minute Drill

Division
Single Digit, Horizontal
Long Division
5 Minute Drill

Mixed Problems
Mixed Problems

Fractions
Least Common Multiple
Reduce to Lowest Terms

Measurement
Reading a Tape Measure

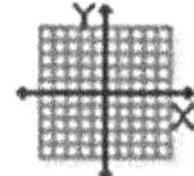

Graphing
Number Lines
Coordinate Plane

Telling Time
Telling Time

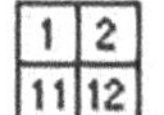

One Hundred Chart
One Hundred Chart

Print a worksheet and see if the child is able to successfully complete the worksheet correctly in five minutes. Work on those problems where the child is experiencing difficulty by doing the problems on a multiplication worksheet.

For example:

If the child is having difficulty with the division problem 56 ÷ 8 = ?, then create a multiplication worksheet where the child does problem with eight as a factor.

Multiplication: Single Digit Horizontal

Each problem will have one factor from the selections on the left and one factor from the selections on the right. If there are no factors selected in one of the lists, the numbers 0 through 9 will be used.

Number of problems

(●) 10 problems
( ) 16 problems
( ) 20 problems

Multiply These Numbers...

[ ] 0 [ ] 1 [ ] 2
[ ] 3 [ ] 4 [ ] 5
[ ] 6 [ ] 7 [x] 8
[ ] 9 [ ] 10 [ ] 11
[ ] 12
All 0-9 Clear

By These Numbers.

[ ] 0 [x] 1 [x] 2
[x] 3 [x] 4 [x] 5
[x] 6 [x] 7 [x] 8
[x] 9 [x] 10 [ ] 11
[ ] 12
All 0-9 Clear

[ ] Include Answer Key

Create It

A division problem can be expressed three different ways. The first is with the division sign ($\div$).

$$20 \div 5 = 4$$

The second way will look like a fraction. In this case the fraction bar means divide.

$$\frac{20}{5} = 4$$

The final way is long division. This is where the divisor is on the outside of the division box. The dividend is on the inside of the box.

$$5\overline{)20}$$

In this case the dividend is twenty and the divisor is five. The quotient will go on top like this:

$$\begin{array}{r} 4 \\ 5\overline{)20} \end{array}$$

Once the child has mastered the division facts then it will be time to teach the child long division. This will be done in several small steps.

However, before beginning long division there is one very important item to stress to the child that will become crucial as the child advances in mathematics. This rule is that no number can ever be divided by zero.

$$X \div 0$$

In the above problem X can be considered any number. The above problem can never happen. At this time the child is not ready for an explanation. This will be discussed once the child is enrolled in an algebra class.

When teaching long division explain to the child that it is a four step process that will be repeated until the problem is complete. These four steps are:

Divide
Multiply
Subtract
Bring Down

Example:

$$3\overline{)78}$$

The first step is to divide. Since the divisor is three, check to see if the divisor can go into the first digit of the dividend, which is seven. Since the three is less than the seven it can go in at least one time. The three will go into the seven twice so write a two above the seven.

$$\begin{array}{r} 2 \\ 3\overline{)78} \end{array}$$

The next step is to multiply. The three will be multiplied by the number on top, which is two. The product of three and two is six, so write a six under the seven.

$$\begin{array}{r} 2 \\ 3\overline{)78} \\ 6 \end{array}$$

The next step is to subtract. Draw a line under the six. Subtract the six from seven to get a difference of one and write a one below the line that is under the six.

$$\begin{array}{r} 2 \\ 3\overline{)78} \\ \underline{6} \\ 1 \end{array}$$

The next step is to bring down. To bring down is to go to the next digit in the problem, which is eight. Write an eight to the right of the difference in the subtraction step, which is one. The result is eighteen.

$$\begin{array}{r} 2 \\ 3\overline{)78} \\ \underline{6} \\ 18 \end{array}$$

The first four step process is complete. Since the division problem is not finished the four step process needs to be repeated. Once again the first step is to divide, so it is necessary to determine how many times three will go into to new number after the eight is brought down, which is eighteen. Three will go into eighteen six times so write a six above the eight in the box.

$$\begin{array}{r} 26 \\ 3\overline{)78} \\ \underline{6} \\ 18 \end{array}$$

Next multiply the three and the six to get a product of eighteen. Write an eighteen below the eighteen.

```
   26
3 )78
   6
   18
   18
```

The next step is to draw a line under the eighteen and subtract to get a difference of zero.

```
   26
3 )78
   6
   --
   18
   18
   --
    0
```

Since there is not another number to bring down, the problem is complete. The answer is the number on the top of the box, which is twenty-six.

Sometimes there will be a remainder when a divisor will not go into a dividend evenly. In this case the problem will be solved with the same four steps. The difference is on the final subtraction step the difference will not be zero. This number will be the remainder.

As an example, do the same problem but with a divisor of four.

```
4 )78
```

The first step is to divide. Since four is less than seven, four will go into seven at least once. It will not go in twice so write a one on top of the box above the seven.

```
   1
4 )78
```

The next step is to multiply. The product of four and one is four. Write a four under the seven and draw a line under the four.

```
   1
4 )78
   4
   -
```

Now on the subtraction step, subtract four from seven to get a difference of three. Write the three below the line that is under the four.

```
    1
4 )78
   4
   3
```

Now bring down the eight to make thirty-eight.

```
    1
4 )78
   4
   38
```

That completes the first set of four steps. Now repeat by determining how many times four goes into thirty-eight. Since thirty is close to forty that suggests four will go into thirty-eight close to ten times. The number closest to ten is nine, so write a nine above the eight in the box.

```
   19
4 )78
   4
   38
```

The next step is to multiply the four by the nine to get a product of thirty-six. Write thirty-six under the thirty-eight and draw a line to subtract.

```
   19
4 )78
   4
   38
   36
```

Now subtract thirty-six from thirty-eight to get a difference of two. Write the two under the six.

```
   19
4 )78
   4
   38
   36
    2
```

At this point there is no other number to bring down. Since there is a two that was the difference to the final subtraction step, the two will be a remainder, so on the top line write, "R. 2."

```
    19 R.2
4 )78
   4
   38
   36
    2
```

The answer is nineteen with a remainder of two.

Sometimes the divisor is larger than the first digit of the dividend. If that is the case then it is necessary to determine how many times the divisor will go into the first two digits of the dividend.

Example:

```
6 )258
```

The first step is to divide. For this problem the divisor, which is six, is larger than the first digit of the dividend, which is two. When this is the case it is necessary to determine how many times the divisor will go into the first two digits of the divisor, which is twenty-five.

Since six goes into twenty-five at least four times, write a four above the five. It is very important to line up the numbers properly when doing long division.

```
     4
6 )258
```

Writing the four above the proper place, which is above the five will decrease confusion as the child works to solve the problem. The next step is to multiply, so multiply six and four to get a product of twenty-four. Write the twenty-four under the twenty-five.

```
     4
6 )258
   24
```

The next step is to subtract. Draw a line under the twenty-four and subtract it from twenty-five to get a difference of one.

```
    4
6 )258
   24
    1
```

Now bring down the eight to make eighteen.

```
    4
6 )258
   24
    18
```

The first set of four steps is complete, so begin the second set of four steps by determining how many times six will go into eighteen, which of course is three. Write a three above the eight.

```
    43
6 )258
   24
    18
```

Now continue to the second step and multiply six and three to get a product of eighteen.

```
    43
6 )258
   24
    18
    18
```

Subtract the two eighteens to get a difference of zero.

```
    43
6 )258
   24
    18
    18
     0
```

Since there are no more numbers to bring down and there is no remainder, the problem is complete and the answer is forty-three.

The key challenge for children when learning long division is determining a number that goes into the dividend. Sometimes the number that is first chosen will either be too small or too large. Once a child determines that a number is either too small or too large, another number must be tried.

For example, in the previous problem look what happens when a number that is too small is selected.

$$6\overline{)258}$$

If instead of four a three is selected, then when six is multiplied by the three then the result is a product of eighteen, which will be written below the twenty-five.

$$\begin{array}{r} 3 \\ 6\overline{)258} \\ 18 \end{array}$$

When the subtraction step is completed in this case the difference is seven.

$$\begin{array}{r} 3 \\ 6\overline{)258} \\ \underline{18} \\ 7 \end{array}$$

Since the difference, which is seven, is greater than the divisor, which is six, then the number selected to divide is too small. The child should retry the division step with a number larger than three.

Retry the same problem but instead choose five.

$$\begin{array}{r} 5 \\ 6\overline{)258} \end{array}$$

When six is multiplied by five, the result is a product of thirty.

$$\begin{array}{r} 5 \\ 6\overline{)258} \\ 30 \end{array}$$

Since the thirty is greater than twenty-five, that means it is too large. A smaller number must be tried.

The more that a child practices long division, the more that the child will be able to choose the correct number in the division step. When dividing by a two digit divisor, it is probably necessary to try more than one number in the division step. However, before working on two digit divisors, it is necessary for the child to practice long division with a one digit divisor.

Go to themathworksheetsite.com to create worksheets for daily practice. Look under the "Division," heading, select, "Long Division."

Addition
Single Digit, Horizontal
Single Digit, Vertical
Multiple Digit
5 Minute Drill

Subtraction
Single Digit, Horizontal
Single Digit, Vertical
Multiple Digit
5 Minute Drill

Multiplication
Single Digit, Horizontal
Single Digit, Vertical
Multiple Digit
5 Minute Drill

Division
Single Digit, Horizontal
Long Division ←
5 Minute Drill

Mixed Problems
Mixed Problems

Fractions
Least Common Multiple
Reduce to Lowest Terms

Measurement
Reading a Tape Measure

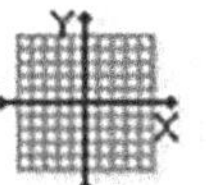

Graphing
Number Lines
Coordinate Plane

Telling Time
Telling Time

One Hundred Chart
One Hundred Chart

Be sure to select "1" in the drop down box for "Number of Digits in Divisor." For "Number of Digits in Quotient," select "2". Check the "Mixed," button and check the "Include Answer Key," box. Finally for "Answer key Remainders as:" select the "Remainders," button. The fractions will be learned later.

The
Math Worksheet Site.com

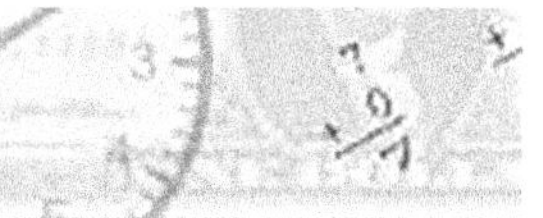

On-line Math Worksheet Generator

Long Division

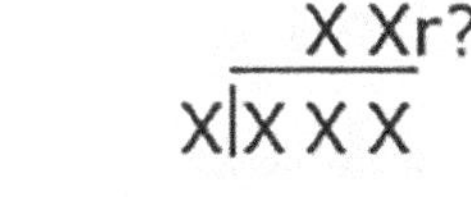

Number of Digits in Divisor

1

Number of Digits in Quotient

2

- ◯ With Remainders
- ◯ Without Remainders
- ◉ Mixed

☑ Include Answer Key

Answer Key Remainders as:

- ◉ Remainders
- ◯ Fractions

Create It

This will create a worksheet of nine problems. The answer sheet will show how the problem is solved so the child can review the steps after completing the worksheet. If any problems were answered incorrectly, the child can determine where the mistake in solving the problem was made. The goal is to correctly complete these problems in fifteen minutes or less.

Once the child can consistently solve these problems in fifteen minutes then create worksheets with "3" in the dropdown box for "Number of Digits in Quotient."

The Math Worksheet Site.com

On-line Math Worksheet Generator

Long Division

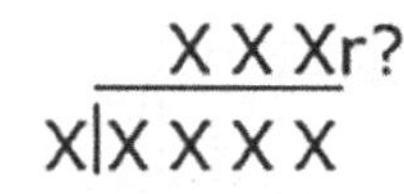

Number of Digits in Divisor

Number of Digits in Quotient

- With Remainders
- Without Remainders
- Mixed

Include Answer Key

Answer Key Remainders as:

- Remainders
- Fractions

Create It

This will create a worksheet of six problems. These will take longer to solve so the child should have a goal of fifteen minutes to correctly complete the worksheet in order to achieve mastery. After a few weeks of successful completion of these worksheets the child should be taught long division with a two digit divisor.

When teaching the child division with a two digit divisor, explain that there will be an element of trial and error when attempting to determine the number to be used on the first step. Sometimes the number selected will be wrong and a new number must be attempted. Also explain that it is best to use a pencil when solving math problems so that such errors can be erased.

While at first long division with a two digit divisor may be overwhelming to the child, calmly explain that the ten's digit of the divisor will be used to determine the number used in the first step. That digit will be compared to the first digit of the dividend.

Example:

```
23)73
```

The first step is to divide. Instead of trying to figure out how many times twenty-three will go into seventy-three, take the first digit of each and try to figure out how many times two will go into seven. Well two will go into seven three times. Instead of immediately writing a three above the box, multiply three by the divisor (23) and see if that number is larger than the dividend (73).

```
 23
x 3
 69
```

Since sixty-nine is less than seventy-three, go back to the problem and write a three-above the three.

```
    3
23)73
```

Now the next step is to multiply and that has already been completed. Just write sixty-nine under the seventy-three.

```
    3
23)73
   69
```

Now subtract.

```
    3
23)73
   69
    7
```

Since there are no more numbers to bring down, the remainder is seven.

```
    3 R.7
23)73
   69
    7
```

The problem is complete.

Now do a similar problem. It will almost be the same as the previous problem except the divisor will be twenty-six instead of twenty-three.

$$26\overline{)73}$$

Once again look at the first digit in the divisor and the dividend to determine the number to be used in the first step. Since two goes into seven three times, multiply the whole divisor by three.

$$\begin{array}{r} 26 \\ \underline{\times 3} \\ 78 \end{array}$$

Notice that this result is larger than the dividend, which means that three is too large, so a smaller number is necessary. Retry using two.

$$\begin{array}{r} 26 \\ \underline{\times 2} \\ 52 \end{array}$$

Now this number is smaller than the divisor, so write a two above the three.

$$\begin{array}{r} 2 \\ 26\overline{)73} \end{array}$$

The next step is to multiply. That has been done so write fifty-two under the seventy-three.

$$\begin{array}{r} 2 \\ 26\overline{)73} \end{array}$$

Now subtract.

$$\begin{array}{r} 2 \\ 26\overline{)73} \\ \underline{52} \\ 21 \end{array}$$

Since the difference is smaller than the divisor, two is the right number for the divide step. Since there is not a number to bring down, twenty-one is the remainder.

$$\begin{array}{r} 2 \text{ R. } 21 \\ 26\overline{)73} \\ \underline{52} \\ 21 \end{array}$$

The problem is complete.

It must be noted that the remainder can never be larger than the divisor.

Sometimes a zero will be in the quotient (answer to a division problem). This will happen after the bring down step results in a number that is smaller than the divisor. When this happens place a zero in the quotient and bring down the next number.

Example:

$$3\overline{)625}$$

The first step is to divide. Since three is less than six, three will go into six at least once. Three goes into six twice so write two above the six.

$$\begin{array}{r} 2 \\ 3\overline{)625} \end{array}$$

The next step is to multiply. Multiply three and two to get a product of six. Write the six below the six and draw a line under the six.

$$\begin{array}{r} 2 \\ 3\overline{)625} \\ \underline{6} \end{array}$$

Subtract to get a zero.

$$\begin{array}{r} 2 \\ 3\overline{)625} \\ \underline{6} \\ 0 \end{array}$$

Now bring down the two.

$$\begin{array}{r} 2 \\ 3\overline{)625} \\ \underline{6} \\ 02 \end{array}$$

The first set of four steps is complete, so start the next first step, which is to divide. Since two is less than three the division step cannot take place at this time. To continue, place a zero above the two.

$$\begin{array}{r} 20 \\ 3\overline{)625} \\ \underline{6} \\ 02 \end{array}$$

Instead of multiplying the three by zero and writing the zero under the two and subtracting to get two, just bring down the five.

```
    20
 3 )625
    6
    025
```

Start the process again with the first step. Three will go into twenty-five, eight times. Write an eight above the five.

```
    208
 3 )625
    6
    025
```

Multiply the three and the eight to get a product of twenty-four.

```
    208
 3 )625
    6
    025
     24
```

Subtract to get a difference of one.

```
    208
 3 )625
    6
    025
     24
      1
```

Since no other number can be brought down the problem is complete.

```
    208 R. 1
 3 )625
    6
    025
     24
      1
```

Now here is an example of a problem with a two digit divisor and a zero in the quotient.

```
25 ⟌7642
```

The first step is to divide. Twenty-five will not go into seven, but will go into seventy-six. (An easy way to work when twenty-five is a divisor is to think in terms of quarters.) Twenty-five will go into seventy-six three times. (Three quarters), so write a three above the six.

```
     3
25 ⟌7642
```

The next step is to multiply. The product of twenty-five and three is seventy-five. Write a seventy-five beneath the seventy-six and then draw a line under the seventy-five.

```
     3
25 ⟌7642
    75
    --
```

Now subtract to get a difference of one.

```
     3
25 ⟌7642
    75
    --
     1
```

Next bring down the four to make fourteen.

```
     3
25 ⟌7642
    75
    --
     14
```

The first set of four steps is complete. Begin the second set of four steps by dividing. Since fourteen is less than twenty-five that step cannot be done. Write a zero above the four.

```
     30
25 ⟌7642
    75
    --
     14
```

Now bring down the two to make one-hundred forty-two.

```
     30
25 ⟌7642
    75
    --
     142
```

Now divide twenty-five into one-hundred forty-two. Cover up the five in twenty-five and the two in the one-hundred forty-two. Now the question is how many times does two go into fourteen. The answer is seven, so try seven by multiplying twenty-five by seven off to the side.

```
 25
 x 7
175
```

Since one-hundred seventy-five is greater than one-hundred forty-two, it is necessary to try a number less than seven. Try the next lowest number is six.

```
          25       25
_____     x 6      x 7
         150      175
```

One-hundred fifty is still greater than one-hundred forty-two, so once again multiply by a smaller number, which will be five.

```
 25    25    25
 x 5   x 6   x 7
125   150   175
```

Now it looks like five is the number, so write five above the two.

```
     305
25)7642
    75
     142
```

The next step is to multiply, which was already done, so write one-hundred twenty-five below the one-hundred forty-two, and then draw a line under the one-hundred twenty-five.

```
     305
25)7642
    75
     142
     125
```

Subtract to get a difference of seventeen.

```
     305
 25)7642
    75
     142
     125
      17
```

Since there are no more numbers to bring down, the problem is complete with a remainder of seventeen.

```
    305 R. 17
 25)7642
    75
     142
     125
      17
```

Note: Instead of multiplying the child could have guessed that five quarters would work in the final division step. The multiplication was shown as a way to solve the problem if the number used to divide is not obvious to the child.

Go to themathworksheetsite.com and create a worksheet with two divisors, alternate between one, two, and three digits in the quotient. This will create a worksheet containing twelve to four problems depending on the number of digits selected to be in the quotient. The goal is to complete the problems correctly in fifteen minutes to achieve mastery.

Once the child has achieved mastery in long division, it will be necessary to explain word problems involving division. If such a word problem that requires division has a remainder, the correct answer will depend on the nature of the problem. The following two word problems will be solved exactly the same way, but will have different correct answers based on the nature of the problem. Sometimes a simple picture can be drawn to solve the problem.

Example word problem number one:

A length of ribbon is fifty-five inches long. How many strips of ribbon that are a foot in length can be cut from the ribbon?

Example word problem number two:

Fifty-five people are scheduled to go on a field trip. They will travel in small buses that hold a maximum of twelve passengers each. How many buses are necessary?

Both problems will be solved by the following division problem:

```
12)55
```

Notice in the first problem that the child needs to know that there are twelve inches in a foot. The solved problem will look like this:

```
     4  R. 7
12)55
   48
   --
    7
```

The key to answering problem correctly is to properly interpret what to do with the remainder. It is also to understand what the problem is asking.

The first problem asks, "How many ribbons that are a foot in length can be cut from this ribbon?"

To answer the question, draw a simple picture on a piece of paper.

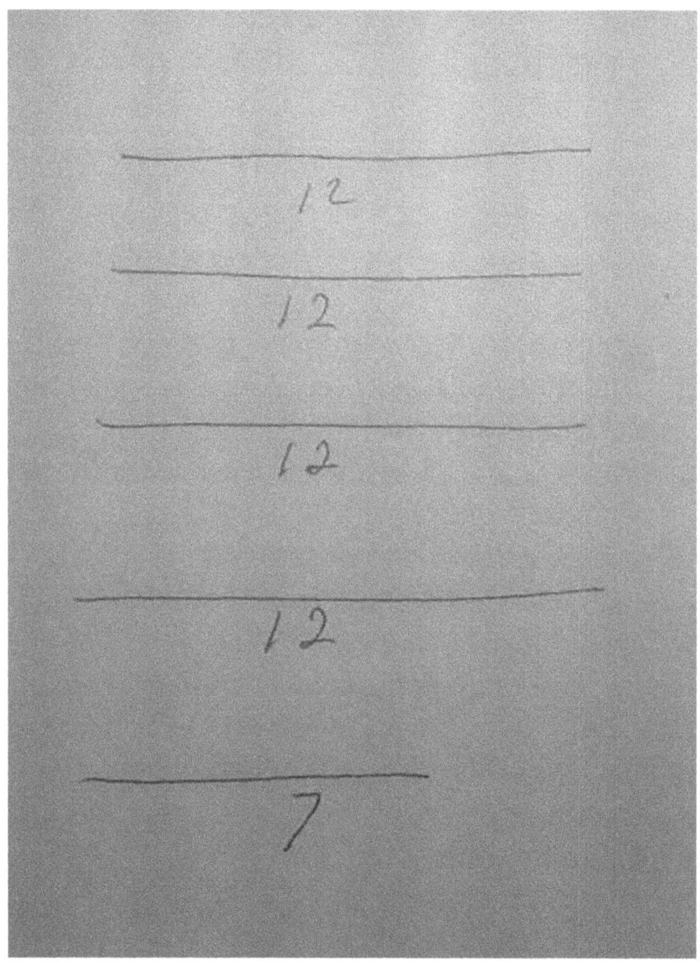

The picture shows the correct answer is four. The remainder in this case will be the seven inches of ribbon that is left over once the four pieces of ribbon that are a foot in length are cut.

The second problem asks, "How many busses are necessary?"

To answer this question, draw a picture on a piece of paper.

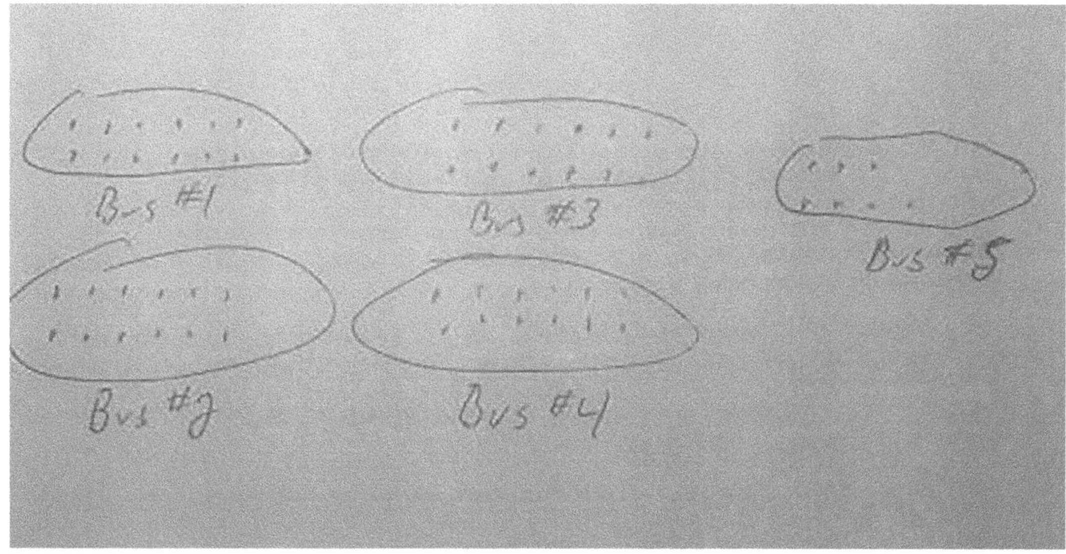

The picture shows the correct answer is five. The remainder in this case will be seven extra people that will not fit into the full buses so another bus is needed.

Notice that the drawings are very simple. The child should be to draw pictures to solve these types of problems. This requires critical thinking on the part of the child. This critical thinking can be developed and improved through practice.

By having strong mastery of the four basic computational skills, (addition, subtraction, multiplication, and division), the child will be extremely well prepared to take on and master advanced mathematical concepts. The child should be confident going forward in mathematical studies and find math to be something that is fascinating instead of something that is frustrating.

TEACHING ORDER OF OPERATIONS

A very important concept to teach the child after the child achieves mastery over the four basic operations, which are addition, subtraction, multiplication and division, is the concept of order of operations. This is where a series of operations must be completed in a proper order.

At this point the idea of exponents will be excluded. Exponents and their role in the order of operations will be addressed at a later time.

The first consideration for order of operations is grouping symbols. Grouping symbols will either be parenthesis, brackets, or braces.

Parenthesis will look like this:

( )

Brackets will look like this:

[ ]

Braces will look like this:

{ }

Example:

Solve: 10 x (4 + 3)

To solve it is necessary to work the operation inside the parenthesis. Since 4 + 3 = 7, rewrite the problem as:

10 x 7

Now this is a simple problem that the child should be able to complete. Since 10 x 7 = 70, the answer is seventy.

It is best to explain to the child to work down. For the rest of the discussion on order of operations, the operation to be done in a certain step will be shown in red.

10 x (4 + 3)
10 x (4 + 3)
10 x 7
70

Example:

8 x (6 - 4)

To solve:

$$8 \times (6 - 4)$$
$$8 \times 2$$
$$16$$

Notice that the operation in the parenthesis is done first. Once that is complete then the next step is a simple multiplication problem.

Once the operation in the grouping symbols is completed, multiplication and division is done next and finally addition and subtraction. It is important to stress that multiplication is not done before division; the two operations have the same priority. Likewise addition is not done before subtraction. The order that the operations of the same priority are completed is determined by their place in the problem.

Example:

$$6 \times 3 \div 2$$

In this case the multiplication is done before the division because it comes before division in the problem. Or it can be stated that since the multiplication symbol is to the left of the division symbol the multiplication operation is done first.

$$6 \times 3 \div 2$$
$$6 \times 3 \div 2$$
$$18 \div 2$$
$$9$$

If the operation signs were switched the problem would look like this:

$$6 \div 3 \times 2$$

In this case the division is done first because the division symbol is to the left of the multiplication symbol.

$$6 \div 3 \times 2$$
$$2 \times 2$$
$$4$$

The same goes for addition and subtraction. For example look at the following problem:

$$10 - 4 + 3$$

In this case the subtraction operation is done first because the subtraction symbol is to the left of the addition symbol. The problem will be solved as follows:

$$10 - 4 + 3$$
$$6 + 3$$
$$9$$

Now switch the operation symbols and the problem will look like this:

$$10 + 4 - 3$$

To solve:

$$10 + 4 - 3$$
$$14 - 3$$
$$11$$

Look at this problem:

$$4 + 3 \times 2$$

In this case the multiplication operation will be done first even though the addition symbol is to the left of the multiplication symbol.

$$4 + 3 \times 2$$
$$4 + 6$$
$$10$$

Look at this problem with four numbers:

$$3 \times 4 + 6 \div 2$$

In this case there are three operations, multiplication, addition and division. The multiplication and division operations will be completed before the addition operation. What determines the first operation to be completed between multiplication and division is to order of the symbols in the problem. Since the multiplication symbol comes before the division symbol the multiplication operation will be completed before the division operation.

$$3 \times 4 + 6 \div 2$$
$$12 + 6 \div 2$$
$$12 + 3$$
$$15$$

Here is another problem:

$$6 - 10 \div 5 + 3$$

Again there are three operational signs, subtraction, division, and addition. The division operation will be done first, followed by the subtraction operation and finally the addition operation.

$$6 - 10 \div 5 + 3$$
$$6 - 2 + 3$$
$$4 + 3$$
$$7$$

Look at this problem that contains a set of parenthesis:

$$(6 + 5) - 4 \times 2$$

In this problem the operation in the parenthesis is completed first. Once this is completed the multiplication operation will be completed and finally the subtraction operation.

$$(6 + 5) - 4 \times 2$$
$$11 - 4 \times 2$$
$$11 - 8$$
$$3$$

Now here is a more complex problem with brackets and parenthesis:

$$5 \times [4 + (8 + 3 \times 2) \div 7]$$

While at first glance this problem looks difficult, it is actually fairly easy once the child understands how order of operations work. The problem inside the parenthesis will be solved first. The result of that will be fourteen.

$$8 + 3 \times 2$$
$$8 + 6$$
$$14$$

Look at it in the context of the whole problem.

$$5 \times [4 + (8 + 3 \times 2) \div 7]$$
$$5 \times [4 + (8 + 6) \div 7]$$
$$5 \times [4 + 14 \div 7]$$

Now the problem in the brackets can be solved. Since there are two operations, addition and division, the division operation must be completed first.

$$5 \times [4 + 14 \div 7]$$
$$5 \times [4 + 2]$$
$$5 \times 6$$
$$30$$

Once the problem in the brackets is complete, the brackets are removed, and work on the problem continues until completion.

Practice a few problems once a week on the back of an envelope to maintain and improve the child's skills in order of operations. Be sure that any operation involving division will not result in a remainder.

Proper understanding of order of operations is very important in high school mathematics. Order of operations will be revisited once the child learns about exponents.

TEACHING AREA AND PERIMETER

The concept of area and perimeter uses addition and multiplication. They are two different measurements that children sometimes confuse. To begin teaching these concepts use just squares and rectangles. Later the perimeter and area of triangles will be discussed.

Perimeter is a linear distance around the outside of a figure. In squares and rectangles it will be the total of the length of the four sides.

Example:

What is the perimeter of the rectangle shown below?

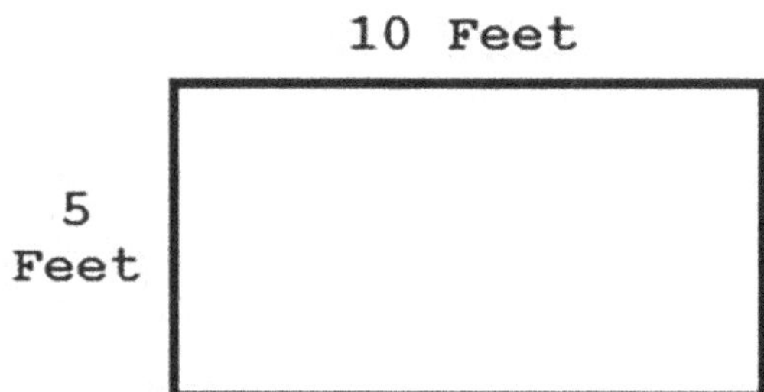

Solution:

Since the opposite sides of a rectangle are the same length, so the lengths of the four sides are: five feet, ten feet, five feet, and ten feet. Thus in order to solve, add the four numbers.

$$5 + 10 + 5 + 10$$

The answer is thirty feet.

$$5 + 10 + 5 + 10 = 30$$

Anytime the child answers a perimeter question the answer usually has a unit measure. In the previous example the unit was feet, so the answer is not expressed as thirty, but thirty feet. Other units used could be inches, yards, miles or metric measures such as centimeters, meters, or kilometers.

In perimeter problems that involve a square, usually only the length of one side is given. The child is expected to know that each side of a square has the same length.

Example:

What is the perimeter of the square shown below?

Solution:

Since one side of the square is seven yards in length, then all four sides of the square are seven yards in length. In order to figure out the perimeter the child can either add seven four times or multiply seven by four.

$$7 + 7 + 7 + 7$$
$$7 \times 4$$

The answer is twenty-eight yards.

$$7 + 7 + 7 + 7 = 28$$
$$7 \times 4 = 28$$

Occasional practice by drawing either a square or rectangle on the back of an envelope and assigning numbers to the side to indicate their length will help the child maintain and improve this skill. Remember for a square just give the length of one side and for a rectangle give the length of one of the long sides and one of the short sides. It should not take the child longer than a minute to do a problem.

Area is a two dimensional measurement that is expressed in square units, such as square inches, square feet, square yards or square miles. One way to explain the concept of square feet to the child is to use vinyl record albums because they are very close to a square foot.

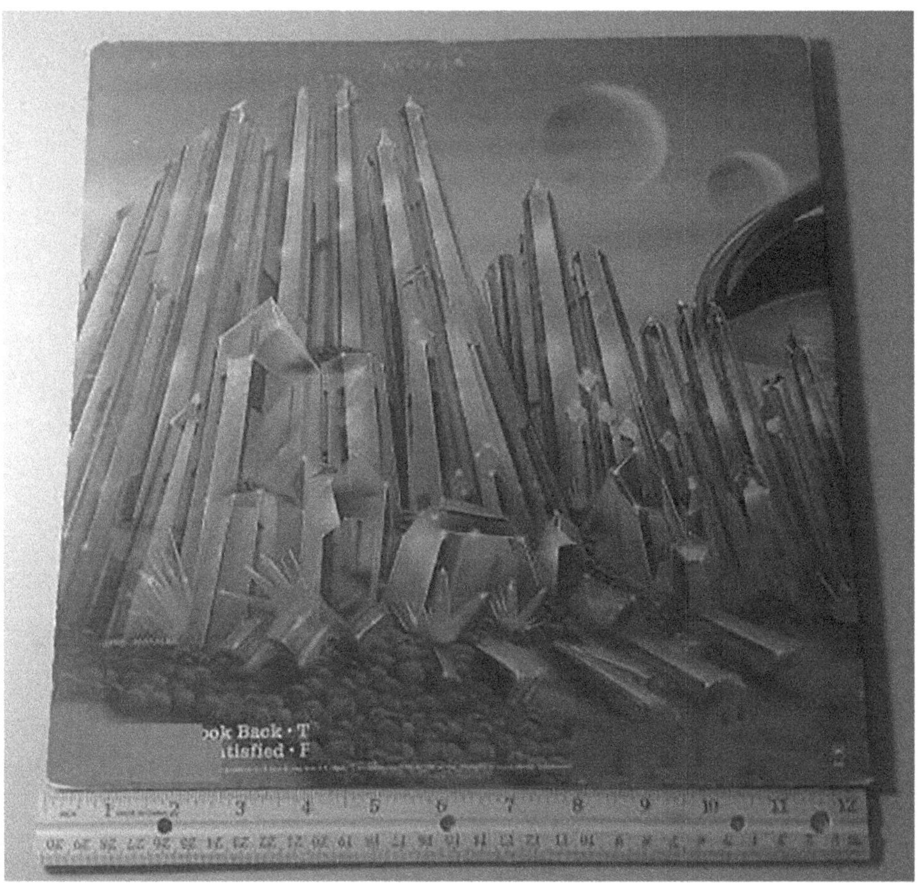

Explain to the child that since the sides of the album cover is one foot the area of the album cover is one square foot. Next place two albums down and explain to the child that the area of this rectangle is two square feet.

The child can count the two album covers to determine that the area is two square feet. Next arrange four album covers to make a large square.

Have the child count the four albums. The area of the large square is four square feet. Next arrange six albums in two rows of three.

Count the album covers so that the child knows that the area of the rectangle is six square feet. Next ask the child to guess the area of a room. Once the child gives an answer, explain that it is not easy to place album covers all over the floor and count them to determine the area of a room.

Go back to the six album covers and show that the area can be found by taking the length of one side, which will be three feet, and multiplying it by the other side, which will be two feet, to get an area of six square feet. Thus the area of any rectangle can be determined by multiplying the length and the width.

Example:

What is the area of the rectangle shown below?

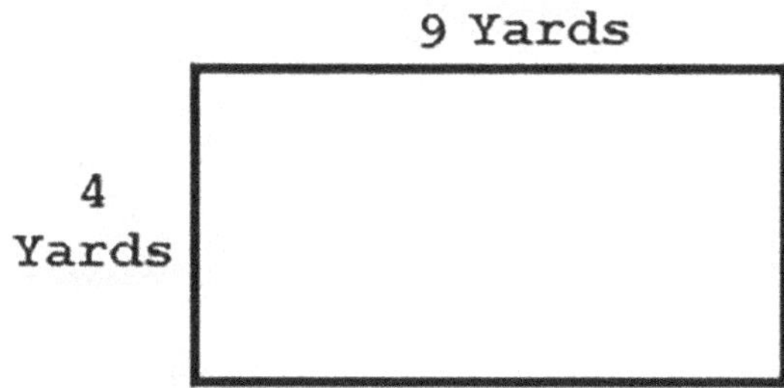

Since the length is nine yards and the width is four yards, the area will be the product of these two numbers.

$$9 \times 4 = 36$$

The answer is thirty-six square yards.

Example:

What is the area of the square shown below?

Solution:

Since all sides of a square are the same length, the area of this square will be eight multiplied by eight, which is sixty-four square inches.

$$8 \times 8 = 64$$

Sometimes the length and width of a rectangle will be expressed in different units. When this is the case, one side must be converted to the units of the other.

Example:

What is the area of the rectangle shown below?

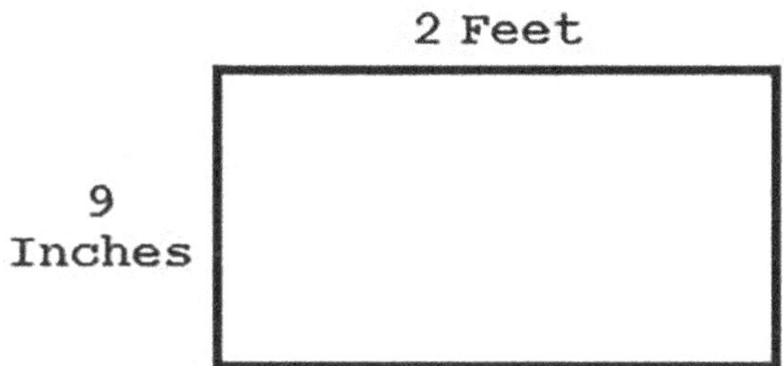

Solution:

In this case one side is expressed in inches and the other side is expressed in feet. In order to solve this problem either the inches must be converted to feet or the feet converted to inches. The problem is best solved by converting the feet to inches. Since each foot has twelve inches, the side that is two feet in length will be converted to inches by multiplying twelve and two to get a length of twenty-four inches.

12 x 2 = 24

So now the problem looks like this:

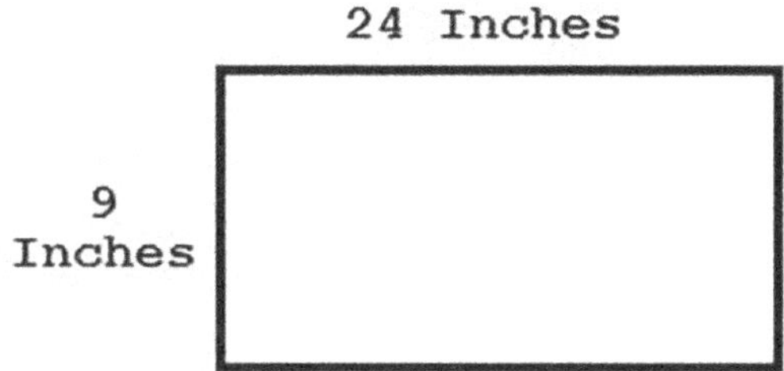

Now that both sides are expressed in the same unit of measurement (inches), the problem can be solved by multiplying nine and twenty-four.

$$\begin{array}{r} 24 \\ \underline{\times\ 9} \\ 216 \end{array}$$

Thus the answer is two-hundred sixteen square inches.

Now the child should understand and be able to determine perimeter and area as it pertains to rectangles and squares. Occasionally include these concepts with the child's daily practice. Now it is time to teach perimeter and area of triangles.

To figure out the perimeter of a triangle should be very easy for the child. All that is necessary is to add the lengths of the three sides.

Example:

What is the perimeter of the triangle below?

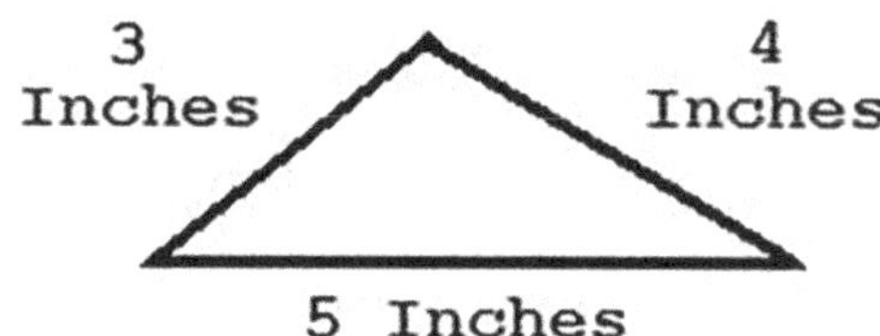

Solution:
When the three sides are added the sum is twelve, so the answer is twelve inches.

$$3 + 4 + 5 = 12$$

To teach the child how to calculate the area of a triangle, start with a rectangle that measures five by ten. In this case use feet for the unit of measurement. (Any unit can be used. Feet are used in this example.)

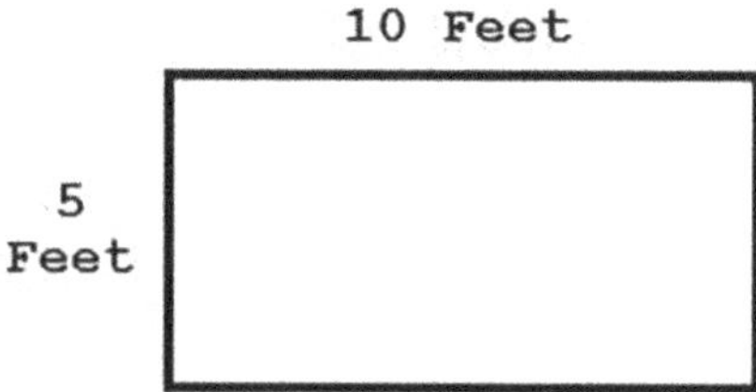

Ask the child, "What is the area of the rectangle?" and the child should answer, "Fifty square feet." Now draw a diagonal like this:

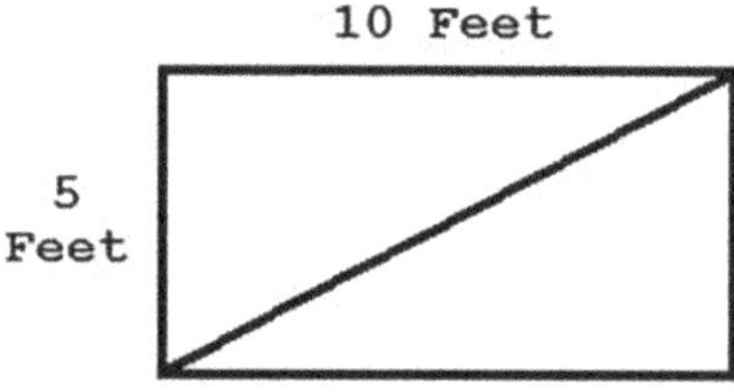

Now erase two of the sides to make a triangle.

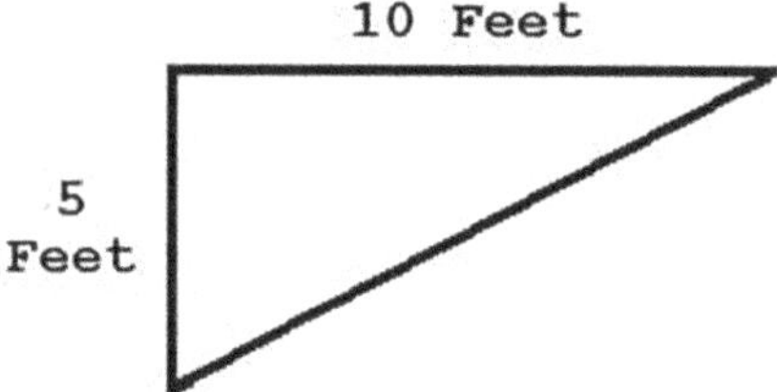

Since the area of a triangle is half of a rectangle, it is necessary to divide the area of a rectangle by two. Fifty divided by two is twenty-five. Therefore the area of the triangle is twenty-five square feet. So explain to the child that in order to find the area of a triangle multiply the length of the base by the height to get a product and then divide that product by two.

It is extremely important to explain to the child that the base and height are not always two sides of a triangle. The base and height will meet at right angles. This will be shown by a little square when the two sides meet.

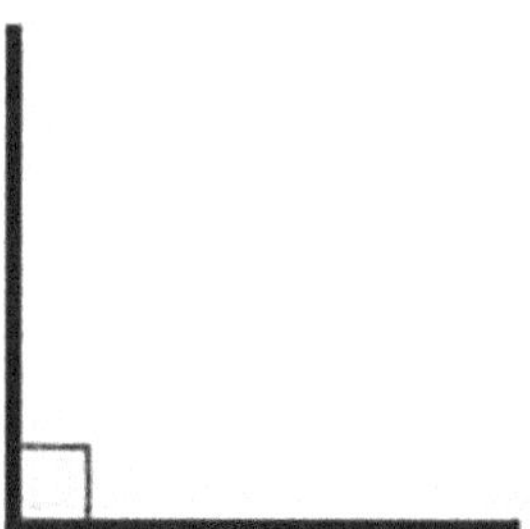

Example:

What is the area of the triangle shown below?

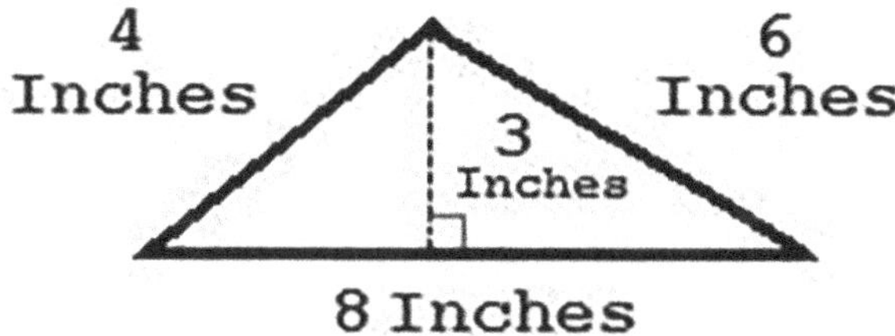

Solution:

The base of the triangle is eight inches. The other two sides are four inches and six inches in length; and those two sides will not be used to calculate the area of this triangle. The height is taken from a line that begins at the corner opposite the base and ends at a right angle that intersects with the base, which in this case has a length, or height, of three, so to calculate the area, multiply eight and three to get a product of twenty-four and divide the twenty-four by two to get a quotient of twelve.

$$8 \times 3 = 24$$
$$24 \div 2 = 12$$

Therefore the answer is twelve square inches.

Perimeter and area are rather simple concepts once they are explained and understood by the child. Remember that to calculate perimeter, addition is required; and to calculate area, multiplication is required (plus an extra division step in regards to triangles).

TEACHING FACTORS AND MULTIPLES

The next subject to teach the child is the concept of factors and multiples. These concepts will later be used to teach fractions and other advanced concepts. The terms factors and multiples are used in similar situations, but they are different and can be confused by the child if these concepts are not properly taught. However, once mastered, these concepts will help the child with more advanced mathematical concepts.

To begin teaching these concepts, use the number ten. Multiples of ten are easily taught, since it is a simple matter of counting by ten.

Write the multiples of ten on a piece of paper like this:

10
20
30
40
50
60
70
80
90
100

Have the child count by ten and explain that these numbers are multiples of ten. Then write down in front of the numbers the factors of ten that make the numbers on the list.

10 x 1 = 10
10 x 2 = 20
10 x 3 = 30
10 x 4 = 40
10 x 5 = 50
10 x 6 = 60
10 x 7 = 70
10 x 8 = 80
10 x 9 = 90
10 x 10 = 100

Once this is explained have the child write down the first six multiples of the following numbers: two, three, five, and eight. It should look like this:

2	3	5	8
4	6	10	16
6	9	15	24
8	12	20	32
10	15	25	40
12	18	30	48

It should not take the child more than a day for the child to understand what a multiple of a number is. Once this is fully understood and mastered, it will be time to teach the child the concept of factors.

To help understand the concepts of factors, show the child this basic equation:

Factor x Factor = Product

Therefore, in order to understand what the factors of ten are, it is necessary to show how ten becomes a product of two numbers. In case of ten, the two equations are as follows:

$$1 \times 10 = 10$$
$$2 \times 5 = 10$$

For now exclude the negative numbers. This will be learned by the child at a later time.

It is not feasible to try and list the equations for a specific number, such as was done with ten shown above. A different approach is needed.

Fortunately an easier way is available. Begin with one and the number (in this case ten), and list them apart on the paper. Then increase by one on the left side until the first number on the right is reached. This sounds confusing, but once an example is shown, it will be easy to understand and use.

Example:

What are the factors of ten?

Solution:

To solve, write ten in the middle of the paper.

10

Now write a one on the far left of the next line.

10
1

The child knows that when one is multiplied by a number will equal that number, so one multiplied by ten will equal ten. Write ten on the far right of the line that contains the one.

10

1 10

Now work toward the middle. The next number after one is two. Ask if two is a factor of ten. The answer is yes, so write two next to the one.

10

1, 2 10

Since two has to be multiplied by five to get a product of ten, write a five in front of the ten.

10

1, 2 5, 10

The next number after two is three. Since three is not a factor of ten, do not write it down. The next number after three is four. Since four is not a factor of ten, do not write it down. The next number after four is five. Since five is one the other side (the right), that means that all the whole number factors of ten are listed.

10

1, 2 5, 10

Therefore, the factors of ten are one, two, five and ten. Notice that one will always be a factor of any whole number, and the number itself will be a factor. These two numbers will be placed on the opposite ends when trying to determine the factors of a particular number. Once this is done, go to the next number (two) and work toward the middle. Once the first number on the right is reached the exercise is complete and all of the whole number factors of that number will be listed.

Example:

What are the factors of twenty-four?

Solution:

Set up the problem by writing a twenty-four in the middle of the paper. On the next line write a one and a twenty-four on opposite side like this:

24

1 24

Work toward the middle. The next number after one is two. Since two will go into twenty-four twelve times, write a two after the one on the left and a twelve in front of the twenty-four on the right side.

24

1, 2 12, 24

The next number after two is three. Three goes into twenty-four eight times. Write a three after the two on the left and an eight in front of the twelve on the right.

24

1, 2, 3 8, 12, 24

The next number after three is four. Four goes into twenty-four six times. Write a four after the three on the left and a six in front of the eight on the right.

24

1, 2, 3, 4 6, 8, 12, 24

The next number after four is five. Five does not go into twenty-four evenly so it is not written down. Since five is not written down, go on to the next number, which is six. Six is on the right side, so the problem is complete. The eight numbers on the line are the factors of twenty-four.

Answer:

The factors of twenty-four are: 1, 2, 3, 4, 6, 8, 12 and 24.

We see this as follows:

1 x 24 = 24	3 x 8 = 24
2 x 12 = 24	4 x 6 = 24

This method is easy to use. Mastery of this exercise will allow the child to progress on to advanced mathematical concepts with confidence.

Example:

What are the factors of thirty-six?

Solution:

Once again set up the problem.

36

1 36

The next number after one is two. Two goes into thirty-six eighteen times. Work toward the middle by writing the two numbers in the appropriate places.

36

1, 2 18, 36

The next number after two is three. Three goes into thirty-six twelve times. Write the three and the twelve.

36

1, 2, 3   12, 18, 36

The next number after three is four. Four goes into thirty-six nine times. Write the four and the nine.

36

1, 2, 3, 4   9, 12, 18, 36

The next number after four is five. Five does not go into thirty-six evenly, so it is skipped for the next number. After five is six and six goes into thirty-six six times. Since it is the same number, write the six in the middle.

36

1, 2, 3, 4,   6,   9, 12, 18, 36

In the case of a perfect square (6 x 6 = 36), the number that is multiplied by itself; in this case six, will be the last factor.

Answer:

The factors of thirty-six are: 1, 2, 3, 4, 6, 9, 12, 18 and 36.

Example:

What are the factors of fifteen?

Solution:

Set up the problem.

15

1   15

The number after one is two. Two will not go into fifteen evenly so it is skipped and the next number is tried, which is three. Three will go into fifteen five times. Write the three and the five.

15

1, 3   5, 15

The next number after three is four. Four will not go into fifteen evenly. In fact no even number will go into an odd number evenly, so if two will not go into a certain number, then all even numbers after two will be skipped. The number after four is five. Since five is on the right, this exercise is complete.

Answer:

The factors of fifteen are: 1, 3, 5 and 15.

Example:

What are the factors of seven?

Solution:

Set up the problem.

7

1 7

The number after one is two. Two does not go into seven evenly, so it will be skipped and the next number will be tried, which is three. Three will not go into seven, so it will be skipped and the next number tried, which is four. Four will not go into seven evenly, and neither will five or six. After six is seven and seven is on the right so this exercise is complete.

Answer:

The factors of seven are 1 and 7.

Any number that has only one and itself as factors is a prime number. This will be discussed later in the book.

Revisit the difference between multiples and factors with the last two examples. The first six multiples of seven and fifteen are as follows:

7	15
14	30
21	45
28	60
35	75
42	90

The factors of seven and fifteen are as follows:

7	15
1	5
	3
	1

When it comes to multiples the number in question will always be the smallest multiple. For instance in these two examples, seven is the smallest multiple of seven and fifteen is the smallest multiple of fifteen. There is also no fixed number of multiples. In each case just the first six multiples are listed. The list of multiples does not actually end.

For factors each number is its greatest factor. In these two examples, seven is the greatest factor of seven and fifteen is the greatest factor of fifteen. There are also a fixed number of whole number factors for each number. The number seven has only two whole number factors while fifteen has only four whole number factors.

TEACHING DIVISIBILITY RULES

One of the most interesting and fascinating aspects of mathematics are the various divisibility rules for single digit whole numbers. Knowledge of these rules will not only give the child a quick way to determine if a number is divisible by another number, but hopefully instill in the child a sense of curiosity and wonderment about mathematics. Also the child's confidence in the ability to learn and apply mathematics will increase. Some of these shortcuts for single digit whole numbers and ten will be very easy, while others will be a bit more challenging for the child. However, all of these rules are capable of being understood and mastered by children during their late elementary years. Some of the more challenging rules will be learned last by the child, so that confidence in learning these concepts is maintained and increased.

Begin with the number two. Since the child should have the concept of even and odd numbers mastered, the child should quickly master the divisibility rule of two.

Divisibility rule of two:

A number is divisible by 2 if the one's digit of that number is 0, 2, 4, 6, or 8.

Example:

Which of the following numbers are divisible by two?

3,619

4,278

25,796

Solution:

All that is necessary is for the one's digit to be a 0, 2, 4, 6, or 8.

3,619

The one's digit is a nine so the number is not divisible by two.

4,278

The one's digit is an eight so the number is divisible by two.

25,796

The one's digit is a six so the number is divisible by two.

In summary:

Number	One's Digit	Divisible by 2?
3,619	9	No
4,278	8	Yes
25,796	6	Yes

It does not matter how large a number is, all that is necessary is to look at the one's digit in order to determine if that number is divisible by two.

Next teach the child the divisibility rule of five. This is very similar to the rule of two as only the one's digit needs to be considered.

Divisibility rule of five:

A number is divisible by 5 if the one's digit is a 0 or 5.

Example:

Which of the following numbers are divisible by five?

356

740

855

922

Solution:

All that is necessary is for the one's digit to be a 0 or 5.

356

The one's digit is a six so the number is not divisible by five.

740

The one's digit is a zero so the number is divisible by five.

855

The one's digit is a five so the number is divisible by five.

922

The one's digit is a two so the number is not divisible by five.

Review:

Number	One's Digit	Divisible by 5?
356	6	No
740	0	Yes
855	5	Yes
922	2	No

As with the number two, for the number five just a quick look at the one's digit is necessary to determine divisibility.

The next divisibility rule to learn is the divisibility rule of three. This rule will take a little bit of work on the part of the child to determine if a number is divisible by three.

Divisibility rule of three:

The sum of the digits of the number must be divisible by 3.

To help explain this take the first three multiples of three, which are 3, 6 and 9 and understand that most two digit multiples of three will have the two digits add up to either of these three numbers. The next multiple of three is 12. The digits of 12 are 1 and 2. The sum of 1 and 2 is 3. Since three is a multiple of three, thus twelve is a multiple of three.

Examples:

Which of the following numbers are divisible by three?

643

644

645

Solution:

Take each number and add the digits.

643

6 + 4 + 3 = 13

Since thirteen is not a multiple of three that means that 643 is not divisible by three.

644

6 + 4 + 4 = 14

Since fourteen is not a multiple of three that means that 644 is not divisible by three.

645

6 + 4 + 5 = 15

Since fifteen is a multiple of three that means that 645 is divisible by three.

Review:

Number	Sum of Digits	Multiple of 3?	Divisible by 3?
643	13	No	No
644	14	No	No
645	15	Yes	Yes

The stronger the child's addition skills are the easier it will be for the child to quickly determine if a number is divisible by three. That is why daily practice on these skills is important.

The next divisibility rule for the child to learn is the divisibility rule for the number six. This rule is easy to understand and learn because the child has previously learned the prerequisite to this rule.

Divisibility rule of six:

The number must satisfy the divisibility rules for both 2 and 3.

Thus a number must have a one's digit of 0, 2, 4, 6, or 8; and the sum of the digits must be a multiple of 3.

Example:

Which of the following are divisible by six?

456

741

862

822

Solution:

First check the one's digit. The one's digit in this case is 6, so it satisfies the divisibility rule for 2. Next add the digits to get a sum of 15 (4 + 5 + 6 = 15). Since 15 is a multiple of 3, the number 456 is divisible by 3. The number 456 thus satisfies the rules of divisibility of both 2 and 3, so it is divisible by 6.

For the next number 741, check the one's digit. Since the one's digit is 1, that means that the number is not divisible by 2. Now once it is determined that a number is not divisible by 2, it is certain that the number is not divisible by 6, thus 741 is not divisible by 6.

For 862 check the one's digit, which is 2. This satisfies the conditions for the rule of divisibility for 2. Now add the digits to get a sum of 16 (8 + 6 + 2 = 16). Since 16 is not a multiple of 3, the number 862 is not divisibility by 6.

For 822, check the one's digit, which is 2. This satisfies the condition for being divisible by 2. Now add the digits to get a sum of 12 (8 + 2 + 2 = 12). Since 12 is a multiple of 3, that satisfies the divisibility rule of 3. The number 822 satisfies both the divisibility rules of 2 and 3; it is therefore divisible by 6.

Review:

Number	Divisible by 2?	Divisible by 3?	Divisible by 6?
456	Yes	Yes	Yes
741	No	?	No
862	Yes	No	No
822	Yes	Yes	Yes

Notice on the number 741, it was unnecessary to add the digits because it was not divisible by 2. If a number is not divisible by 2, then it will not be divisible by 6.

The next divisibility rule for the child to learn is the divisibility rule for the number nine. This rule is similar to the divisibility rule for three.

Divisibility rule for nine:

The sum of the digits must be divisible by 9.

The child should have learned that for the first ten multiples of nine the sum of the two digits are always nine.

9 x 1 = 9	9 = 9
9 x 2 = 18	1 + 8 = 9
9 x 3 = 27	2 + 7 = 9
9 x 4 = 36	3 + 6 = 9
9 x 5 = 45	4 + 5 = 9
9 x 6 = 54	5 + 4 = 9
9 x 7 = 63	6 + 3 = 9
9 x 8 = 72	7 + 2 = 9
9 x 9 = 81	8 + 1 = 9
9 x 10 = 90	9 + 0 = 9

When nine is multiplied by eleven, the product is ninety-nine.

9 x 11 = 99 9 + 9 = 18

Eighteen is not nine, but eighteen is a multiple of nine. Thus it can be explained to the child that the divisibility rule for nine is very similar to the divisibility rule for three.

Example:

Which of the following numbers are divisible by nine?

528

792

426
864
Solution:
Add the digits of the numbers.

$$5 + 2 + 8 = 15$$
$$7 + 9 + 2 = 18$$
$$4 + 2 + 6 = 12$$
$$8 + 6 + 4 = 18$$

Since 18 is a multiple of 9 and 12 and 15 are not multiples of 9; 792 and 864 are divisible by 9, while 528 and 426 are not divisible by 9.

Once again if the child has strong math skills that have been improved through daily practice, the child can quickly and easily determine if a number is divisible by nine.

The next divisibility rule for the child to learn is the divisibility rule of four. While the rule is easy to remember, the method for determining if a particular number is divisible by four will take some critical thinking on the part of the child. It is important to remember that in order for a number to be divisible by four it must also be divisible by two.

Divisibility rule of four:

The last two digits of a number must be divisible by 4.

To help explain to the divisibility rule of four, show the child these four multiplication facts:

$$4 \times 25 = 100$$
$$4 \times 50 = 200$$
$$4 \times 75 = 300$$
$$4 \times 100 = 400$$

Explain that every number that is divisible by one-hundred is divisible by four. It is as if the two digit part of the number resets in respect to multiples of four. For instance:

$$4 \times 26 = 104$$
$$4 \times 51 = 204$$
$$4 \times 76 = 304$$
$$4 \times 101 = 404$$

As the child can see the last digit is four and is a multiple of four. The next set of two digit numbers will be eight, twelve, and then sixteen. With this explanation the child should now understand why the last two digits of a number determine whether that number is divisible by four.

Also explain that every other even number will be divisible by four. The method used to quickly determine whether an even number is divisible by four will be determined by whether the ten's digit is even or odd.

If the ten's digit is even and the one's digit is 0, 4 or 8, then the number is divisible by 4. Some examples of this are: 8, 24, 40 and 64. Notice that the ten's digit is even in these cases. (For the number 8, the ten's digit is assumed to be 0, which is an even number.)

If the ten's digit is odd and the one's digit is either a 2 or a 6, then the number is divisible by 4. Some examples of this are the numbers: 16, 32, 56 and 72. Notice that the ten's digit is odd in these cases.

Example:

Which of the following numbers are divisible by four?

1,284
24,345
54,226
578,692

Solution:

For the number 1,284 the key is the last two digits or 84. The first check is the one's digit, which is 4. It is even so then the ten's digit is checked. The ten's digit is even. Therefore in order for the number to be divisible by 4, the one's digit must be a 0, 4 or 8. Since the one's digit is a 4, this satisfies the rule of divisibility by 4, so the number 1,284 is divisible by 4.

For the number 24,345 a quick check determines that it is not divisible by 2 because the one's digit is 5. Since it is not divisible by 2, it cannot be divisible by 4.

For the number 54,226 the key is the last two digits or 26. The one's digit is divisible by 2, so look at the ten's digit, which is even. In order to be divisible by 4, the one's digit must be a 0, 4 or 8. Since the one's digit is 6, the number is not divisible by 4.

For the number 578,692 the last two digits are 92. The number is even and the ten's digit is odd. In order to be divisible by 4, the one's digit must be either a 2 or 6. Since the one's digit is 2, the number 578,692 is divisible by 4.

Review:

Ten's Digit	One's Digit
Even	0, 4 or 8
Odd	2 or 6

Number	Last two Digits	Divisible by 4?
1,784	84	Yes
24,345	45	No
54,226	26	No
578,692	92	Yes

To apply this rule requires critical thinking on the part of the child. With practice the child should become proficient in using this rule and thus gaining increased confidence in mathematical ability.

The next divisibility rule for the child to learn is the divisibility rule for eight. This rule has similar characteristics to the divisibility rule for four. It is easy to memorize the rule, but challenging to use. The child will need to do more critical thinking in order to determine if a number is divisible by eight than any of the previously discussed single digit divisibility rules. Explain to the child that in order to be divisible by eight a number must be divisible by two and four. Thus a child can eliminate any odd number from being divisible by eight.

Divisibility rule of eight:

The last three digits must be divisible by 8.

A simple explanation that was used for teaching the divisibility rule for four can be used for teaching the divisibility rule for eight.

8 x 125 = 1,000	8 x 126 = 1,008
8 x 250 = 2,000	8 x 251 = 2,008
8 x 375 = 3,000	8 x 376 = 3,008
8 x 500 = 4,000	8 x 501 = 4,008

In order to be able to determine if a large number is divisible by eight, the child must have single digit multiplication by eight totally mastered. In addition the child needs these multiplication facts mastered:

8 x 11 = 88 8 x 12 =96

Now when the hundreds digit is even and the final two digits are a multiple of eight, then the whole number is divisible by eight. Thus the following numbers are divisible by eight.

256 – Hundred's digit even (2), 56 (multiple of eight)
432 – Hundred's digit even (4), 32 (multiple of eight)

When the hundred's digit is odd, the last two digits must be a multiple of four, but not a multiple of eight. The following numbers are divisible by eight:

104 – Hundred's digit odd (1), 4 (multiple of four, but not a multiple of eight)

328 – Hundred's digit odd (3), 28 (multiple of four, but not a multiple of eight)

To determine if a number is divisible by eight, have the child go through the following checklist:

Is the number even?

If the answer is no, then the number is not divisible by eight. If the answer is yes, continue to the next question of the checklist.

Are the last two digits divisible by four?

If the answer is no, then the number is not divisible by eight. If the answer is yes continue to the next question of the checklist.

Is the hundreds digit even or odd?

If the hundreds digit is even, then the number will be divisible by eight if the last two digits are divisible by eight. If the hundreds digit is odd, then the number will be divisible by eight if the last two digits are not divisible by eight.

Example:

Which of the following numbers are divisible by 8?

1,284

1,384

Solution:

To solve the first problem check to see if the number is odd or even. Since it is even (4), then check to see if the last two digits are divisible by 4. 84 is divisible by 4, continue and check the hundred's digit. The hundred's digit is even (2), so the last two digits must be divisible by 8. Since 84 is not divisible by 8, the number 1,284 is not divisible by 8.

To solve the second problem check to see if the number is odd or even. Since it is even (4), then check to see if the last two digits are divisible by 4. 84 is divisible by 4, continue and check the hundred's digit. The hundred's digit is odd (3), so the last two digits must not be divisible by 8. Since 84 is not divisible by 8, 1,384 is divisible by 8.

Review:

Number:	1,284	1,384
Even?	Yes	Yes
Last two digits divisible by 4?	Yes	Yes
Hundred's Digit:	Even	Odd
Last two digits divisible by 8?	No	No
Number divisible by 8?	No	Yes

While the child can quickly determine whether a number is divisible by two, and this ability will be necessary when the child starts to work with fractions. Practice in determining whether or not a number is divisible by eight is an excellent way for the child to develop and improve critical thinking skills.

Seven is the final single digit for the child to learn. It is often necessary for the child to understand the concept of negative numbers in order to use the divisibility rule of seven because it will sometimes require subtracting a larger number from a smaller number. The rule itself is confusing, but once a few examples are shown to the child it can be understood.

Division rule for seven:

The difference of the digits besides the one's digit and the one's digit doubled must be divisible by seven.

While this seems confusing, it only takes three steps to implement.

Remove the one's digit from the number.

Then double the one's digit.

Finally subtract the doubled one's digit from the rest of the number.

For instance 7 x 13 = 91 and to see how this rule works, explain it with the number 91.

First remove the one's digit (1) from the number.

Second, double the one's digit to get 2.

Finally, subtract the doubled number (2) from the rest of the number (9).

$$\begin{array}{r} 9 \\ \underline{-2} \\ 7 \end{array}$$

Since seven is a multiple of seven, the number ninety-one is divisible by seven.

Example:

Is the number 371 divisible by 7?

Solution:

Take the one's digit, which is 1, and double it to get 2. Next subtract the 2 from the rest of the number to get a difference of 35. Since 35 is a multiple of 7, the number 371 is divisible by 7.

The divisibility rule for seven is one of the most fascinating aspects of mathematics. Not very many people know or understand this most unusual divisibility rule.

Before moving on to other concepts, one last division needs to be discussed. This rule is extremely easy to remember and use. This is the divisibility rule of ten.

Divisibility rule of ten:

The number must have a one's digit of 0.

For practice go to themathworksheetsite.com and choose Long Division. Then choose "1" for "Number of Digits in Divisor" and "2" for "Number of Digits in Quotient." Select "Mixed" and Include an Answer Key.

This will produce a worksheet of nine problems. Instead of having the child solve the problems, have the child determine if the dividend is divisible by the divisor.

Example:

$$6\overline{)570}$$

The child is to determine if the dividend (570) is divisible by the divisor (6).

Solution:

Since 570 is divisible by 2 and 3 (5 + 7 + 0 = 12), then the number 570 is divisible by 6.

This exercise should not take longer than a few minutes to complete. Armed with the knowledge of these divisibility rules and how to use them, the child's skills and ability in mathematics will increase along with the child's confidence.

TEACHING PRIME AND COMPOSITE NUMBERS

It is very important for the child to understand prime and composite numbers. This knowledge will strengthen the child's mathematical skills and will help the child master future mathematical concepts.

The definition of a prime number is any number that has only itself and one as factors. A composite number is a number that has more than itself and one as a factor. The first six prime numbers are: 2, 3, 5, 7, 11 and 13. The number 1 is considered to be neither prime nor composite.

When the child learned how to determine the factors of a certain number, an example of seven was used and the factors of seven were one and seven. The same exercise can be used for any number.

During late elementary school a child needs to be able to determine if a certain number that is less than one-hundred is prime or composite. Being able to quickly do this will be helpful when the child learns about fractions and decimals. The tool to do this will be the divisibility rules that the child previously mastered.

Begin with the first prime number, which is two. If any number is divisible by two, then that number is not a prime number. Thus a child can quickly see that two is the only even prime number. Any other even number is a composite number.

The second prime number is three. The child knows that three times three is nine so nine is a composite number. Any two digit number that the sum of the digits is a multiple of three is divisible by three and not a prime number.

The next number after three is four. Since four is an even number and divisible by two, it is not a prime number. Four is a composite number.

The next number after four is five. Five is a prime number because it has only one and itself as factors. Also it can be determined to be a prime number because it is not divisible by any prime number of lesser value (two or three). Any number that has a five in its one digit is divisible by five and thus not a prime number.

After five is six. Six is an even number so it is a composite number.

After six is seven. Seven is a prime number because it only has one and itself as factors. Also it is not divisible by any prime number of lesser value. Multiples of seven are not prime numbers. The first six multiples of seven are as follows:

7 x 1 = 7
7 x 2 = 14
7 x 3 = 21

7 x 4 = 28
7 x 5 = 35
7 x 6 = 42

Each of these numbers (besides the 7) can be determined to be composite by checking the divisibility rules of the previous three prime numbers (two, three and five).

14 – even
21 – sum of digits multiple of 3 (2 + 1 = 3)28–even
35 – one's digit a 5
42 – even

The next multiple of seven is forty-nine (7 x 7), which must be memorized by the child as a composite number.

To quickly continue with the next five numbers:

8 – even
9 – divisible by 3
10 – even
11 – not divisible by 2, 3, 5, or 7 – prime number

Eleven is a prime number because it is not divisible by any previous prime number. It is not even, so it is not divisible by two. Its digits add up to two, so it is not divisible by three. Its one's digit is a one, s it is not divisible by five. It is also not divisible by seven.

At this point the child has all the knowledge necessary to determine if a certain number less than one-hundred is prime or composite. However, show the child the following multiples of seven:

7 x 11 = 77
7 x 13 = 91

So seven has three multiples, (49, 77, and 91) that do not fall under the rules of divisibility for two, three and five that will determine if a number is prime or composite.

Here is a quick checklist to determine if a number is prime or composite. If a number satisfies any of these then it is a composite number. If it satisfies none of these then it is a prime number. Remember, this is only for numbers less than one-hundred.

1. Even (One's digit a 0, 2, 4, 6, or 8)
2. One's digit a five
3. The sum of the two digits is a multiple of three
4. The number is 49, 77, or 91

   Example:

   Which of the following numbers are prime numbers?

29, 57, 64, 83, 91

Solution:

For the first number, 29, it is determined to be odd, so it is not divisible by 2. Its one's digit is a 9, so it is not divisible by 5. The sum of the digits (2 + 9 = 11) is 11, so it is not divisible by 3. It is not 49, 77 or 91, so it is not divisible by 7. 29 is a prime number.

For the second number, 57, it is determined to be odd, so it is not divisible by 2. Its one's digit is 7, so it is not divisible by 5. The sum of its digits (5 + 7 = 12) is 12, so it is divisible by 3. 57 is not a prime number; it is a composite number.

For the third number, 64, it is determined to be even, and thus divisible by 2. 64 is not a prime number; it is a composite number.

For the forth number, 83, it is determined to be odd, so it is not divisible by 2. Its one's digit is 3, so it is not divisible by 5. The sum of its digits (8 + 3 = 11) is 11, so it is not divisible by 3. It is not 49, 77, or 91, so it is not divisible by 7. 83 is a prime number.

The last number, 91, is determined to be odd, so it is not divisible by 2. Its one's digit is 1, so it is not divisible by 5. The sum of its digits (9 + 1 = 10) is 10, so it is not divisible by 3. It is one of the three numbers (49, 77, or 91). 91 is divisible by 7, so it is not a prime number; it is a composite number.

To incorporate the recognition of prime numbers into the child's daily practice, once again use a deck of playing cards. Separate the cards into two decks, one of black cards and one of red cards. Remove the face cards and the tens. Use the black cards as the ten's digit and the red cards as the one's digit. When the cards are turned over, the child should quickly determine if the number is a prime number.

Example:

If a black eight and a red three are turned over, consider that an eighty-three. Eighty-three is a prime number.

The understanding and recognizing prime numbers is a key skill for a late elementary school student to master. The knowledge of prime numbers will be used in more advance topics of mathematics.

TEACHING PRIME FACTORIZATION

Prime factorization is the process of determining the prime factors of a composite number. The use of factor trees is a common method of prime factorization. Use the first few prime numbers (2, 3, 5, 7 and 11) and the divisibility rules to break down a number to its prime factors. A child can always rely on this method, but can also use the multiplication facts previously learned as well. When using factor trees, continue until a prime number is reached and circle the prime number.

Example:

What is the prime factorization of 24?

First Solution:

First write a twenty-four in the middle of the paper.

24

Now go through the prime numbers. The first prime number is two. Check to see if twenty-four is divisible by two. Since the one's digit is four, twenty-four is divisible by two. Two will go into twenty-four twelve times. Make the tree with two and twelve as shown below and circle the two because it is a prime number.

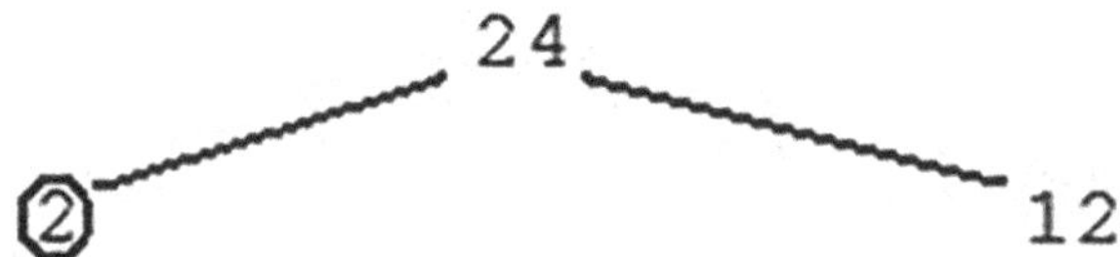

Since twelve is not a prime number, check to see if it is divisible by two. The one's digit is two, so it is divisible by two and two will go into twelve six times. From the twelve make a tree with a two and a six. Circle the two because it is a prime number.

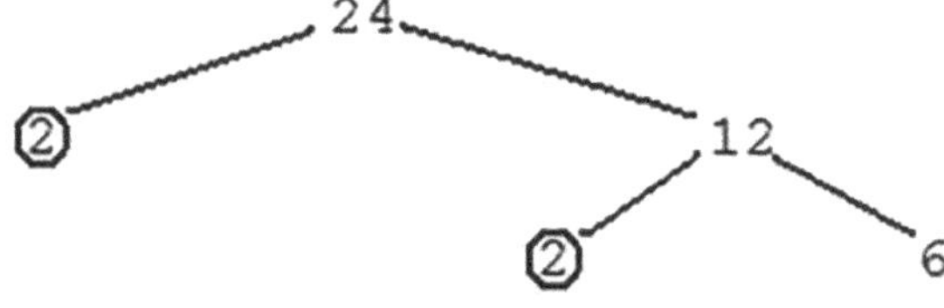

Six is not a prime number and two will go into six three times. Make a tree with the two and three. Circle both numbers because they are both prime numbers.

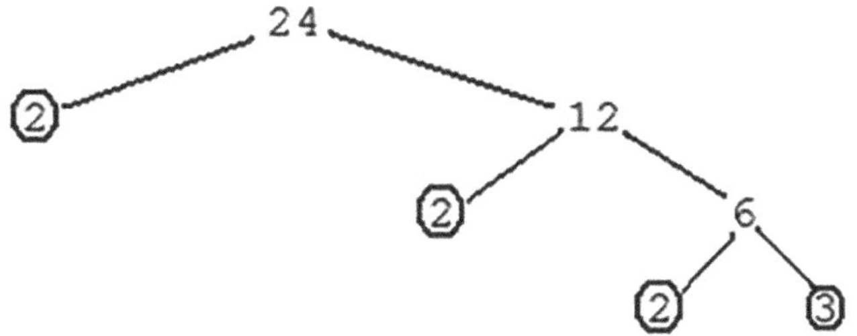

Since all of the numbers at the ends are circled and thus prime numbers, the factorization part of the problem is complete. Next list the prime numbers.

2, 2, 2, 3

Thus the prime factorization of 24 is:

24 = 2 x 2 x 2 x 3

Second Solution:
Once again start by writing a twenty-four in the center of the paper.

24

Now suppose the child recognizes that 4 x 6 = 24, and then uses those two factors as the legs of the tree.

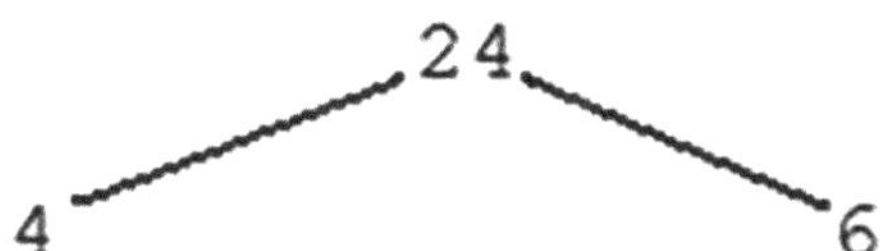

Since both numbers are not prime numbers, they have to be factored. Four will be factored with two times two, while six will be factored with two times three. Continue the tree and circle all the prime numbers.

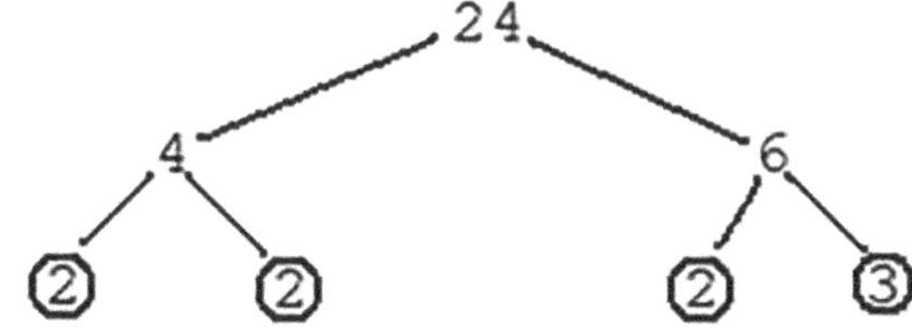

Since all of the numbers at the end are circled, the factorization part of the problem is complete.
Thus the prime factorization of 24 is:

24 = 2 x 2 x 2 x 3

Notice that both ways give the same answer. Neither way is incorrect. The second way is quicker but the first way can be used if the child cannot see two factors that can be used.

Example:

What is the prime factorization of 36?

First Solution:

36

Divide by 2:

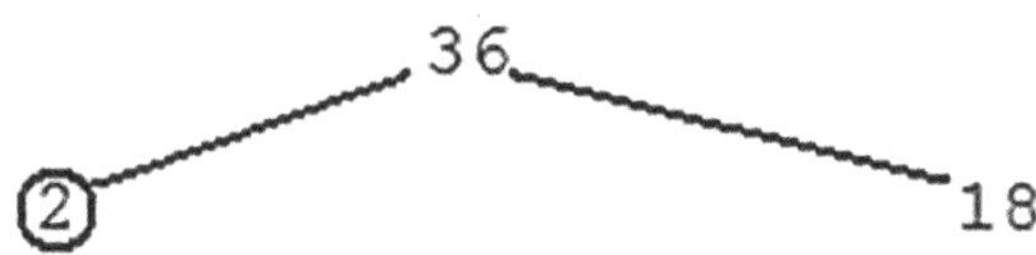

Divide by 2:

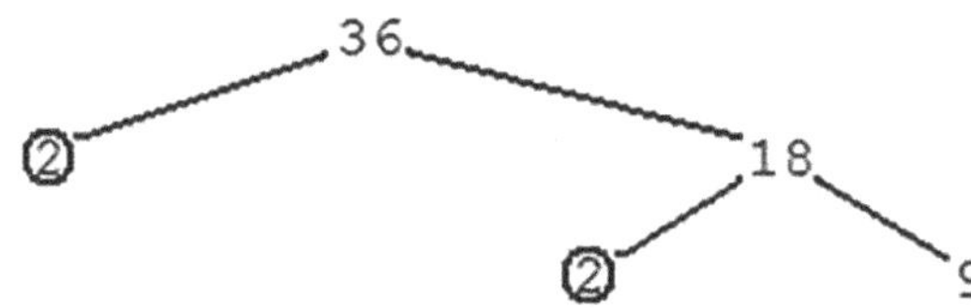

Divide by 3:

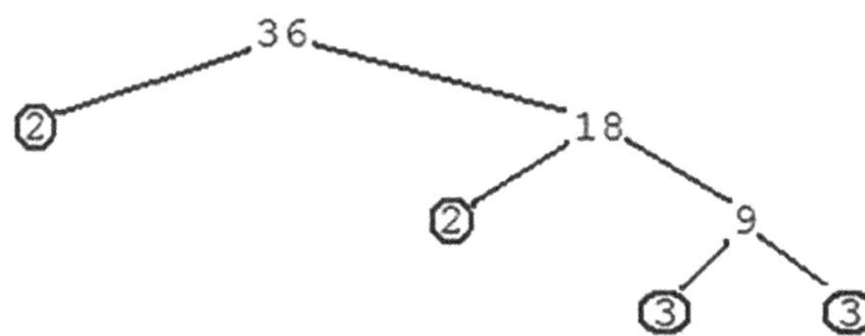

The prime factorization of 36 is:

36 = 2 x 2 x 3 x 3

Second Solution:

36

Recognize and use 6 x 6

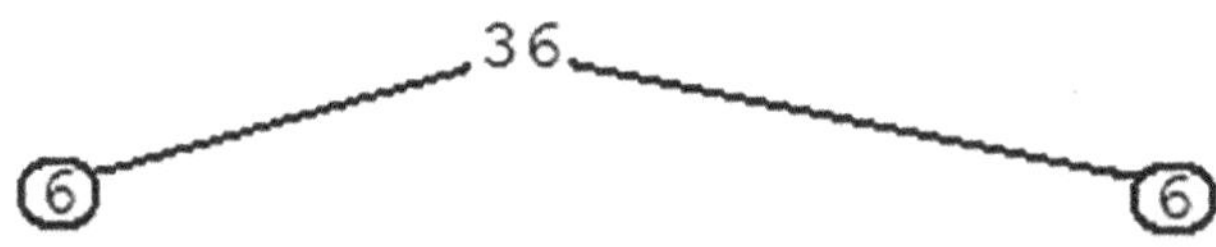

Use 2 x 3 for both numbers

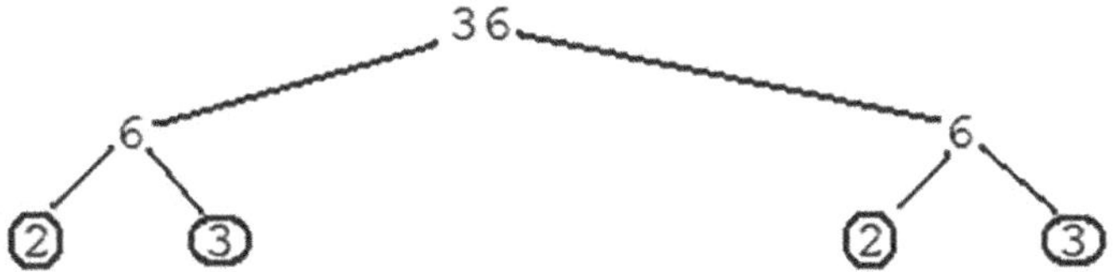

The prime factorization for 36 is:

36 = 2 x 2 x 3 x 3

Once again both ways results in the same answer.

Example:

What is the prime factorization of 480?

Once again start by writing the number in the middle of the paper.

480

Anytime a number has zero as the one's digit, it is divisible by ten. In this case ten will go into the number forty-eight times.

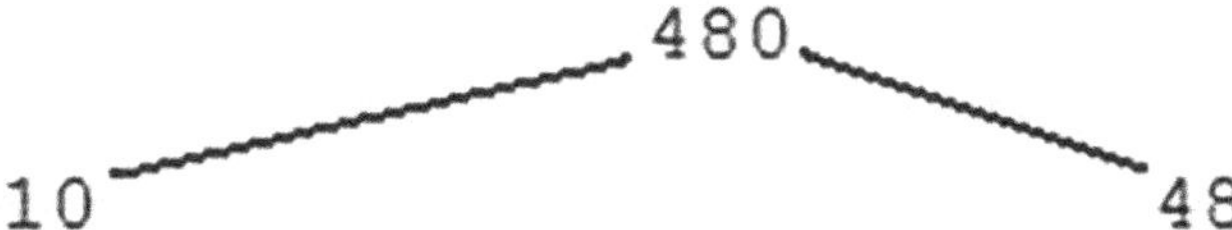

Neither number is a prime number. Ten will be factored with two and five. These are both prime numbers so circle them. Forty-eight can be factored with six and eight neither of which is a prime number.

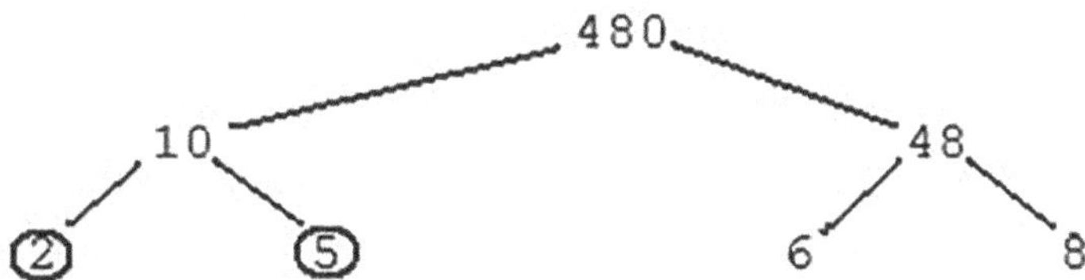

Six can be factored into two and three, while eight can be factored into two and four. Circle the prime numbers.

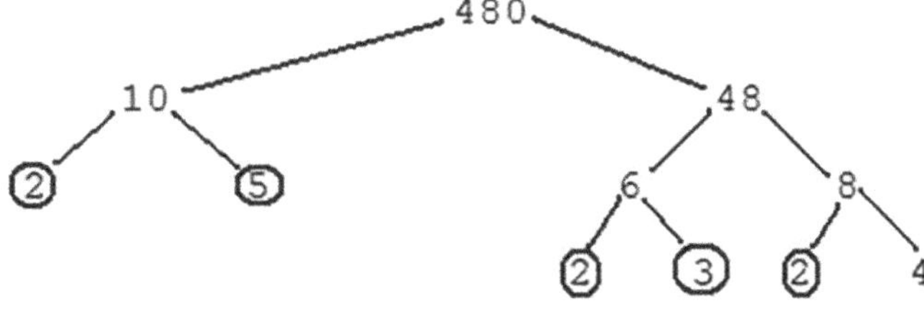

Finally four can be factored with two and two.

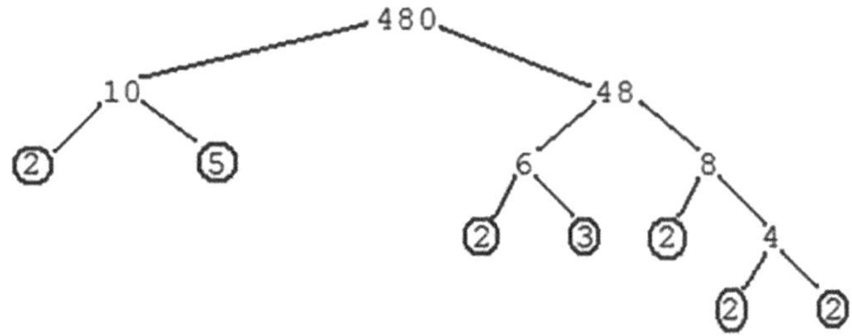

Now all the bottom numbers are circled and thus prime numbers. The prime factorization of 480 is:

$$480 = 2 \text{ x } 2 \text{ x } 2 \text{ x } 2 \text{ x } 2 \text{ x } 3 \text{ x } 5$$

For practice, log on to themathworksheetsite.com and select "Long Division." On the drop down boxes select "1" for "Number of Digits in Divisor" and "2" for "Number of Digits in Quotient." It is important to select "Without Remainders". Hit the "Create It" button and this will create a worksheet of twelve problems. Have the child do prime factorization on the dividend.

Example:

The child sees the problem:

$$4\overline{)140}$$

Have the child do a prime factorization of 140.

With daily practice the child should easily master prime factorization. This will add another skill to help the child to obtain above average proficiency in mathematics.

TEACHING GREATEST COMMON FACTOR

Learning and mastering the concept of greatest common factor will be helpful to the child in both reducing fractions and developing critical thinking skills. The skills of determining factors and prime factorization will be used to determine the greatest common factor between two numbers.

Previously the child learned the factors of 24 and 36.

The factors of 24 are:

1, 2, 3, 4, 6, 8, 12 and 24

The factors of 36 are:

1, 2, 3, 4, 6, 9, 12, 18 and 36

List the factors of both numbers and circle the factors that appear in both lists.

24: 1, 2, 3, 4, 6, 8, 12, 24
36: 1, 2, 3, 4, 6, 9, 12, 18, 36

The common factors of 24 and 36 are:

1, 2, 3, 4, 6 and 12

Since twelve is the largest number it is called the greatest common factor.

There will always be a greatest common factor between two numbers. In many cases the greatest common factor will be one. This will happen if both numbers are prime numbers.

Example:

What is the greatest common factor of 19 and 29?

Solution:

Since both numbers are prime numbers, the factors are as follows:

19: 1, 19
29: 1, 29

If the common factors are circled, only one will be shown to be a common factor. Therefore the greatest common factor of 19 and 29 is 1.

To list all of the factors of two numbers is not always an efficient way of determining the greatest common factor of those two numbers. This is especially true if the numbers are large. However, prime factorization can be used to determine the greatest common factor between two numbers. This is done in three steps.

The first step is to write the prime factors of the two numbers, one above the other.

The second step is to circle the common factors of both numbers.
The third step is to multiply the common prime factors to get the greatest common factor.
Once again look at 24 and 36. The first step is to list the prime factor of both numbers.

24 = 2 x 2 x 2 x 3
36 = 2 x 2 x 3 x 3

The second step is to circle the common prime numbers. In this case there is a pair of twos and a single three.

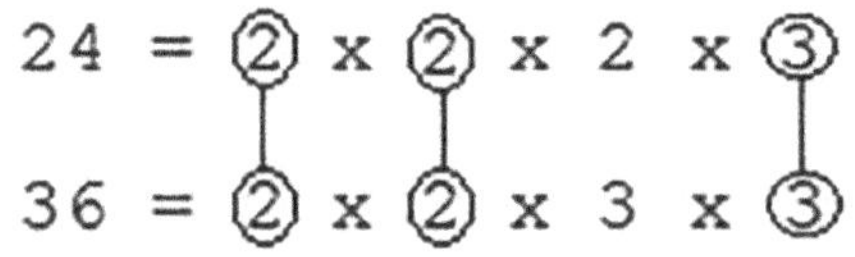

24 = ② x ② x 2 x ③

36 = ② x ② x 3 x ③

The final step is to multiply the circled numbers.

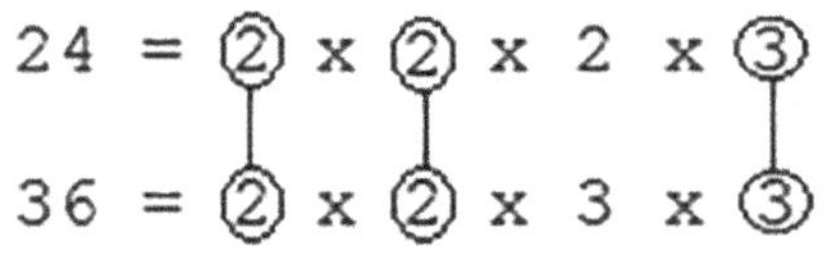

24 = ② x ② x 2 x ③

36 = ② x ② x 3 x ③

GCF = 2 x 2 x 3 = 12

Again the greatest common factor of 24 and 36 is shown to be 12.
Example:
What is the greatest common factor of 45 and 72?
Solution:
List the prime factors of both numbers.

45 = 3 x 3 x 5
72 = 2 x 2 x 2 x 3 x 3

The second step is to circle the common prime numbers, in this case a pair of threes.

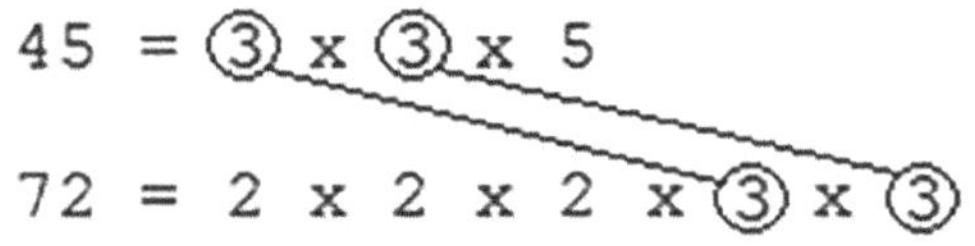

45 = ③ x ③ x 5

72 = 2 x 2 x 2 x ③ x ③

The third step is to multiply the pair of threes to get a product of nine.

3 x 3 = 9

The greatest common factor of 45 and 72 is 9.
Example:

What is the greatest common factor of 14 and 84?
First write the prime factors for both numbers.

14 = 2 x 7
84 = 2 x 2 x 3 x 7

Second circle the common prime factors.

14 = (2) x (7)
84 = (2) x 2 x 3 x (7)

Third multiply the common prime factors.

2 x 7 = 14

Sometimes the smaller number will be the greatest common factor of two numbers. This happens when the larger number is divisible by the smaller number.

Example:

What is the greatest common factor of 6 and 54?

Solution:

In this case the larger number, 54, is divisible by the smaller number, 6. Therefore it is unnecessary to do prime factorization in order to determine the greatest common factor. The greatest common factor of 6 and 54 is 6.

For practice use the list of the following numbers:

12	24	30	40	54
18	25	32	42	60
20	28	36	50	72

Choose any two numbers and have the child determine the greatest common factor. This exercise should take less than a minute for any two numbers in the group. Have the child do one or two of these a night for daily practice until mastery is achieved.

After that, then have the child determine the greatest common factor for two pairs of numbers once a week to maintain proficiency. Themathworksheetsite.com can be used for practice after the child achieves mastery with the above numbers. Choose "Long Division", and then select "1" for both "Number of Digits in Divisor" and "Number of Digits in Quotient". Also select "Mixed" for the remainders. This will create a work sheet with sixteen division problems. Pick any two problems and have the child find the greatest common factor among the dividends.

Example:
For the two following division problems:

$$8\overline{)66} \quad \text{and} \quad 6\overline{)24}$$

Have the child find the greatest common factor of 66 and 24.

Practicing finding the greatest common factor not only helps the child with future math concepts, it also develops critical thinking skills that will be useful in both school and life.

TEACHING LEAST COMMON MULTIPLE

When working with fractions the concept of least common multiple is useful when trying to figure out a common denominator. The least common multiple of two or more numbers is the smallest number that is a common multiple between those numbers.

For instance to find the least common multiple of 6 and 8 list the first several multiples of each number.

6: 6, 12, 18, 24, 30, 36, 42, 48
8: 8, 16, 24, 32, 40, 48, 56, 64

Now circle the common multiples.

6: 6, 12, 18, (24), 30, 36, 42, (48)

8: 8, 16, (24), 32, 40, (48), 56, 64

The common multiples are 24 and 48. However, if the list of multiples is extended, then there are an infinite number of common multiples. What is important is the smallest or least common multiple, which in this case is 24.

As in the case of determining the greatest common factor, prime factorization can be used to determine the least common multiple of two numbers. The steps are similar, but the final step is to multiply all numbers that are not circled.

The first step is to write the prime factors of the two numbers, one on top of the other.

The second step is the circle the common prime factors of both numbers.

The third step is to multiply the circled prime factors.

The forth step is to then multiple the product of the circled prime factors to the prime factors that were not circled.

Once again look at 6 and 8. The first step is to list the prime factors of both numbers.

6 = 2 x 3
8 = 2 x 2 x 2

The second step is to circle the common prime factors. In this case only a single 2 is circled.

$$6 = \textcircled{2} \times 3$$
$$8 = \textcircled{2} \times 2 \times 2$$

The third step is to multiply the circled factors, which will only be the 2.

2

Now multiply the 2 by all of the prime factors that were not circled, which were a 2, a 2 and a 3.

2 x 2 x 2 x 3 = 24

Thus the least common multiple of 6 and 8 is 24.
Example:
What is the least common multiple of 12 and 18?
Solution:
The first step is to list the prime factors of the two numbers.

12 = 2 x 2 x 3
18 = 2 x 3 x 3

The second step is to circle the common prime factors, which are a single two and a single three.

$$12 = \textcircled{2} \times 2 \times \textcircled{3}$$
$$18 = \textcircled{2} \times 3 \times \textcircled{3}$$

The third step is to multiply the circled factors to get a product of six.

2 x 3 = 6

The fourth step is to multiply the six by the factors that were not circled, which was a two in the twelve and a three in the eighteen.

6 x 2 x 3 = 36

Thus the least common multiple of 12 and 18 is 36.
Example:
What is the least common multiple of 4 and 20?
Solution:
First list the prime factors of both numbers.

4 = 2 x 2
20 = 2 x 2 x 5

Second, circle the common prime factors.

$$4 = (2) \times (2)$$
$$20 = (2) \times (2) \times 5$$

Third, multiply the common prime factors to get a product of four.

$$2 \times 2 = 4$$

Fourth, multiply four by the factors that are not circled. For this example there is only a five that a prime factor that is not circled.

$$4 \times 5 = 20.$$

Thus the least common multiple of 4 and 20 is 20.

In the previous example the larger number was the least common multiple of the two numbers. This always happens when the larger number is divisible by the smaller number.

Example:

What is the least common multiple of 5 and 15?

Solution:

In this case the larger number, 15, is divisible by the smaller number, which is 5. Therefore the least common multiple is the larger number, which is 15.

In the case of two prime numbers, the least common multiple is the product of the two numbers.

Example:

What is the least common multiple of 7 and 11?

Solution:

Since both numbers are prime numbers, the least common multiple is the product of those two numbers.

$$7 \times 11 = 77$$

Thus the least common multiple of 7 and 11 is 77.

Also if the larger of the two numbers is a prime number, then the least common multiple is the product of the two numbers.

Example:

What is the least common multiple of 6 and 13?

Solution:

First list the prime factors of six. Since thirteen is a prime number it cannot be factored, so it is just thirteen.

$$6 = 2 \times 3$$
$$13 = 13$$

Since no prime factors are the same, no numbers are circled. So the least common multiple is the product of all the prime factors, or the two numbers.

$$6 \times 13 = 78$$

Thus the least common multiple of 6 and 13 is 78.

For practice take a deck of cards and separate it into two decks; one of black cards and one of red cards. Remove the ace, jack, queen, and king. Flip over a card from both decks and have the child determine the least common multiple of the two numbers. Do about five every day for the child's daily practice. Once the child has this mastered, the addition and subtraction of fractions will be easy for the child because of the strength in math skills developed before learning fractions.

TEACHING FRACTION CONCEPTS

When introducing fractions concepts to the child begin with the concept of one-half. This can be done in different ways. The first is to take a circle and divide it into two equal parts.

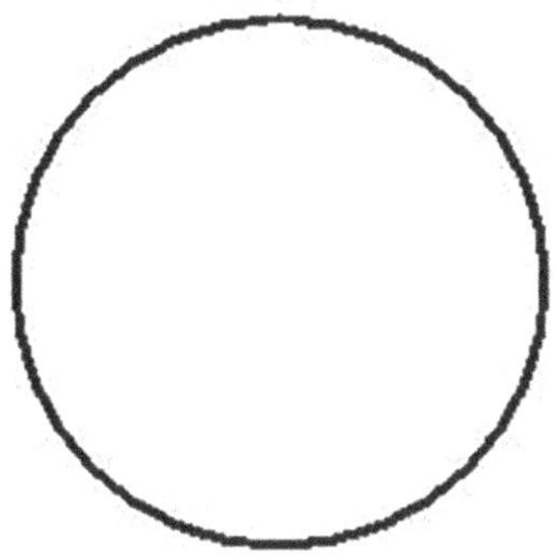

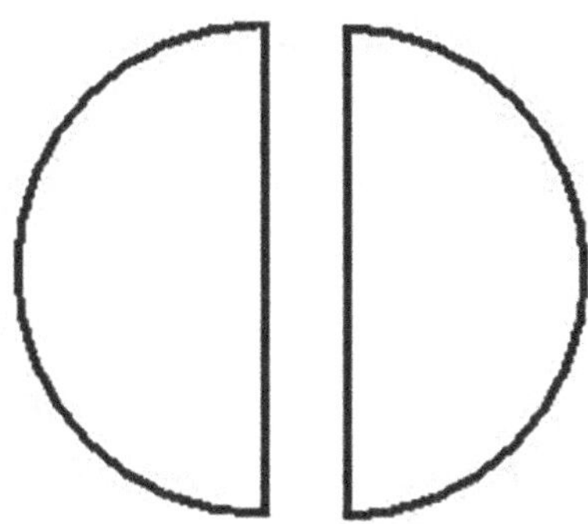

Other items can be a pizza.

A sandwich,

Four quarters, (two quarters make a half dollar)

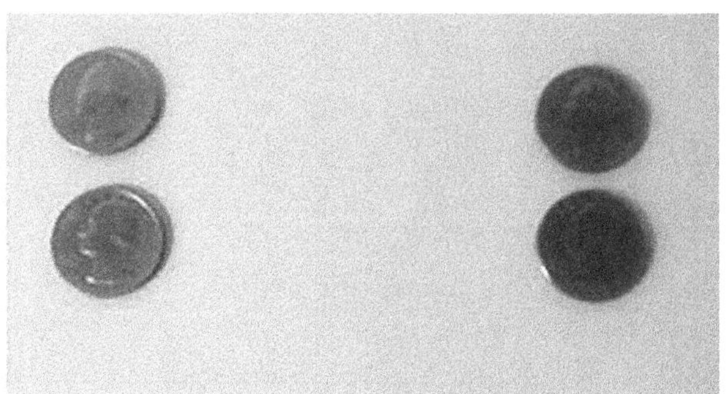

Or a line divided in two equal parts.

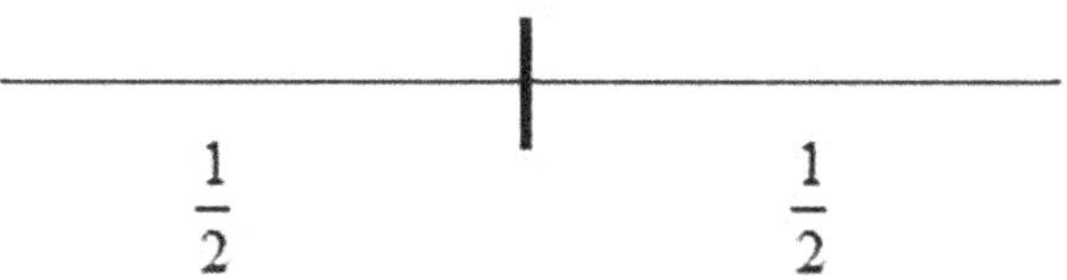

Explain that two halves make a whole.

A fraction is written with one number one top of another. For instance the fraction one-half is written as follows:

$$\frac{1}{2}$$

The top number is, in this case the one, is called the numerator. The bottom number, in this case the two, is called the denominator.

Explain to the child that anytime the numerator and the denominator are the same, the amount will be one.

$$\frac{2}{2} = 1$$

Now explain the concept of fourths. This can be done using four quarters. Explain to the child that since four quarters equals one dollar then one quarter equals one fourth of a dollar. It is written as:

$$\frac{1}{4}$$

Thus three quarters is three-fourths of a dollar.

$$\frac{3}{4}$$

Next explain that since ten dimes make a dollar, so one dime is one tenth of a dollar.

$$\frac{1}{10}$$

Now explain that three dimes equals three tenths of a dollar.

$$\frac{3}{10}$$

Then explain that ten tenths is one whole.

$$\frac{10}{10} = 1$$

For practice take some pennies and ask the child what fraction are heads. For example if seven pennies are displayed on the table and two of them are showing heads, ask the child, "What fraction of the pennies are showing heads?"

The child should answer, "Two-sevenths." Also the child could write down the fraction on a piece of paper.

$$\frac{2}{7}$$

It should not take long for the child to master the concept of fractions after practicing with a different amount of pennies (denominator) that have a different amount showing heads (numerator). Once this concept is mastered, then it is time to teach the child about equivalent fractions.

TEACHING EQUIVALENT FRACTIONS

Equivalent fractions is an important concept for the child to master in order to do operations with fractions. When two fractions represent the same amount but the fractions have different numbers for the numerator and denominator, the fractions are equivalent.

For instance take a circle into two equal parts and shade one of the parts.

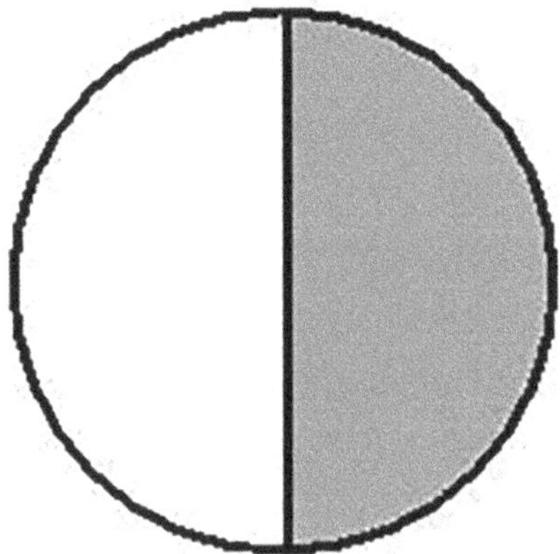

The shaded part is one half of a circle. Now take a circle and divide it into eight equal parts and shade four of the parts.

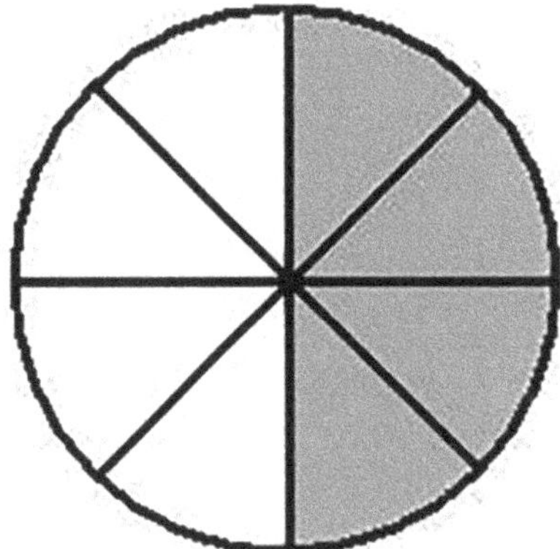

In the first instance one-half of the circle is shaded and in the second instance four-eighths of the circle are shaded. Both fractions represent the same amount of area shaded in the circle, thus the fractions are equivalent.

$$\frac{1}{2} = \frac{4}{8}$$

Now explain to the child that if the numerator and the denominator are multiplied by the same number the result will be an equivalent fraction. For example in the fraction shown above, both the numerator and the denominator are both multiplied by four.

$$\frac{1 \times 4}{2 \times 4} = \frac{4}{8}$$

Conversely if the numerator and the denominator of a fraction are divided by the same number the result is an equivalent fraction.

$$\frac{4 \div 4}{8 \div 4} = \frac{1}{2}$$

Example: Are the fractions below equivalent fractions?

$$\frac{2}{3} \qquad \frac{8}{12}$$

Solution:

First look at the numerator of both fractions, which are two and eight. Since two times four equals eight, this means that the four is the number to be multiplied by the smaller denominator, which is three.

2 x 4 = 8
3 x 4 = ?

Since three times four equals twelve and twelve is in the denominator of the second fraction, the fractions are equivalent.

2 x 4 = 8
3 x 4 = 12

$$\frac{2}{3} = \frac{8}{12}$$

Example: Are the fractions below equivalent fractions?

$$\frac{4}{5} \qquad \frac{12}{16}$$

Solution:

Since four times three equals twelve, the denominator in the first fraction, which is five, will be multiplied by three.

4 x 3 = 12
5 x 3 = ?

Since five times three equals fifteen, and the denominator of the second fraction is sixteen, the fractions are not equivalent fractions.

$$4 \times 3 = 12$$
$$5 \times 3 = 15$$
$$\frac{4}{5} \neq \frac{12}{16}$$

For practice write two fractions on a piece of paper. In order to write equivalent fractions multiply the numerator and denominator by the same number. For instance to have the child practice determining if a fraction is equivalent to two-thirds multiply both the denominator by the same number. In the example use five.

$$\frac{2}{3}$$

Since:

$$2 \times 5 = 10$$
$$3 \times 5 = 15$$

Write down these two fractions:

$$\frac{2}{3} \qquad \frac{10}{15}$$

Ask the child if the two fractions are equivalent fractions. The child should answer, "Yes."

Take the same fraction and multiply the numerator and denominator by six, but then add two to the result of the denominator.

$$2 \times 6 = 12$$
$$3 \times 6 = 18$$
$$18 + 2 = 20$$

So write the following two fractions on a piece of paper:

$$\frac{2}{3} \qquad \frac{12}{20}$$

Ask the child if the two fractions are equivalent fractions. The child should answer, "No."

Practice for a few days and then teach the child how to reduce a fraction to its simplest form.

TEACHING SIMPLEST FORM

Reducing a fraction to its simplest form is a key skill for the child to master. This skill will use previously learned concepts as well as provide a foundation to master more advanced mathematical concepts.

A fraction is in its simplest form when one is the only common factor of the numerator and the denominator. Any fraction that has any other common factor in the numerator and the denominator is a fraction that is not in its simplest form and can be reduced.

For instance examine the fraction:

$$\frac{3}{5}$$

This is a fraction in its simplest form.

The factors of the numerator (3) are 1 and 3.

The factors of the denominator (5) are 1 and 5.

Since 1 is the only common factor of the numerator and the denominator, this fraction is in its simplest form.

Now examine the fraction:

$$\frac{6}{8}$$

This is not a fraction that is in its simplest form.

The factors of the numerator (6) are 1, 2, 3 and 6.

The factors of the denominator (8) are 1, 2, 4 and 8.

Since 1 and 2 are common factors of both the numerator and the denominator, this fraction is not in its simplest form and can be reduced.

There are a few quick ways to determine if a fraction is in its simplest form. If any of these conditions exist then the fraction is in its simplest form and no further calculating is necessary.

1. The fraction has a numerator of one.
2. The denominator of the fraction is a prime number.
3. The numerator of the fraction is one less than the denominator.

4. The numerator is a prime number and the denominator is not a multiple of the numerator.

Some examples of the first type of fractions are as follows:

$\frac{1}{2}$ $\frac{1}{8}$ $\frac{1}{12}$ $\frac{1}{19}$

Some examples of the second type of fraction are as follows:

$\frac{3}{5}$ $\frac{5}{7}$ $\frac{6}{13}$ $\frac{14}{17}$

Some examples of the third type of fraction are as follows:

$\frac{8}{9}$ $\frac{13}{14}$ $\frac{23}{24}$ $\frac{29}{30}$

Some examples of the fourth type of fraction are as follows:

$\frac{3}{8}$ $\frac{5}{16}$ $\frac{7}{20}$ $\frac{11}{25}$

It is also important for the child to recognize when a fraction is not in its simplest form. Use of the previously learned divisibility rules will allow a child to quickly determine is a fraction can be reduced.

If both the numerator and the denominator are even numbers, then the fraction can be reduced by dividing both numbers by two.

An example of such a fraction is:

$$\frac{6}{8}$$

This fraction can be reduced by dividing both the numerator and the denominator by two.

$6 \div 2 = 3$ $8 \div 2 = 4$

$$\frac{3}{4}$$

Since three is one less than four, this fraction is in its simplest form.

If both the numerator and the denominator have digits that produce a sum of three, then both the numerator and denominator can be divided by three.

An example of such a fraction is:

$$\frac{12}{21}$$

The fraction can be reduced by dividing both the numerator and denominator by three.

$12 \div 3 = 4$ $21 \div 3 = 7$

$$\frac{4}{7}$$

Since the denominator is a prime number, this fraction is in its simplest form.

If both the numerator and the denominator end in a five or a zero then both the numerator and the denominator can be divided by five.

An example of such a fraction is:

$$\frac{15}{60}$$

The fraction can be reduced by dividing both the numerator and the denominator by five.

$15 \div 5 = 3$ $60 \div 5 = 12$

$$\frac{3}{12}$$

Since both the numerator and the denominator are divisible by three, the fraction is not in its simplest form. Therefore it is necessary to divide both the numerator and the denominator by three.

$3 \div 3 = 1$ $12 \div 3 = 4$

$$\frac{1}{4}$$

Since the numerator is one, this fraction is now in its simplest form.

Another way to solve the previous example is to divide both the numerator and the denominator by the greatest common factor of both numbers. The greatest common factor of 15 and 60 is 15.

$15 \div 15 = 1$ $60 \div 15 = 4$

This is another way to reduce the fraction to its simplest form. With practice the child can quickly determine the greatest common factor of the numerator and the denominator and then divide those two numbers by the greatest common factor to obtain the simplest form of a fraction.

Example:
What is the simplest form of the following fraction?

$$\frac{18}{81}$$

The greatest common denominator of the numerator and the denominator is nine. Therefore divide both numbers by nine.

$18 \div 9 = 2$ $81 \div 9 = 9$

Thus the fraction in its simplest form is:

$$\frac{2}{9}$$

Remember if the greatest common factor of both the numerator and the denominator is one, then the fraction is in its simplest form. Some examples of these are:

$$\frac{4}{15} \quad \frac{9}{16} \quad \frac{8}{21} \quad \frac{11}{15}$$

In the final example the numerator is a prime number. If the numerator is a prime number the fraction can only be reduced if the denominator is a multiple of the numerator.

For example if the numerator is eleven, then the following fractions can be reduced:

$$\frac{11}{22} \quad \frac{11}{55} \quad \frac{11}{77} \quad \frac{11}{99} \quad \frac{11}{121}$$

These fractions can be reduced because the denominators are all multiples of eleven.

The following fractions cannot be reduced, and therefore are in their simplest form:

$$\frac{11}{19} \quad \frac{11}{35} \quad \frac{11}{48} \quad \frac{11}{65} \quad \frac{11}{72}$$

In these fractions, none of the denominators are the multiple of the numerator, which is a prime number.

For practice, go to themathworksheetsite.com and select "Reduce to Lowest Terms," under the heading "Fractions."

Now select "20" for "Number of Problems"; "1" for "Difficulty"; and "No" for "Improper Fractions."

Have the child practice daily with this worksheet until the child can correctly reduce all of the fractions in less than five minutes. Once this is achieved then select "28" for the number of problems and continue until the child can correctly reduce all of the fractions in less than six minutes. Once this is mastered change the difficulty setting to "2" and repeat with twenty problems. The goal is to get the child to correctly reduce twenty fractions on the difficulty setting of "4" in less than five minutes.

Once mastery is achieved a worksheet can set at difficulty setting "4" and used for practice. Practice once every week or two weeks to maintain proficiency at reducing fractions.

TEACHING LOWEST COMMON DENOMINATOR

When comparing two fractions with different denominators it is necessary to convert both fractions to equivalent fractions with the same denominator. This denominator is called a common denominator. While there will be an infinite number of common denominators it is important to find the lowest common denominator.

The same technique for finding the least common multiple is used to find the lowest common denominator. Once the lowest common denominator is determined, then both fractions will be converted to equivalent fractions with the lowest common denominator.

For example to compare the following fractions:

$$\frac{1}{3} \quad \frac{1}{2}$$

It will be necessary to convert both fractions to have the same denominator. Although there are several common denominators, the lowest common denominator of the two fractions is what is desired.

The least common multiple of two and three is six. Therefore the lowest common denominator is six. For the first fraction the thought process is as follows:

$$\frac{1}{3} = \frac{?}{6}$$

What is three multiplied by in order to get a product of six. The answer is two.

3 x 2 = 6

In order to make an equivalent fraction the numerator must be multiplied by the same number that was multiplied by the denominator.

1 x 2 = 2

Thus:

$$\frac{1}{3} = \frac{2}{6}$$

Now take the next fraction and convert it to a fraction that has a denominator of six.

$$\frac{1}{2} = \frac{?}{6}$$

What is two multiplied in order to get a product of six? The answer is three.

$$2 \times 3 = 6$$

So multiply the numerator by the same number.

$$1 \times 3 = 6$$

Thus:

$$\frac{1}{2} = \frac{3}{6}$$

So the fractions:

$$\frac{1}{3} \quad \frac{1}{2}$$

Are rewritten with the lowest common denominator to get:

$$\frac{2}{6} \quad \frac{3}{6}$$

Thus it is easy to see that one-half is greater than one-third.

Also note that the following fractions that are equivalent to one-third and one-half and have a common denominator.

$$\frac{4}{12} \qquad \frac{6}{12}$$

$$\frac{6}{18} \qquad \frac{9}{18}$$

$$\frac{8}{24} \qquad \frac{12}{24}$$

This list could go on forever, but it is important to find the two fractions with the lowest common denominator.

Review the section on teaching the least common multiple to help with the converting of two fractions to equivalent fractions with the lowest common denominator. Practice by writing a few fractions on a piece of paper and have the child convert them to equivalent fraction with the lowest common denominator. This skill is very important when the child needs to add and subtract fractions.

TEACHING HOW TO CONVERT A MIXED NUMBER TO AN IMPROPER FRACTION

When teaching how to convert a mixed number to an improper fraction, it is important to know what a mixed number is and what an improper fraction is. A mixed number is a whole number and a fraction. An improper fraction is a fraction that has the numerator that is greater than the denominator.

An example of a mixed number is:

$$3\frac{2}{3}$$

An example of an improper fraction is:

$$\frac{11}{3}$$

The process of converting a mixed number to an improper fraction is easy.
First, multiply the denominator by the whole number to get a product.
Second, add this product to the numerator to get a sum.
Third, write this sum as the new numerator.
Finally, write the original denominator as the denominator.
Example:
Convert the following mixed number to an improper fraction:

$$3\frac{2}{3}$$

Solution:
The first step is to multiply the denominator (3) by the whole number (3).

3 x 3 = 9

The second step is to take this product (9) and add it to the numerator (2).

9 + 2 = 11

The third step is to write the sum (11) as the new numerator.

<u>11</u>

The final step is to write the original denominator (3) under the new numerator (11).

$$\frac{11}{3}$$

Thus:

$$3\frac{2}{3} = \frac{11}{3}$$

A quick visual to help the child remember the process is as follows:

Then add

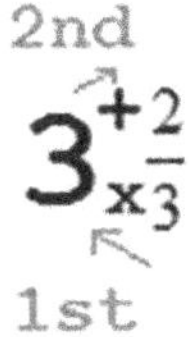

First multiply

For practice write a few mixed numbers on a piece of paper for the child to convert into improper fractions. The child should be able to correctly convert five mixed numbers to improper fractions in less than a minute.

TEACHING HOW TO CONVERT AN IMPROPER FRACTION TO A MIXED NUMBER

The process of converting an improper fraction to a mixed number is very easy if the child has mastered long division. The steps are exactly the same except that the remainder will become the numerator and the divisor will become the denominator. It is also important to understand that the fraction bar is the same as a division sign.

Thus:

$$\frac{18}{3} = 18 \div 3 = 3\overline{)18}$$

Once this is understood, converting an improper fraction to a mixed number is a matter of completing a long division problem.

Example:

Convert the following improper fraction to a mixed number:

$$\frac{35}{8}$$

Solution:

Rewrite the fraction as a division problem. The numerator will go inside and become the dividend and the denominator will go outside and become the divisor.

$$8\overline{)35}$$

Solve the division problem.

$$\begin{array}{r} 4 \\ 8\overline{)35} \\ \underline{32} \\ 3 \end{array}$$

At this point, instead of labeling the remainder as three make a fraction with the remainder as the numerator and the divisor as the denominator.

$$\frac{3}{8}$$

Thus:

$$\begin{array}{r} 4\frac{3}{8} \\ 8\overline{)35} \\ \underline{32} \\ 3 \end{array}$$

$$\frac{35}{8} = 4\frac{3}{8}$$

Go to themathworksheetsite.com in order to create some practice fractions. To do this, select “Long Division” under the “Division” heading. Select “1” for “Number of Digits in Divisor” and “1” for “Number of Digits in Quotient”. Choose the button, “With Remainders” and “Fractions”.

On-line Math Worksheet Generator

Long Division

Number of Digits in Divisor

1 ▾

Number of Digits in Quotient

1 ▾

X r X
X|X X

◉ With Remainders
○ Without Remainders
○ Mixed

☐ Include Answer Key

Answer Key Remainders as:

○ Remainders
◉ Fractions

Create It

This will create a worksheet of twelve division problems. Change them to improper fractions. For instance a division problem that looks like:

$$5\overline{)31}$$

Change it to look like:

$$\frac{5}{31}$$

Write five problems on a piece of paper. The child should be able to successfully change the five improper fractions to a missed number in less than a minute.

These skills will be helpful as the child learns operations with fractions.

TEACHING THE ADDITION OF FRACTIONS WITH LIKE DENOMINATORS

Adding two fractions with like denominators is a fairly straightforward process. Once the child has mastered addition of whole numbers, reducing a fraction to its simplest form, and converting an improper fraction to a mixed number; the child has the necessary skills to easily master this new skill.

When two fractions have the same denominator they are said to have like denominators. It is important for the child to understand that the denominator will not change when two fractions are added. It is only the numerator that is added in this process.

There are three steps for the child to complete when adding two fractions with like denominators.

The first step is to add the numerators, while keeping the denominator the same.

The second step is to reduce the fraction to its lowest terms, if necessary.

The final step is if the fraction is an improper fraction, to convert it to a mixed number.

Example:

Add the following two fractions and write the sum in its simplest form.

$$\frac{1}{8} + \frac{5}{8}$$

Solution:

The first step is to add the numerators.

$$1 + 5 = 6$$

This sum is the new numerator. The denominator (8) is not changed.

$$\frac{1}{8} + \frac{5}{8} = \frac{6}{8}$$

The second step is to reduce the fraction to its simplest form. Since both the numerator and the denominator are divisible by two, the fraction can be reduced by dividing both six and eight by two.

$$6 \div 2 = 3 \qquad 8 \div 2 = 4$$

$$\frac{3}{4}$$

Since the fraction is not an improper fraction, the problem is complete.

$$\frac{1}{8} + \frac{5}{8} = \frac{6}{8} = \frac{3}{4}$$

Example:
Add the following two fractions and write the sum in its simplest form.

$$\frac{7}{9} + \frac{5}{9}$$

Solution:
The first step is to add the two numerators.

$$7 + 5 = 12$$

This is the new numerator. The denominator stays the same.

$$\frac{7}{9} + \frac{5}{9} = \frac{12}{9}$$

The second step is to reduce the fraction to its simplest form. Since both the numerator and the denominator are divisible by three, the fraction can be reduced by dividing both twelve and nine by three.

$$12 \div 3 = 4 \qquad 9 \div 3 = 3$$

$$\frac{4}{3}$$

Since the fraction is an improper fraction it is necessary to convert it to a mixed number by division.

$$\frac{4}{3} = 3\overline{)4}$$

Divide:

$$\begin{array}{r} 1\frac{1}{3} \\ 3\overline{)4} \end{array}$$

Thus:

$$\frac{7}{9} + \frac{5}{9} = \frac{12}{9} = \frac{4}{3} = 1\frac{1}{3}$$

For practice pick a number between two and twenty as a denominator. Then select two numbers that are less than the denominator and make two fractions for the child to add. It is important to vary the types of numbers that are used as denominators between odd and even numbers so that the child will have to reduce some problems and not others. Having the child do three or four problems a day will be enough for the child to gain mastery in a week or two.

TEACHING THE ADDITION OF FRACTIONS WITH UNLIKE DENOMINATORS

When teaching the addition of two fractions with unlike denominators to the child, stress that once the first step is completed then everything else that needs to be done in order to solve the problem has been previously mastered, so it will be easy. In fact many times when the child is learning a new concept in mathematics, the child will be learning one or two new steps before the child will have a problem that is familiar and therefore simple. Once this is understood by the child, new types of problems can be solved successfully with confidence.

Two fractions that have different numbers as their denominators are said to have unlike denominators. Examples of these types of fractions are as follows:

$$\frac{1}{2} \text{ and } \frac{1}{3}$$

$$\frac{3}{4} \text{ and } \frac{2}{7}$$

$$\frac{3}{8} \text{ and } \frac{5}{6}$$

In order to add two fractions with unlike denominators it is first necessary to convert both fractions to equivalent fractions with the lowest common denominator. This is a skill that has been previously by the child. Once this initial step is completed then the child will do the three steps learned in adding fractions with like denominators. Thus there are four steps to add fractions with unlike denominators.

The first step is to convert both fractions to equivalent fractions with the lowest common denominator.

The second step is to add the numerators, while keeping the denominator the same.

The third step is to reduce the fraction to its lowest terms, if necessary.

The final step is to convert the fraction to a mixed number if the result is an improper fraction.

Notice that the second, third and final steps is the same process of adding two fractions with unlike denominators are the same as the three steps when adding fractions with like denominators. Since the child has previously mastered this process, learning to add two fractions with unlike denominators requires only mastering converting two fractions with unlike fractions to equivalent fractions with the lowest common denominator. Since this has also been previously mastered by the child, the process of adding two fractions with unlike denominators should be mastered by the child with relative ease.

Example:

Solve the following addition problem:

$$\frac{3}{4} + \frac{3}{10}$$

The first step is to convert both fractions to the lowest common denominator. Since the least common multiple of four and ten is twenty, the lowest common denominator is twenty.

$$\frac{3}{4} = \frac{?}{20} \qquad \frac{3}{10} = \frac{?}{20}$$

The problem rewritten with equivalent fractions is as follows:

$$\frac{15}{20} + \frac{6}{20}$$

Once this first step is completed, the child should see that this is a type of problem that has been previously mastered. The second step is to add the two numerators and keep the denominator the same.

$$15 + 6 = 21$$

$$\frac{15}{20} + \frac{6}{20} = \frac{21}{20}$$

The third step is to reduce the fraction if necessary. The child should see that this fraction is in its simplest form and therefore no reduction is needed. The final step is to convert the fraction to a mixed number if the answer is an improper fraction. Since the numerator (21) is greater than the denominator (20), the fraction is and improper fraction and thus can be converted to a mixed number.

$$\frac{21}{20} = 20\overline{)21}$$

Solve the division problem.

$$\begin{array}{r} 1 \\ 20\overline{)21} \\ \underline{20} \\ 1 \end{array}$$

Since the remainder is one, that will be the new numerator.

$$\begin{array}{r} 1\ \frac{1}{20} \\ 20\overline{)21}\phantom{\frac{1}{20}} \\ \underline{20}\phantom{\frac{1}{20}} \\ 1\phantom{\frac{1}{20}} \end{array}$$

Thus:

$$\frac{3}{4} + \frac{3}{10} = \frac{15}{20} + \frac{6}{20} = \frac{21}{20} = 20\overline{)21} = 1\frac{1}{20}$$

For practice take a deck of cards and remove the aces, kings, queens, and jacks. Create two small decks, one of red cards and one of black cards. Turn over two cards from each deck and make two fractions with the four cards. The smaller number red and black cards will be the numerator and the larger number on the red and black cards will be the denominator. Have the child add the two fractions.

Example:

Suppose the two red cards that are drawn are a three and a five, and the two black cards drawn are an eight and a nine, the fraction problem will be as follows:

$$\frac{3}{5} + \frac{8}{9}$$

The child should be able to consistently do a problem such as this correctly in less than one minute to achieve mastery.

TEACHING THE ADDITION OF MIXED NUMBERS

When teaching the child addition of mixed numbers, it will be exactly like the addition of two fractions with like or unlike denominators. There is just one more very easy extra step, which is the addition of whole numbers, a skill that the child has previously mastered.

It will be easier for the child if the two mixed numbers are added vertically, because this allows room for the equivalent fractions when they are converted to the lowest common denominator.

Example:

Add the following mixed numbers:

$$3\frac{2}{5} + 5\frac{8}{9}$$

Solution:

First have the child rewrite the problem vertically.

$$3\frac{2}{5}$$

$$+\ 5\frac{8}{9}$$

Now have the child convert the two fractions to equivalent fractions with the lowest common denominator. In this case the least common multiple of five and nine is forty-five, so that is the number that is used for the lowest common denominator. Write two fractions to the right of the original fractions with a denominator of forty-five.

$$3\frac{2}{5} \quad \frac{}{45}$$

$$+\ 5\frac{8}{9} \quad \frac{}{45}$$

The two new numerators are eighteen and forty, respectively, so write above the denominator.

$$
\begin{array}{rl}
3\frac{2}{5} & \frac{}{45} \\[2ex]
+\,5\frac{8}{9} & \frac{}{45} \\
\hline
\end{array}
$$

Now add the fractions with the like denominators.

$$
\begin{array}{rl}
3\frac{2}{5} & \frac{18}{45} \\[2ex]
+\,5\frac{8}{9} & \frac{40}{45} \\
\hline
 & \frac{58}{45}
\end{array}
$$

This fraction cannot be reduced, so it is in its simplest form. However, this fraction is an improper fraction so it must be converted to a mixed number by division.

$$\frac{58}{45} = 45\overline{)58}$$

Divide.

$$
\begin{array}{r}
1\,\frac{13}{45} \\
45\overline{)58} \\
\underline{45} \\
13
\end{array}
$$

In this case the whole number part of the mixed number (1) will be carried. Write the fraction part under the original fraction.

carried whole number part → 1

$$\begin{array}{rcc} & 3\frac{2}{5} & \frac{18}{45} \\ + & 5\frac{8}{9} & \frac{40}{45} \\ \hline & \frac{13}{45} & \frac{58}{45} \end{array}$$

↖ fraction part

Now add the three whole numbers (1 + 3 + 5) to get a total of nine and write that in front of the fraction.

$$\begin{array}{rcc} & 1 & \\ & 3\frac{2}{5} & \frac{18}{45} \\ + & 5\frac{8}{9} & \frac{40}{45} \\ \hline & 9\frac{13}{45} & \frac{58}{45} \end{array}$$

The answer is $9\frac{13}{45}$.

Notice that only the last step is different from what the child has done before. A quick way to complete the problem if the resultant fraction is an improper fraction without division is to subtract the denominator from the numerator. The difference will be new numerator.

$$\frac{58}{45}$$

$$\begin{array}{r} 58 \\ \underline{-45} \\ 13 \end{array}$$

$$1\frac{13}{45}$$

Carry the one to add to the whole numbers in the problem.

Practice by using the cards just like was done when the child was learning to add fractions with unlike denominators, only include a single digit whole number in front of each fraction to make two mixed numbers. The child should consistently solve adding two mixed numbers within two minutes to achieve mastery.

TEACHING THE SUBTRACTION OF FRACTIONS WITH LIKE DENOMINATORS

The teaching of subtraction of two fractions with like denominators should be fairly easy. Since the child has previously mastered addition of two fractions with like denominators and understands how to subtract whole numbers, all that should be needed is to show a few examples and a little practice for the child to obtain mastery of this skill.

There are only two steps in order to subtract two fractions with like denominators.

First subtract the two numerators while keeping the denominator the same. The difference will be the numerator in the answer.

The second step is to reduce the difference to its simplest form if necessary.

Example:

Solve the following problem:

$$\frac{5}{6} - \frac{1}{6}$$

Solution:

Since the fractions have the same denominator, just subtract the numerators.

$$5 - 1 = 4$$

Thus:

$$\frac{5}{6} - \frac{1}{6} = \frac{4}{6}$$

The next step is to reduce the fraction to its simplest form if necessary. Since both the numerator and denominator are divisible by two, the fraction can be reduced.

$$4 \div 2 = 2 \qquad 6 \div 2 = 3$$

$$\frac{4}{6} = \frac{2}{3}$$

Thus:

$$\frac{5}{6} - \frac{1}{6} = \frac{4}{6} = \frac{2}{3}$$

For practice pick two numbers between three and twenty as denominators. Then select two numbers that are less than the denominator as numerators to make two fractions for the child to subtract. The child should master this skill in a few days of practice doing three to four problems a day.

TEACHING THE SUBTRACTION OF FRACTIONS WITH UNLIKE DENOMINATORS

Subtraction of fractions with unlike denominators is very similar to the addition of two fractions with unlike denominators. Once the lowest common denominator is found and the fractions are converted into equivalent fractions, the problem becomes simple. There are three steps to the skill of subtracting fractions with unlike denominators.

The first step is to find the lowest common denominator and convert the two fractions into equivalent fractions with the lowest common denominator.

The second step is to subtract the numerators. The denominator will not change. The difference will be the numerator in the answer.

The final step is to reduce the fraction to its lowest terms if necessary.

Example:

Subtract the following two factions.

$$\frac{2}{3} - \frac{1}{4}$$

The first step is to find the lowest common denominator and convert both fractions to equivalent fractions with the lowest common denominators. The least common multiple of three and four is twelve.

Since the three needs to be multiplied by four to get twelve, the two in the numerator needs to be multiplied by four; also, the four needs to be multiplied by three in order to get twelve so the one in the numerator must be multiplied by three.

$2 \times 4 = 8$ $1 \times 3 = 3$

Thus:

$$\frac{2}{3} = \frac{8}{12} \qquad \frac{1}{4} = \frac{3}{12}$$

So, rewrite the problem.

$$\frac{8}{12} - \frac{3}{12}$$

The second step is to subtract the numerators.

$$8 - 3 = 5$$

Thus:

$$\frac{8}{12} - \frac{3}{12} = \frac{5}{12}$$

The final step is to reduce the fraction to its simplest form if necessary. Since the fraction cannot be reduced it is in its simplest form, and the problem is complete.

$$\frac{2}{3} - \frac{1}{4} = \frac{8}{12} - \frac{3}{12} = \frac{5}{12}$$

For practice take a deck of cards and remove the aces, kings, queens, and jacks. Create two small decks, one of red cards and one of black cards. Turn over two cards from each deck and make two fractions with the four cards. The smaller number red and black cards will be the numerator and the larger number on the red and black cards will be the denominator. Have the child subtract the two fractions. The child should be able to consistently do a problem correctly in less than one minute to achieve mastery.

TEACHING THE SUBTRACTION OF MIXED NUMBERS WITH LIKE DENOMINATORS

Subtracting mixed numbers with like denominators is very similar to adding mixed numbers with like denominators. The exception is that it is sometimes necessary to borrow from the whole number part of the mixed number if the fraction part of the mixed number in the minuend is smaller than the fraction part of the mixed number in the subtrahend. If this is not the case, then the subtracting will be a very straightforward process that the child will find very easy.

Example:

Solve the following problem:

$$9\frac{5}{7} - 5\frac{3}{7}$$

Solution:

First rewrite the mixed numbers vertically.

$$9\frac{5}{7}$$

$$-5\frac{3}{7}$$

The first step is to subtract the fractions. In this case the fraction part of the minuend is greater the fraction part of the subtrahend, so no borrowing is necessary.

$$\begin{array}{r} 9\frac{5}{7} \\ -5\frac{3}{7} \\ \hline \frac{2}{7} \end{array}$$

Once that is complete subtract the whole numbers.

$$\begin{array}{r} 9\frac{5}{7} \\ -5\frac{3}{7} \\ \hline 4\frac{2}{7} \end{array}$$

Such a problem should be solved in less than five seconds.

However, if the fraction parts of the mixed numbers are reversed then borrowing is necessary. For instance, if the problem was:

$$9\frac{3}{7} - 5\frac{5}{7}$$

The fraction part of the minuend is less than the fraction part of the subtrahend, therefore borrowing is necessary.

In order to understand how to borrow in the subtraction of mixed numbers, the child needs to know the fact that if the numerator and the denominator of any fraction are equal then that fraction is equal to one.

$$1 = \frac{2}{2} = \frac{3}{3} = \frac{4}{4} = \frac{5}{5} = \frac{6}{6} = \frac{7}{7} = \frac{8}{8} = \frac{9}{9} = \frac{10}{10}$$

In order to borrow, reduce the whole number part of the minuend by one and then add a fraction that is equivalent to one to the fraction part of the minuend. Now the fraction part of the minuend will be greater than the fraction part of the subtrahend and the problem can be easily solved.

Example:

Solve the following problem:

$$9\frac{3}{7} - 5\frac{5}{7}$$

Solution:

First rewrite the problem vertically.

$$\begin{array}{r} 9\frac{3}{7} \\ -5\frac{5}{7} \\ \hline \end{array}$$

Since the fraction part of the minuend ($3/7$) is less than the fraction part in the subtrahend ($5/7$) it will be necessary to borrow. Cross out the nine to make eight.

$$\begin{array}{r} 8 \\ \not{9}\frac{3}{7} \\ -5\frac{5}{7} \\ \hline \end{array}$$

Since the denominator of the fractions is seven, use an equivalent fraction with seven as the denominator.

$$1 = \frac{7}{7}$$

Add that fraction to the fraction part of the minuend.

$$\frac{3}{7} + \frac{7}{7} = \frac{10}{7}$$

Write this new fraction to the right of the original fraction in the minuend.

$$\not{8}\frac{3}{7} \quad \frac{10}{7}$$

$$-5\frac{5}{7}$$

Now complete the problem by subtracting the fractions and then subtracting the whole number.

$$\frac{10}{7} - \frac{5}{7} = \frac{5}{7}$$

So:

$$\not{8}\frac{3}{7} \quad \frac{10}{7}$$

$$-5\frac{5}{7}$$

$$\overline{}$$

$$\frac{5}{7}$$

Then subtract the whole numbers.

$$8 - 5 = 3$$

$$\begin{array}{r} 8 \\ \not{9}\frac{3}{7} \quad \frac{10}{7} \\ -5\frac{5}{7} \\ \hline 3\frac{5}{7} \end{array}$$

Thus, the answer:

$$9\frac{3}{7} - 5\frac{5}{7} = 3\frac{5}{7}$$

Example:
Solve the following problem:

$$7\frac{3}{8} - 2\frac{5}{8}$$

Solution:
First rewrite the problem vertically.

$$\begin{array}{r} 7\frac{3}{8} \\ -2\frac{5}{8} \\ \hline \end{array}$$

Since the fraction part of the minuend ($3/8$) is less than the fraction part in the subtrahend ($5/8$) it will be necessary to borrow. Cross out the seven to make six.

Since eight is the denominator.

$$1 = \frac{8}{8}$$

Add this to the fraction part of the minuend.

$$\frac{3}{8} + \frac{8}{8} = \frac{11}{8}$$

$$\begin{array}{l} \quad 6 \\ \not{7}\frac{3}{8} \quad \frac{11}{8} \\ -2\frac{5}{8} \\ \hline \end{array}$$

Now subtract the fractions and then the whole numbers.

$$\frac{11}{8} - \frac{5}{8} = \frac{6}{8}$$

$$6 - 2 = 4$$

Thus:

$$\begin{array}{r} 6 \\ \not{7}\frac{3}{8} \;\; \frac{11}{8} \\ -2\frac{5}{8} \\ \hline 4\frac{6}{8} \end{array}$$

The fraction part of the answer can be reduced since both the numerator, and the denominator are divisible by two.

$6 \div 2 = 3$ $\quad\quad$ $8 \div 2 = 4$

$$\frac{6}{8} = \frac{3}{4}$$

$$\begin{array}{r} 6 \\ \not{7}\frac{3}{8} \;\; \frac{11}{8} \\ -2\frac{5}{8} \\ \hline 4\frac{6}{8} = 4\frac{3}{4} \end{array}$$

Thus:

$$7\frac{3}{8} - 2\frac{5}{8} = 4\frac{6}{8} = 4\frac{3}{4}$$

Sometimes the minuend will be a whole number, and the subtrahend will be a mixed number. When this is the case, borrow from the whole number to make a fraction equivalent to one in the minuend.

Example:

Solve the following problem:

$$8 - 3\frac{4}{9}$$

Solution:

First rewrite the problem vertically.

$$\begin{array}{r} 8 \\ -3\frac{4}{9} \end{array}$$

The denominator of the fraction part of the subtrahend is nine, so nine will be used as the fraction equivalent to one in the minuend.

$$1 = \frac{9}{9}$$

Borrow from the eight.

$$\begin{array}{r} 7 \\ \cancel{8}\,\frac{9}{9} \\ -3\frac{4}{9} \\ \hline \end{array}$$

Now simply subtract the fractions and the whole numbers.

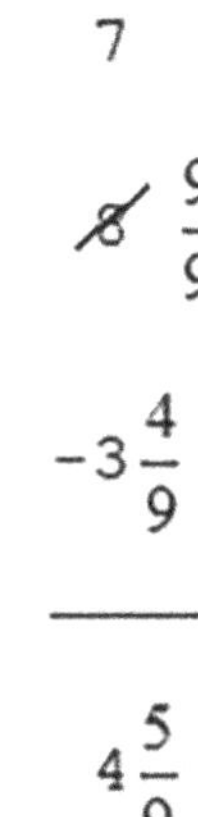

Thus:

$$8 - 3\frac{4}{9} = 4\frac{5}{9}$$

For practice make up three problems with mixed numbers that have the same denominator. Have the problems where the numerator in fraction part of the minuend is less than the numerator in fraction part of the subtrahend. This will force the child to borrow. The child should be able to consistently answer correctly three such problems in less than a minute to achieve mastery.

TEACHING THE SUBTRACTION OF MIXED NUMBERS WITH UNLIKE DENOMINATORS

Once the child has mastered the subtraction of mixed numbers with like denominators, it is only a matter of converting two fractions to equivalent fractions with the lowest common denominator in order for the child to easily solve the subtraction of mixed numbers with unlike denominators.

After the subtraction problem is rewritten vertically, the child has five steps to solve a subtraction problem with mixed numbers and unlike denominators.

The first step is to convert the two fractions in the mixed numbers to equivalent fractions with the lowest common denominator.

The second step is to borrow if necessary.

The third step is to subtract the fraction portion of the mixed numbers.

The fourth step is to subtract the whole number portion of the mixed numbers.

The final step is to reduce the fraction to its simplest form if necessary.

Example:

Solve the following problem:

$$9\frac{2}{3} - 5\frac{3}{4}$$

Rewrite the problem vertically.

$$9\frac{2}{3}$$

$$-5\frac{3}{4}$$

$$\overline{}$$

Since the fractions have unlike denominators it will be necessary to convert them to equivalent fractions with the lowest common denominator. The least common multiple of three and four is twelve, so the fractions need to be converted to equivalent fractions with a denominator of twelve, which is the lowest common denominator.

$$\frac{2}{3} = \frac{8}{12} \qquad\qquad \frac{3}{4} = \frac{9}{12}$$

Write these two fractions to the right of the fractions in the problem.

$$\begin{array}{rr} 9\frac{2}{3} & \frac{8}{12} \\ -5\frac{3}{4} & \frac{9}{12} \\ \hline \end{array}$$

The second step is to borrow, if necessary. Since the fraction portion of the minuend is less than the fraction portion of the subtrahend, it will be necessary to borrow. In this case the denominator of the fraction is twelve, so use a fraction with a denominator of twelve that is equivalent to one.

$$1 = \frac{12}{12}$$

Add this to the fraction portion in the minuend while crossing out the nine to make eight.

$$\frac{8}{12} + \frac{12}{12} = \frac{20}{12}$$

$$\begin{array}{rrr} 8 & & \\ \not{9}\frac{2}{3} & \frac{8}{12} & \frac{20}{12} \\ -5\frac{3}{4} & \frac{9}{12} & \end{array}$$

The third step is to subtract the subtraction portion of the problem.

$$\begin{array}{lll} \overset{8}{\not{9}}\frac{2}{3} & \frac{8}{12} & \frac{20}{12} \\ -5\frac{3}{4} & \frac{9}{12} & \\ \hline & \frac{11}{12} & \end{array}$$

The fourth step is to subtract the whole number portion of the problem.

$$\begin{array}{lll} \overset{8}{\not{9}}\frac{2}{3} & \frac{8}{12} & \frac{20}{12} \\ -5\frac{3}{4} & \frac{9}{12} & \\ \hline 3 & \frac{11}{12} & \end{array}$$

The final step is to reduce the fraction to its simplest form, if necessary. Since the fraction is in its simplest form no reduction is necessary, so the problem is complete.

Thus:

$$9\frac{2}{3} - 5\frac{3}{4} = 3\frac{11}{12}$$

Example:

Solve the following problem:

$$7\frac{1}{2} - 4\frac{5}{6}$$

Rewrite the problem vertically.

$$7\frac{1}{2}$$

$$-4\frac{5}{6}$$

The first step is to convert both fractions into equivalent fractions with the lowest common denominator if necessary. Since the fractions have unlike denominators this is necessary. The least common multiple of two and six is six, so the lowest common denominator of the equivalent fractions will be six.

$$\frac{1}{2} = \frac{3}{6} \qquad \frac{5}{6} = \frac{5}{6}$$

Since the second fraction has a denominator of six the fraction will stay the same. Write these fractions to the right of the original fractions.

$$7\frac{1}{2}\ \frac{3}{6}$$

$$-4\frac{5}{6}\ \frac{5}{6}$$

Note: rewriting $\frac{5}{6}$ is optional.

The second step is to borrow if necessary. Since the fraction portion of the minuend is less than the fraction portions of the subtrahend, it will be necessary to borrow.

$$1 = \frac{6}{6}$$

$$\frac{3}{6} + \frac{6}{6} = \frac{9}{6}$$

Cross out the seven and replace it with six.

$$\begin{array}{l} \quad 6 \\ \not{7}\frac{1}{2}\ \frac{3}{6}\ \frac{9}{6} \\ -4\frac{5}{6}\ \frac{5}{6} \\ \hline \end{array}$$

The third step is to subtract the fraction portion of the mixed numbers.

$$\begin{array}{l} \quad 6 \\ \not{7}\frac{1}{2}\ \frac{3}{6}\ \frac{9}{6} \\ -4\frac{5}{6}\ \frac{5}{6} \\ \hline \quad \frac{4}{6} \end{array}$$

The fourth step is to subtract the whole number portion of the mixed numbers.

$$\begin{array}{l} \quad 6 \\ \not{7}\frac{1}{2}\ \frac{3}{6}\ \frac{9}{6} \\ -4\frac{5}{6}\ \frac{5}{6} \\ \hline \quad 2\frac{4}{6} \end{array}$$

The final step is to reduce the fraction portion of the mixed number to its simplest form, if necessary. Since both the numerator and the denominator are divisible by two, the fraction can be reduced.

$4 \div 2 = 2 \qquad 6 \div 2 = 3$

$$\frac{4}{6} = \frac{2}{3}$$

Write the reduced fraction in the problem.

$$\begin{array}{r} 6 \phantom{\frac{1}{2}\ \frac{3}{6}\ \frac{9}{6}} \\ \not{7}\frac{1}{2}\ \ \frac{3}{6}\ \ \frac{9}{6} \\ -4\frac{5}{6}\ \ \frac{5}{6}\phantom{\ \ \frac{9}{6}} \\ \hline 2\frac{4}{6}\ \ \frac{2}{3}\phantom{\ \ \frac{9}{6}} \end{array}$$

Thus:

$$7\frac{1}{2} - 4\frac{5}{6} = 2\frac{4}{6} = 2\frac{2}{3}$$

For practice make up two problems with mixed numbers that have unlike denominators. The child should be able to consistently answer correctly two such problems in less than a minute to achieve mastery.

TEACHING THE MULTIPLICATION OF FRACTIONS

When teaching the multiplication or the division of fractions to the child there will be no need to have a common denominator. Multiplying fractions is quite easy. There are only three steps.

The first step is to multiply the numerators to get a product. This product will be the new numerator.

The second step is to multiply the denominators to get a product. This product will be the new denominator.

The third step is to reduce the fraction to its simplest form, if necessary.

That's it!

Example:

Solve the following problem:

$$\frac{1}{2} \text{ x } \frac{1}{3}$$

This problem will show just how easy multiplying fractions will be for the child.

Solution:

The first step is to multiply the numerators.

$$1 \text{ x } 1 = 1$$

The numerator in the answer will be one.

The second step is to multiply the denominators.

$$2 \text{ x } 3 = 6$$

The denominator in the answer will be six.

Thus:

$$\frac{1}{2} \text{ x } \frac{1}{3} = \frac{1}{6}$$

Since the answer is in its simplest form, the problem is complete.

Example:

Solve the following problem:

$$\frac{2}{3} \text{ x } \frac{9}{10}$$

Solution:

The first step is to multiply the numerators.

$$2 \times 9 = 18$$

The second step is to multiply the denominators.

$$3 \times 10 = 30$$

So, the product is:

$$\frac{2}{3} \times \frac{9}{10} = \frac{18}{30}$$

The third step is to reduce the fraction to its simplest form, if necessary. Since both the numerator and the denominator are divisible by six, (The greatest common factor of eighteen and thirty is six.) divide both numbers by six.

$$18 \div 6 = 3 \qquad 30 \div 6 = 5$$

Thus:

$$\frac{18}{30} = \frac{3}{5}$$

So:

$$\frac{2}{3} \times \frac{9}{10} = \frac{18}{30} = \frac{3}{5}$$

It is also possible to reduce before multiplying the fractions through a process called cross cancellation. This is usually preferable because the numbers that the child has to reduce are smaller. This will be shown with the previous problem.

Example:

Solve the following problem and cross cancel if required:

$$\frac{2}{3} \times \frac{9}{10}$$

In order to cross cancel, look at the first numerator, which is two, and see if it has a common factor with one of the denominators. In this problem the two has a common denominator with the denominator ten. The greatest common factor of two and ten is two, so divide both numbers by two.

$$2 \div 2 = 1 \qquad 10 \div 2 = 5$$

On the problem, cross out the two and replace it with a one; and cross out the ten and replace it with a five.

$$\frac{\overset{1}{\cancel{2}}}{3} \times \frac{9}{\underset{5}{\cancel{10}}}$$

Now look at the second numerator, which is nine and see if it has a common factor with one of the denominators. The denominator, three shares a common factor with the numerator, nine. The greatest common factor of both numbers is three, so divide both numbers by three.

$9 \div 3 = 3$ $3 \div 3 = 1$

On the fraction cross out the nine and replace it with a three; and cross out the three and replace it with a one.

$$\frac{\overset{1}{\cancel{2}}}{\underset{1}{\cancel{3}}} \times \frac{\overset{3}{\cancel{9}}}{\underset{5}{\cancel{10}}}$$

Now multiply the numerators and the denominators.

$1 \times 3 = 3$ $1 \times 5 = 5$

Thus:

$$\frac{\overset{1}{\cancel{2}}}{\underset{1}{\cancel{3}}} \times \frac{\overset{3}{\cancel{9}}}{\underset{5}{\cancel{10}}} = \frac{3}{5}$$

The same answer.

Also, when the word of is used in a fraction problem it mean the same thing as multiply.

Example:

$$\text{What is } \frac{7}{8} \text{ of } \frac{11}{14}?$$

Solution:

Rewrite the problem as a multiplication problem.

$$\frac{7}{8} \times \frac{11}{14}$$

Look at the first numerator, which is seven, to see if it has a common factor with one of the denominators. Seven and fourteen have common factors. The greatest common factor of seven and fourteen is seven, so divide both numbers by seven.

$7 \div 7 = 1 \qquad\qquad 14 \div 7 = 2$

On the problem cross out the seven and replace it with a one; and cross out the fourteen and replace it with a two.

$$\frac{\overset{1}{\cancel{7}}}{8} \times \frac{11}{\underset{2}{\cancel{14}}}$$

Now look at the second denominator, which is eleven, and see if it has a common factor with any of the denominators. Neither the eight nor the two has a common factor with the eleven, so the cross-cancellation process is complete. Multiply the numerators and the denominators.

$1 \times 11 = 11 \qquad\qquad 8 \times 2 = 16$

Thus:

$$\frac{\overset{1}{\cancel{7}}}{8} \times \frac{11}{\underset{2}{\cancel{14}}} = \frac{11}{16}$$

Notice if cross cancellation did not take place the product would be:

$$\frac{77}{112} = \frac{(7 \times 11)}{(8 \times 14)}$$

Now this fraction can be reduced by dividing both the numerator and the denominator by seven. However, the child will usually find it easier to cross cancel before multiplying the fractions.

To review:

Originally there were three steps to the process of multiplying fractions. Those were, first multiply the two numerators, second multiply the two denominators, and finally reduce the product to its simplest form, if necessary. After cross cancellation is understood, the process will change to first cross cancel, if necessary, second multiply the numerators, and finally multiply the denominators.

For practice, use the deck of cards just as it was used for practice in the addition of fractions with unlike denominators. That is to make a fraction with two red cards and another fraction with two black cards. The child then would multiply the two fractions. The child should be able to do consistently answer four problems correctly in a minute in order to achieve mastery.

TEACHING THE MULTIPLICATION OF FRACTIONS AND WHOLE NUMBERS

Once the child has mastered the multiplication of fractions, learning how to multiply a fraction and a whole number will be fairly easy. All that the child needs to learn is how to convert a whole number into a fraction, which can be taught in less than ten seconds.

In order to convert a whole number to a fraction, write a fraction with the whole number as the numerator and one as the denominator.

Here are some examples of whole numbers and an equivalent fraction with a denominator of one.

$$2 = \frac{2}{1} \quad 8 = \frac{8}{1} \quad 15 = \frac{15}{1}$$

Once the whole number is converted to a fraction the child will cross cancel, if necessary. After the child multiplies the numerator and the denominator, there is the possibility of the product being an improper fraction. If this is the case the child needs to convert the improper fraction to a mixed number. This process can be broken down into the following five steps:

The first step is to convert the whole number into a fraction by writing the whole number over one.

The second step is to cross cancel, if necessary.

The third step is to multiply the numerators.

The fourth step is to multiply the denominators.

The fifth and final step is to convert the product to a mixed number if the product is an improper fraction.

Notice that after the first step where the whole number is converted to a fraction, ever other step in the process of solving a problem is something that the child has previously mastered.

Example:

What is $\frac{5}{6}$ of 9?

Recall that when the word of is in a problem involving fractions, the problem is a multiplication problem.

$$\frac{5}{6} \text{ x } 9$$

The first step is to convert the whole number to a fraction.

$$\frac{5}{6} \times \frac{9}{1}$$

The second step is to cross cancel if necessary. The first numerator is five and the five does not share a common factor with either denominator, so no reduction can take place. The second numerator is nine and the nine shares a common factor with the six. The greatest common factor of nine and six is three, so divide both numbers by three.

$9 \div 3 = 3$ $\qquad$ $6 \div 3 = 2$

So, cross out the nine and replace it with a three, and then cross out the six and replace it with a two.

$$\frac{5}{\cancel{6}_{2}} \times \frac{\cancel{9}^{3}}{1}$$

The third step is to multiply the numerators.

5 x 3 = 15

The fourth step is to multiply the denominators.

2 x 1 = 2

$$\frac{5}{\cancel{6}_{2}} \times \frac{\cancel{9}^{3}}{1} = \frac{15}{2}$$

The fifth and final step is to convert the product to a mixed number if it is an improper fraction. In this case the numerator is greater than the denominator, so such a conversion is necessary by division.

$$\frac{15}{2} = 2\overline{)15}$$

Divide.

$$\begin{array}{r} 7\frac{1}{2} \\ 2\overline{)15} \\ \underline{14} \\ 1 \end{array}$$

Thus:

$$\frac{5}{6} \text{ of } 9 \text{ is } 7\frac{1}{2}$$

For practice, create a fraction with red cards to be multiplied by a single black card to represent the whole number. The child should be able to consistently answer two problems correctly in less than two minutes to achieve mastery.

TEACHING THE MULTIPLICATION OF MIXED NUMBERS

By this time the child has mastered all the component skills required to multiply mixed numbers. The conversion of a mixed number to an improper fraction is a previously learned skill that will be included with everything learned concerning the multiplication of fractions. There are five steps to multiply mixed numbers.

The first step is to convert the mixed numbers to improper fractions.

The second step is to cross cancel, if necessary.

The third step is to multiply the numerators.

The fourth step is to multiply the denominators.

The fifth and final step is to convert the product from an improper fraction to a mixed number.

Example:

Find the product of the following:

$$1\frac{2}{5} \times 3\frac{1}{3}$$

Solution:

The first step is to convert the mixed number to an improper fraction. Recall that this is a two-step process of multiplying the denominator and the whole number to get a product; and then adding the numerator to get the new numerator.

$$1\frac{2}{5} = \frac{7}{5} \qquad 3\frac{1}{3} = \frac{10}{3}$$

So now the problem is stated as a multiplication problem of two improper fractions.

$$\frac{7}{5} \times \frac{10}{3}$$

The second step is to cross cancel if necessary. The first numerator is seven, and the seven does not share a common factor with either denominator. The second numerator is the ten and the ten shares a common factor with the denominator five. The greatest common factor of ten and five is five, so divide both numbers by five.

$$10 \div 5 = 2 \qquad 5 \div 5 = 1$$

Cross out the ten in the problem and replace it with a two; and then cross out the five and replace it with a one.

$$\frac{7}{\cancel{5}_{1}} \times \frac{\cancel{10}^{2}}{3}$$

The third step is to multiply the numerators.

7 x 2 = 14

The fourth step is to multiply the denominators.

1 x 3 = 3

So, the problem now looks like this:

$$\frac{7}{\cancel{5}_{1}} \times \frac{\cancel{10}^{2}}{3} = \frac{14}{3}$$

The final step is to convert the improper fraction to a mixed number.

$$\frac{14}{3} = 3\overline{)14}$$

Divide.

$$\begin{array}{r} 4\frac{2}{3} \\ 3\overline{)14} \\ \underline{12} \\ 2 \end{array}$$

Thus:

$$1\frac{2}{5} \times 3\frac{1}{3} = 4\frac{2}{3}$$

Example:
Find the product of $2\frac{1}{2} \times 3\frac{1}{5}$
Solution:
The first step is to convert the mixed numbers to improper fractions.

$$\frac{5}{2} \times \frac{16}{5}$$

The second step is to cross cancel if necessary. The first numerator is five, and the five shares a common factor with the denominator five. The greatest common factor of five and five is five, so divide both by five to get a result of one.

$$5 \div 5 = 1$$

The second numerator is the sixteen and the sixteen shares a common factor with the denominator two. The greatest common factor of sixteen and two is two, so divide both numbers by two.

$$16 \div 2 = 8 \qquad 2 \div 2 = 1$$

Cross out both fives in the problem and replace them with ones. Cross out the sixteen in the problem and replace it with an eight; and then cross out the two and replace it with a one.

$$\frac{\overset{1}{\cancel{5}}}{\underset{1}{\cancel{2}}} \times \frac{\overset{8}{\cancel{16}}}{\underset{1}{\cancel{5}}}$$

The third step is to multiply the numerators.

$$1 \times 8 = 8$$

The fourth step is to multiply the denominators.

$$1 \times 1 = 1$$

So, the problem now looks like this:

$$\frac{\overset{1}{\cancel{5}}}{\underset{1}{\cancel{2}}} \times \frac{\overset{8}{\cancel{16}}}{\underset{1}{\cancel{5}}} = \frac{8}{1}$$

The final step is to convert the improper fraction to a mixed number. There is no need to work out the division since the child should recognize that anytime that a fraction has a denominator of one, then it will be equal to the numerator of that fraction.

$$\frac{8}{1} = 8$$

Thus:
The product of $2\frac{1}{2} \times 3\frac{1}{5}$ is 8.

Practice by using the cards just like was done when the child was learning to multiply fractions, only include a single digit whole number in front of each fraction to make two mixed numbers. The child should consistently solve multiplying two mixed numbers within one minute to achieve mastery.

TEACHING THE CONCEPT OF A RECIPROCAL

Before moving on to teach the division of fractions it is important for the child to learn the concept of the reciprocal. This concept is very easy for the child to understand and master. The biggest challenge is to learn the definition and remember the word.

For math a reciprocal is a number that is multiplied by a given number to obtain a product of one.

While at first glance this seems complicated and difficult, in practice it is very simple and easy to figure out what is the reciprocal of a given number. If the number in question is a proper fraction or a whole number, the process can be easily completed in less than five seconds. If the number is a mixed number a little extra time (less than one minute) may be required.

In order to find the reciprocal of a proper fraction, just invert the fraction. This means replacing the numerator with the denominator and the denominator with the numerator.

For instance, the reciprocal of $\frac{2}{3}$ is $\frac{3}{2}$.

When these two numbers are multiplied:

$$\frac{2}{3} \text{ x } \frac{3}{2} = \frac{6}{6} = 1$$

That is how easy it is to find the reciprocal of a proper fraction.

When the number in question is a whole number, it is necessary to remember that a whole number can be easily converted to a fraction by writing a one as the denominator.

Example:

What is the reciprocal of 8?

Solution:

The whole number can be written as a fraction.

$$8 = \frac{8}{1}$$

Then invert.

$$\frac{1}{8}$$

Thus:

The reciprocal of 8 is $\frac{1}{8}$.

Once the child understands this it should take the child less than five seconds to correctly determine the reciprocal of a proper fraction or a whole number. Determining the reciprocal of a mixed number is just as easy but it takes a little more time.

Example:

Find the reciprocal of $4\frac{2}{5}$.

Solution:

First convert the mixed number to an improper fraction. This is a skill that has been previously mastered by the child.

$$4\frac{2}{5} = \frac{22}{5}$$

Then invert the improper fraction.

$$\frac{5}{22}$$

So, the reciprocal of $4\frac{2}{5}$ is $\frac{5}{22}$.

The child should easily master this skill in one day. It is important to master this skill before learning how to divide fractions.

TEACHING THE DIVISION OF FRACTIONS

Once the child has completely mastered multiplication with fractions, it will be very easy to teach the division of fractions. In a problem that requires the division of two fractions, it is just a simple matter of taking the reciprocal of the divisor and then multiplying the fractions.

Consider the following:

$$\frac{1}{2} \div \frac{7}{10} = \frac{1}{2} \text{ x } \frac{10}{7}$$

$$\frac{5}{8} \div \frac{1}{4} = \frac{5}{8} \text{ x } \frac{4}{1}$$

$$\frac{2}{3} \div \frac{3}{10} = \frac{2}{3} \text{ x } \frac{10}{3}$$

Dividing by a fraction is the same as multiplying by the reciprocal of the fraction.

Example:

Solve the following problem:

$$\frac{5}{8} \div \frac{5}{6}$$

Solution:

The first step is to change the problem to a multiplication problem with the reciprocal of the divisor.

The reciprocal of $\frac{5}{6}$ is $\frac{6}{5}$.

So, rewrite the problem.

$$\frac{5}{8} \text{ x } \frac{6}{5}$$

Cross cancel and multiply.

$$\frac{\overset{1}{\cancel{5}}}{\underset{4}{\cancel{8}}} \times \frac{\overset{3}{\cancel{6}}}{\underset{1}{\cancel{5}}} = \frac{3}{4}$$

Thus:

$$\frac{5}{8} \div \frac{5}{6} = \frac{5}{8} \times \frac{6}{5} = \frac{3}{4}$$

That is how simple these types of problems are. Take the reciprocal of the divisor and then multiply. Practice by writing a few improper fractions for the child to divide. The child should be able to consistently solve correctly four problems in less than a minute to achieve mastery.

TEACHING DIVISION IN PROBLEMS INVOLVING FRACTIONS AND WHOLE NUMBERS

Once the child has mastered solving problems that involve division of the fractions it will become easy for the child to learn how to solve problems involving fractions and whole numbers. After the child converts the whole number to a fraction, the problem becomes something the child has just previously mastered.

Example:

Solve the following problem:

$$4 \div \frac{5}{9}$$

Solution:

First convert the whole number to a fraction.

$$\frac{4}{1} \div \frac{5}{9}$$

Next take the reciprocal of the divisor and multiply.

$$\frac{4}{1} \times \frac{9}{5}$$

Cross cancel and multiply. In this case no cross cancelling is possible.

$$\frac{4}{1} \times \frac{9}{5} = \frac{36}{5}$$

Since the product is an improper fraction, it is necessary to convert the product to a mixed number.

$$\frac{36}{5} = 5\overline{)36}$$

Divide.

$$\begin{array}{r} 7\frac{1}{5} \\ 5\overline{)36} \\ \underline{35} \\ 1 \end{array}$$

Thus:

$$4 \div \frac{5}{9} = \frac{4}{1} \times \frac{9}{5} = \frac{36}{5} = 7\frac{1}{5}$$

Example:
Solve the following problem:

$$\frac{3}{8} \div 6$$

Solution:
First convert the whole number to a fraction.

$$\frac{3}{8} \div \frac{6}{1}$$

Next take the reciprocal of the divisor and multiply.

$$\frac{3}{8} \times \frac{1}{6}$$

Cross cancel and multiply.

$$\frac{\overset{1}{\cancel{3}}}{8} \times \frac{1}{\underset{2}{\cancel{6}}} = \frac{1}{16}$$

Since the product is a proper fraction, the problem is complete.
Thus:

$$\frac{3}{8} \div 6 = \frac{3}{8} \times \frac{1}{6} = \frac{1}{16}$$

For practice, create a fraction with red cards to be multiplied by a single black card to represent the whole number, alternate between having the whole number the dividend or the divisor. The child should be able to consistently answer two problems correctly in less than two minutes to achieve mastery.

TEACHING THE DIVISION OF MIXED NUMBERS

The child has all the skills necessary to learn how to solve problems involving the division of mixed numbers. It is quite possible that the child could figure out how to do this without being taught based on the mastery of previously learned material. This process will take five steps.

The first step is to convert the mixed numbers to improper fractions.

The second step is to change the problem to a multiplication problem by taking the reciprocal of the divisor.

The third step is to cross cancel if necessary.

The fourth step is to multiply the numerators and the denominators to get a product.

The fifth and final step is to convert the product to a mixed number if it is an improper fraction.

Example:

Solve the following:

$$5\frac{5}{7} \div 4\frac{1}{6}$$

Solution:

The first step is to convert the mixed numbers to improper fractions.

$$\frac{40}{7} \div \frac{25}{6}$$

The second step is to change the problem to a multiplication problem by taking the reciprocal of the divisor.

$$\frac{40}{7} \text{ x } \frac{6}{25}$$

The third step is to cross cancel if necessary. The first numerator is forty. Forty shares a common factor with the denominator twenty-five. The greatest common factor of forty and twenty-five is five, so divide both numbers by five.

$$40 \div 5 = 8 \qquad 25 \div 5 = 5$$

The second numerator is a six. Six does not share a common factor with either denominator. Cross out the forty and replace it with an eight and then cross out the twenty-five and replace it with a five.

$$\frac{\cancel{40}^{8}}{7} \times \frac{6}{\cancel{25}_{5}}$$

The fourth step is to multiply the numerators and the denominators to get a product.

$$\frac{\cancel{40}^{8}}{7} \times \frac{6}{\cancel{25}_{5}} = \frac{48}{35}$$

The fifth step is to convert the product to a mixed number if it is an improper fraction. This is the case because the numerator is greater than the denominator. Use division to convert.

$$\begin{array}{r} 1\frac{13}{35} \\ 35\overline{)48} \\ \underline{35} \\ 13 \end{array}$$

Thus:

$$5\frac{5}{7} \div 4\frac{1}{6} = 1\frac{13}{35}$$

Practice by using the cards just like was done when the child was learning to multiply two mixed numbers. The child should consistently solve the division of two mixed numbers within one minute to achieve mastery.

TEACHING THE BASICS OF DECIMALS

Once the child has mastered all aspects of fractions, the teaching of decimals can begin. Decimals are based on fractions that have a power of ten. To begin, start with those numbers which have just two digits after the decimal. The child will be familiar with these numbers because our monetary system is based on it.

Show the child that one dollar is equal to ten dimes.

Since ten dimes make one dollar, one dime is one-tenth of a dollar. One dollar and one dime is \$1.10. The one to the right of the decimal represents the dime or one-tenth of a dollar, so show the child:

$$\frac{1}{10} = 0.1$$

It is common to write a zero to the left of the decimal point on positive numbers less than one to draw attention to the fact that the number is a decimal number at first glance.

.1 = 0.1

Both numbers represent the same amount. The number on the left (.1) might be mistaken for a whole number at a quick glance. The number on the right (0.1) has a zero in front of the decimal. It looks unusual at first glance and will alert the viewer that the number is a decimal. In textbooks it will be common for decimals to be expressed with a zero in front of the decimal if the number is a positive number that is less than one.

So, show the child all the numbers with one digit to the right of the decimal.

$$0.1 = \frac{1}{10}$$

$$0.2 = \frac{2}{10} = \frac{1}{5}$$

$$0.3 = \frac{3}{10}$$

$$0.4 = \frac{4}{10} = \frac{2}{5}$$

$$0.5 = \frac{5}{10} = \frac{1}{2}$$

$$0.6 = \frac{6}{10} = \frac{3}{5}$$

$$0.7 = \frac{7}{10}$$

$$0.8 = \frac{8}{10} = \frac{4}{5}$$

$$0.9 = \frac{9}{10}$$

Notice how each decimal is equal to a fraction with a denominator of ten. The digit immediately to the right of the decimal is the tenths digit.

Thus, the number 48.3 can be vocalized as "forty-eight and three-tenths.

Also explain to the child that when reading a number containing a decimal, the word "and" is used in place of the decimal.

The second digit to the right of the decimal is the hundredths digit. Since the penny is one-hundredth of a dollar and one-tenth of a dime, show the child that ten pennies equals a dime.

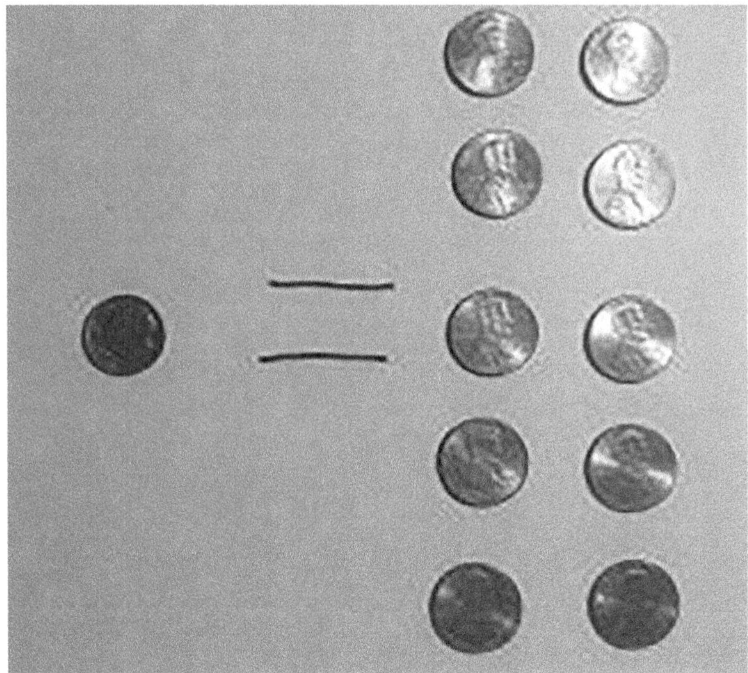

Place three one-dollar bills, two dimes, and four pennies on the table and write down on a piece of paper:

$3.24

The three is in the one's place and represents the whole number. The two is in the tenth's place and represents two-tenths of a dollar. The four is in the hundredth's place and represents four-hundredths of a dollar.

The first nine hundredths are as follows:

$$0.01 = \frac{1}{100}$$

$$0.02 = \frac{2}{100} = \frac{1}{50}$$

$$0.03 = \frac{3}{100}$$

$$0.04 = \frac{4}{100} = \frac{2}{50} = \frac{1}{25}$$

$$0.05 = \frac{5}{100} = \frac{1}{20}$$

$$0.06 = \frac{6}{100} = \frac{3}{50}$$

$$0.07 = \frac{7}{100}$$

$$0.08 = \frac{8}{100} = \frac{4}{50} = \frac{2}{25}$$

$$0.09 = \frac{9}{100}$$

Notice how each decimal is equal to a fraction with a denominator of one hundred. The second digit to the right of the decimal is the hundredths digit. Even if the digit immediately to the right of the decimal is not a zero, if there are two digits after a decimal it is still a denominator of one hundred.

$$0.27 = \frac{27}{100}$$

As the number moves away from the right of the decimal, the number of zeros in the denominator increases.

$$0.1 = \frac{1}{10}$$

$$0.01 = \frac{1}{100}$$

$$0.001 = \frac{1}{1000}$$

$$0.0001 = \frac{1}{10000}$$

$$0.00001 = \frac{1}{100000}$$

This pattern continues indefinitely.

Once the child understands the basics of decimals, it is then necessary to teach the child how to convert a decimal into a fraction.

TEACHING CONVERTING A DECIMAL TO A FRACTION

Converting a decimal to a fraction is quite simple once the child has mastered both the basics of decimals and the reducing of fractions to their simplest form. This will consist of three steps.

The first step is to determine the denominator.

The second step is to write the fraction.

The third step is to reduce the fraction, if necessary.

In order to determine the denominator, count the number of digits to the right of the decimal. The denominator will be a power of ten with the same number of zeros as digits in the decimal.

The first five powers of ten are:

10
100
1000
10000
100000

This series will go on indefinitely.

Example:

What will the denominator be for the decimal 0.327?

Solution:

Since the decimal has three digits after the decimal, the denominator will be the power of ten with three zeros, which is 1000.

Once the child has determined the denominator, the next step is to write the fraction, which is very easy. In order to do this, the number to the right of the decimal will be the numerator. In the previous example, 0.327 will be written as 327 in the numerator.

Thus:

$$0.327 = \frac{327}{1000}$$

It is important to understand that if a zero is to the immediate right of the decimal it still must be counted as a digit to obtain the proper denominator. For instance, 0.027 and 0.007 are both considered three digits for the purposes of determining the denominator, which is 1000.

$$0.027 = \frac{27}{1000}$$

$$0.007 = \frac{7}{1000}$$

Since every denominator of a fraction of a decimal converted to a fraction is a power of ten, the fraction can only be reduced if the numerator is divisible by either two or five. The prime factorizations of the first four powers of ten are as follows:

10 = 2 x 5
100 = 2 x 2 x 5 x 5
1000 = 2 x 2 x 2 x 5 x 5 x 5
10000 = 2 x 2 x 2 x 2 x 5 x 5 x 5 x 5

This means that when the decimal is written as a fraction and the numerator is not divisible by either two or five, the fraction is in its simplest form. In the previous example the fraction has a numerator of 327, and this number is neither divisible by two or five, so the fraction is in its simplest form.

Example:

Convert 0.375 to a fraction in its simplest form.

Solution:

The first step is to determine the denominator. Since there are three digits to the right of the decimal, the denominator will have three zeros. (1000)

The second step is to write the fraction. Convert 0.375 to 375 and write this as the numerator in the fraction.

$$\frac{375}{1000}$$

The third step is to reduce the fraction to its simplest form if necessary. The numerator is divisible by five, so divide both the numerator and the denominator by five to get a simpler fraction.

375 ÷ 5 = 75   1000 ÷ 5 = 200

$$\frac{75}{200}$$

The new numerator is divisible by five and the new denominator is divisible by five. Divide both the numerator and the denominator by five to get a simpler fraction.

75 ÷ 5 = 15   200 ÷ 5 = 40

$$\frac{15}{40}$$

Once again both the numerator and the denominator are divisible by five, so divide both numbers by five.

15 ÷ 5 = 3 40 ÷ 5 = 8

$$\frac{3}{8}$$

Since three is neither divisible by two or five, the fraction is in its simplest form.

$$0.375 = \frac{375}{1000} = \frac{75}{200} = \frac{15}{40} = \frac{3}{8}$$

Instead of dividing by five several times, teach the child that when the original denominator is either twenty-five of seventy-five both the numerator and the denominator can be divided by twenty-five.

Take the fraction from the previous example:

$$\frac{375}{1000}$$

Since the last two digits in the denominator are seventy-five, both the numerator and the denominator can be divided by twenty-five.

375 ÷ 25 = 15 1000 ÷ 25 = 40

$$\frac{15}{40}$$

After that, divide both the numerator and the denominator by five to get the fraction in its simplest form.

It is important for the child to understand that both ways to reduce the fraction are correct. Originally dividing by twenty-five instead of five allows the child to arrive at the simplest form quicker.

For practice, write down four decimal ranging from one to three digits. Vary the final digit so that the child will either have to divide by two, five or not at all in order to reduce the fraction to its simplest form. The goal is to consistently convert the four decimals correctly to fractions in their simplest form in less than two minutes to achieve mastery.

TEACHING CONVERTING A FRACTION TO A DECIMAL

There are two ways to convert a fraction to a decimal. The first way is to divide and the second way is to multiply the numerator and the denominator by the same number that will result in a product in the denominator that will be a power of ten. Both ways will be taught to the child in this section.

It will be different for the child when converting a fraction to a decimal by division because the dividend will be less than the divisor. Place a decimal after the dividend and write a few zeros after the decimal. It is also necessary to place a decimal on the division bar above the decimal in the dividend. The resulting quotient will be a decimal. For the first example, use the fraction from the previous section.

Example:

Convert $\frac{3}{8}$ to a decimal.

Solution:

Recall that the fraction bar means divide.

$$\frac{3}{8} = 3 \div 8 = 8\overline{)3}$$

At first glance this will look strange because the dividend (3) is less than the divisor (8). When this is the case, write a decimal after the divisor and add a few zeros.

$$8\overline{)3.000}$$

Now the problem looks like 3000 ÷ 8 and this will be familiar to the child. It will be necessary to write a decimal on the division bar above the decimal in the dividend.

$$\begin{array}{r} . \\ 8\overline{)3.000} \end{array}$$

Since eight will not go into three, write a zero above the three.

$$\begin{array}{r} 0. \\ 8\overline{)3.000} \end{array}$$

After that, divide as the child has previously mastered. Eight will go into thirty three times, so write an eight above the first zero and continue the division process until completion.

```
   0.375
8 )3.000
   24
    60
    56
     40
     40
      0
```

Thus $\frac{3}{8} = 0.375$

This particular fraction is called a terminating decimal because the decimal ends. Other fractions are called repeating decimals because a number or series of numbers in the quotient will repeat without ending. The next example will be a repeating decimal.

Example:

Convert $\frac{2}{3}$ to a decimal.

Solution:

Rewrite the fraction as a division problem.

```
3 )2
```

Place a decimal after the two and write a few zeros.

```
3 )2.000
```

Place a zero above the two and a decimal above the decimal.

```
   0.
3 )2.000
```

Now divide three into twenty until the problem is complete.

```
   0.666
3 )2.000
   18
    20
    18
     20
     18
      2
```

After a few cycles it is obvious that the division problem will never end. It will repeat the same pattern indefinitely with each digit in the quotient being a six. This is called a repeating decimal. A repeating decimal is written with a line over the digit or digits that repeat.

$$\frac{2}{3} = 0.\overline{6}$$

Here are some common fractions converted to decimals that the child needs to be familiar with due to the frequency the child will encounter them while learning mathematics.

Fraction	Decimal	Type
$\frac{1}{2}$	0.5	Terminating
$\frac{1}{3}$	$0.\overline{3}$	Repeating
$\frac{1}{4}$	0.25	Terminating
$\frac{1}{5}$	0.2	Terminating
$\frac{1}{6}$	$0.1\overline{6}$	Repeating
$\frac{1}{7}$	$0.\overline{142857}$	Repeating
$\frac{1}{8}$	0.125	Terminating
$\frac{1}{9}$	$0.\overline{1}$	Repeating
$\frac{1}{10}$	0.1	Terminating

If the denominator of a fraction in its simplest form only has two or five as its primary factors the decimal will be a terminating decimal. If the denominator in its simplest form has any other prime factor besides two or five then it will have a repeating decimal.

Example:

$4 = 2 \times 2$ (Terminating Decimal)
$6 = 2 \times 3$ (Repeating Decimal)

The a fraction that is in its simplest form that has six as a denominator will be a repeating decimal, even though it has a two in its prime factorization. The fact that it has a three in its prime factorization will mean that when the fraction is converted to a decimal, the decimal will be a repeating decimal.

Sometimes it will be easier to multiply the denominator and the numerator by the same number to get a denominator that is a power of ten. Once that is done then the decimal can be determined by looking at the new numerator.

Example:

Convert $\frac{13}{25}$ to a decimal.

Solution:

The denominator in this case can be multiplied by four to get a product of one-hundred. So multiply both the numerator and the denominator by four to get an equivalent fraction with a denominator of one-hundred.

13 x 4 = 52 25 x 4 = 100

Thus: $\frac{13}{25} = \frac{52}{100}$

Now that the child has a fraction with a denominator that has a power of ten, the decimal can easily be determined.

$$\frac{52}{100} = 0.52$$

So finally:

$$\frac{13}{25} = \frac{52}{100} = 0.52$$

For practice give the child four fractions to convert to decimals. The child should be able to consistently be able to correctly convert four fractions in two minutes in order to achieve mastery of this skill.

TEACHING ROUNDING DECIMALS

When teaching the child how to round decimals it is important to review rounding whole numbers because there is a strong similarity in these two skills. The number five is the key determining digit.

Recall that if 247 or 253 is to be rounded to the nearest hundred, then the determining digit is to the immediate right to the hundreds digit, which in this case is the tens digit. If the tens digit is five or greater than the rounded digit is increased by one, if it is less than five then the rounded digit remains the same.

So:

247 rounded to the nearest hundred is 200.

253 rounded to the nearest hundred is 300.

This same concept applied to decimals as well. The main difference is that there will be no zeros after the rounded digit. The digits after the rounded digit will be dropped.

Example:

Round 57.2894 to the nearest hundredth.

Solution:

The hundredths digit is the second digit to the right of the decimal, in this case the eight. Thus, there are only two possible correct solutions.

57.28
or
57.29

the rounded digit or the thousandths digit. The thousandths digit is nine, which is five or greater, so the rounded digit is increased by one.

Thus:

57.2894 rounded to the nearest hundredth is 57.29.

If the rounded digit is a nine and the determining digit causes the rounded digit to increase, then the rounded digit is changed to zero and the digit to the immediate left of the rounded digit is increased by one.

Example:

Round 16.974 to the nearest tenth.

Solution:

The tenths digit is the first digit to the right of the decimal. Therefore, the hundredths digit is the determining digit. That digit is seven, which means that the rounded digit must be increased by one. Since the rounded digit is nine, it will be changed to zero and the digit to the immediate left, which is the ones digit, will be increased by one.

Thus 19.974 rounded to the nearest tenth is 17.0.

It is important to leave the zero in this case because it shows the number rounded to the nearest tenth. Later when the child studies science; the precision of a measurement will be rounded to a certain digit, and sometimes that digit will be shown with a zero.

For practice, write down ten decimal numbers and have the child round then to various digits. Mastery can be achieved once the child can consistently round ten numbers correctly in a minute.

TEACHING THE ADDITION OF DECIMALS

When teaching the child how to add numbers that contain decimals begin by explaining to the child that only thing different from adding whole numbers is the need to align the decimals. Once this is done, the child will add the numbers just as was previously learned. However, it might be necessary to add zeros to one of the addends to aid the child's understanding.

If zeros are added to the end of a number that contains a decimal it will not change the value of that number. For instance:

$$63.8 = 63.80 = 63.800 = 63.8000$$

Example:
What is the sum of 1.45 and 62.3?
Solution:
Write the two numbers vertically.

$$\begin{array}{r} 1.45 \\ \underline{+62.3} \end{array}$$

The problem as written above is incorrect because the decimals are not aligned. Rewrite the problem with the decimals aligned.

$$\begin{array}{r} 1.45 \\ \underline{+62.3} \end{array}$$

Next write a zero after the three and write a decimal in the sum.

$$\begin{array}{r} 1.45 \\ \underline{+62.30} \\ . \end{array}$$

Finally add from right to left.

$$\begin{array}{r} 1.45 \\ \underline{+62.30} \\ 63.75 \end{array}$$

Thus the sum of 1.45 and 62.3 is 62.75.

It is important for the child to understand that every whole number has an assumed decimal after the one's place that is not normally written.

For instance:

25 can be rewritten as 25. or 25.0 or 25.00 and it will have the same value. This is useful when adding a whole number to a number containing a decimal.

Example:

Find the sum of 26 and 48.23.

Solution:

Rewrite this as an addition problem vertically with 26 as 26.00 and line up the decimals.

$$\begin{array}{r} 26.00 \\ \underline{+48.23} \end{array}$$

Add the two numbers to obtain the sum.

$$\begin{array}{r} 26.00 \\ \underline{+48.23} \\ 74.23 \end{array}$$

Thus the sum of 26 and 48.23 is 74.23.

For practice go to themathworksheetsite.com and click on "Multiple Digit" under the "Addition" heading. Select "3" for "Number of Digits" and "2" for "Number of Addends". Finally select the "Mixed" button. This will create a worksheet of twenty problems. Place decimals in the problem so that the child has to adjust in order to compute the sum. The child should be able to do these problems correctly in ten minutes in order to achieve mastery.

TEACHING THE SUBTRACTION OF DECIMALS

It is very important to add zeros to the end of a number when subtracting numbers with decimals so that both the minuend and subtrahend have the same number of digits. This is especially important when there are more digits in the subtrahend than in the minuend.

Example:

Subtract 346.5 – 261.348

Solution:

First arrange the problem vertically so that the decimals line up.

```
 346.5  (minuend)
-261.348      (subtrahend)
```

Most children when first learning this concept will just write down the last two numbers when they begin to solve the problem. This is incorrect and the proper way needs to be explained to the child so that it is completely understood.

```
  346.5
-261.348
     48
```

The example above is incorrect.

To correctly solve the problem, annex to zeros to the end of the minuend.

```
 346.500
-261.348
```

Then proceed to subtract from right to left and borrow when necessary.

```
 2    49
 3¹46.5̸0̸¹0
-261.348
  85.152
```

Thus:

$$346.5 - 261.348 = 85.152$$

Remember that a whole number is assumed to have a decimal at the end. This will be important when the minuend is a whole number and the subtrahend is a decimal number.

Example:
Subtract 52 – 18.35
Solution:
Rewrite the problem vertically and line up the decimals.

$$\begin{array}{r} 52. \\ \underline{-18.35} \end{array}$$

Next annex zeros at the end of the minuend.

$$\begin{array}{r} 52.00 \\ \underline{-18.35} \end{array}$$

Finally subtract and borrow when necessary.

$$\begin{array}{r} 4\;{}^{1}1\;\;9\; \\ \not{5}\not{2}.{}^{1}\not{0}{}^{1}0 \\ \underline{-18.35} \\ 33.65 \end{array}$$

Thus:

$$52 - 18.35 = 33.65$$

Have the child practice with subtraction problems from themathworksheetsite.com the same way that the child practiced addition problems with decimals. Vary the decimal placement so that the child will be forced to annex zeros. The child should be able to consistently complete a worksheet correctly in twenty minutes to achieve mastery.

TEACHING THE MULTIPLICATION OF DECIMALS

It will be fairly easy for the child to learn and master the multiplication of numbers containing decimals if the child has previously mastered multiplication of whole numbers. The process will be exactly the same except for determining the place of the decimal. In order to do this it is a simple matter of counting the total digits to the right of the decimals in the factors and placing the decimal in the product so that the same number of digits is to the right of the product.

Consider the following multiplication problem:

```
  214
 x 69
```

Now this is how the problem is solved.

```
  214
 x 69
 1926
12840
14766
```

This is a problem that the child should easily be able to correctly complete. Now look at the same problem where each number contains a decimal.

```
 2.14
 X6.9
```

To begin, solve the problem as if the two factors were whole numbers.

```
 2.14
x 6.9
 1926
12840
14766
```

In order to complete the problem, the decimal must be written in the proper place in the product. In order to determine this, count the digits to the right of the decimal in both factors.

```
 2.14       (2 digits)
x 6.9       (1 digit)
```

```
 1926
12840
14766
```

Now add the digits in the factors that are to the right of the decimal (2 + 1 = 3) and write the decimal in the product so that there are three digits to the right of the decimal (between the four and the seven).

```
  2.14      (2 digits)
 x 6.9      (1 digit)
 1926
12840
14.766      (3 digits)
```

That is how easy it is to multiply two numbers that contain decimals. Once the child has multiplied, and the child should have mastered this skill, it takes less than five seconds to determine the place of the decimal.

Sometimes a multiplication problem will have factors and a product less than one.

Example:

Find the product of 0.006 and 0.0008.

Solution:

First arrange the product vertically.

```
   0.006
x 0.0008
```

Now multiply.

```
   0.006
x 0.0008
      48
```

Finally count the digits to the right of the decimal in both of the factors to determine where to place the decimal in the product.

```
   0.006     (3 digits)
x 0.0008     (4 digits)
      48
```

Since 3 + 4 = 7, that means that there are seven digits to the right of the decimal in the product. At this point there are only two digits in the product, so in order to have seven digits to the right of the decimal annex five zeros to the left of the four.

```
   0.006     (3 digits)
x 0.0008     (4 digits)
 0000048
```

Now it is possible to have seven digits to the right of the decimal.

```
  0.006        (3 digits)
x 0.0008       (4 digits)
  .0000048 (7 digits)
```

Write a zero to the left of the decimal (not actually required) to complete the problem.

Thus:

The product of 0.006 and 0.0008 is 0.0000048.

In conclusion, the difference between multiplying whole numbers and multiplying decimal numbers is determining the placement of the decimal in the product. This extra step should take less than five seconds to accomplish.

TEACHING THE DIVISION OF DECIMALS

As with the multiplication of decimals the division of decimals is just a matter of determining the proper placement of the decimal in the quotient. The process of long division that the child has previously learned and mastered will be used when solving division problems with decimals. Teach the child slowly by introducing the concept with three different types of problems.

The first type of problem is when the divisor is a whole number and the dividend is a decimal number.

The second type of problem is when the divisor is a decimal number and the dividend is a whole number.

The third type of problem is when both the divisor and dividend are decimal numbers.

When solving a division when the dividend has a decimal and the divisor is a whole number just one extra step is needed to correctly solve the problem. The extra step is placing the decimal directly above the dividend on the division bar.

Example:

Solve the following division problem:

$$5\overline{)7.45}$$

Solution:

Before working on solving the problem by long division place a decimal on the division bar directly above the decimal in the dividend.

$$\begin{array}{r} . \\ 5\overline{)7.45} \end{array}$$

Now it is just a simple matter of dividing using the four steps that the child has previously learned and mastered.

```
    1.49
 5 )7.45
    5
    24
    20
     45
     45
      0
```

So the quotient is 1.49.

When solving a problem when the dividend is a whole number and the divisor is a decimal number, the decimal in the divisor must be moved to the far right digit of the divisor. When this is done a decimal must be placed at the end of the dividend. Since there are no digits to the right of the decimal in the dividend, zeros must be annexed and then the decimal in the dividend must be moved the same number of places that it was moved in the divisor. Then the decimal needs to be placed on the division bar directly above the place of the moved decimal of the dividend. Once all of these steps are completed, then divide as previously learned.

Example:

Solve the following division problem:

0.12)156

Solution:

In this case the divisor has two digits to the right of the decimal, so the decimal must be moved two places to the right.

0.12‸)156

Since the dividend is a whole number a decimal must be placed at the end of the whole number.

0.12‸)156.

The decimal in the dividend must be moved the same number of places that the decimal was moved in the divisor, which was two places. In order to do this it is necessary to annex zeros at the end of the dividend.

0.12‸)156.0

Now it is possible to move the decimal two places in the dividend.

0.12‸)156.00‸

Thus:

$$0.12_{\wedge}\overline{)156.00_{\wedge}} = 12.\overline{)15600.}$$

Next place a decimal on the division bar directly above where the new decimal in the dividend was placed.

$$12.\overline{)15600.}$$

Once all these steps are completed the division can take place.

```
      1300.
12. )15600.
     12
      36
      36
       0
```

Thus the quotient is 1300.

Once the child has mastered solving division problems where there is a decimal in the divisor and solving division problems where there is a decimal in the dividend, it will then be very easy for the child to learn and master solving division problems where both the divisor and dividend are numbers with decimals. The child will begin by moving the decimal in the divisor and then moving the decimal in the dividend by the same number of places. After these steps are completed the child will then place a decimal on the top of the division bar directly above the place of the new decimal place in the dividend. After this is done, then have the child divide.

Example:

Solve the following division problem:

$$0.24\overline{)28.8}$$

Solution:

In this problem there are two digits to the right of the divisor. Move the decimal right two places so it is to the right of the four in the divisor. Since the decimal was moved two places to the right in the divisor, it must now be moved two places to the right in the dividend. However, there is only one digit to the right of the decimal in the dividend, so it is necessary to annex a zero to the right of the second eight in the dividend in order to move the decimal the required two places to the right. Once this is finished, place a decimal directly above the place of the moved decimal on the division bar.

$$024\overline{)2880.}$$

Now divide.

```
      120.
024 )2880.
     24
      48
      48
       00
```

Thus the quotient is 120.

Sometimes in division problems with decimals it will be necessary to write zeros in the quotient before dividing. Once the decimal is properly placed on the division bar, every place must have a written digit. If the divisor will not go into the dividend, then a zero must be written.

Example:

Solve the following division problem.

$$1.5\overline{)0.14055}$$

Solution:

The first step is to move the decimals in the divisor and dividend and then write the decimal on the division bar.

$$15\overline{)01.4055}$$

Since the fifteen cannot go into either the one or the fourteen, write a zero above each on the decimal bar.

```
    0.0
15 )01.4055
```

Now begin the division by dividing fifteen into one-hundred forty. Continue until the problem is complete.

```
     0.0937
15)01.4055
    135
      55
      45
      105
      105
        0
```

Thus the quotient is 0.0937.

Now that the child has mastered solving division problems with decimals, instead of writing the quotient with a remainder, teach the child how to make the quotient a decimal. To do this annex zeros at the end of the dividend and continue until the subtraction steps results in a difference of zero.

Example:

Solve the following division problem:

```
3.5)27.3
```

Solution:

Move the decimal in both the divisor and the dividend and write a decimal in the appropriate place on the division bar.

```
       .
35.)273.
```

Now divide.

```
       7.
35.)273.
    245
     28
```

Instead of having an answer of seven with a remainder of twenty-eight, annex a zero after the decimal and bring it down.

```
      7.
35.)273.0
    245
     280
```

Now divide thirty-five into two-hundred eighty.

```
       7.8
 35. )273.0
      245
       280
       280
         0
```

Since the difference after the subtraction step is zero, the problem is complete.

Thus the quotient is 7.8.

In some cases the decimal will be long or repeating decimal. It is common to require students to solve these problems by obtaining a quotient rounded to a certain decimal place. To properly solve such problems the child must divide until the determining digit of the quotient is calculated.

Example:

What is the quotient of the following division problem to the nearest hundredth?

$$1.4\overline{)1.38}$$

Solution:

Since the hundredth's place is two digits after the decimal, problem will be calculated to three digits after the decimal. The third digit after the decimal (the thousandth digit) will be the determining digit.

Begin by moving the decimal in the divisor and the decimal in the dividend followed by writing the decimal in the proper place on the division bar.

$$14.\overline{)13.8}$$

Now divide.

```
       0.9
 14. )13.8
      126
       12
```

Since the problem calls for the quotient to be rounded to the nearest hundredth and up to this point the quotient is calculated only to the tenth's place, the student needs two more digits in the quotient. Annex two zeros in the dividend.

```
       0.9
 14. )13.800
      126
       12
```

Bring down the first annexed zero and divide fourteen into one-hundred twenty.

```
      0.98
14.)13.800
    126
     120
     112
       8
```

Bring down the final zero and divide fourteen into eighty.

```
      0.985
14.)13.800
    126
     120
     112
        80
        70
        10
```

It is obvious that this problem will continue, however, the solution only requires it to be solved to the nearest hundredth. The child has worked out the problem to the nearest thousandth's place because the thousandth's digit is the determining digit. Since this is a five the rounded digit, which is the hundredth's digit, must be increased by one to a nine.

Thus the quotient to the nearest hundredth is 0.99.

In conclusion, there are only a few extra steps that make solving problems that involve dividing numbers with decimals different from solving problems that involve dividing whole numbers. First, the number of places that a decimal is moved in a divisor and dividend must be the same. Second, the decimal in the quotient must be directly above the decimal in the dividend. Finally, zeros can be annexed until there is a difference of zero in the subtraction step or enough digits in the quotient so that the quotient can be rounded to the proper digit.

A problem that requires the division of numbers with decimals will usually take a little more time than a division problem with just whole numbers. Once the child masters this skill it will be easier to learn and master the concepts of central tendency, ratios, proportions, and percents.

TEACHING CENTRAL TENDENCY (MEAN, MEDIAN, AND MODE)

Measures of central tendency are key concepts in mathematics. These concepts are used throughout a lifetime, so mastery and understanding of the different measures of central tendency will be used in future applications of mathematics.

The three types of central tendency measurements are the mean, the median and the mode. When teaching the child these measures it will be easier to being with teaching the mode; after that teach the median, and the finally the mean.

The mode is the value in a set of date that occurs most frequently. To determine the mode of a set of data, count the number of occurrences that each value appears. The value that appears the most is the mode.

Example:

A woman runs a child care service out of her home. She has ten children. The ages of these children are 2, 1, 4, 3, 2, 3, 1, 3, 2, and 3. Determine the mode for the age of children under her care.

Solution:

Arrange the data by age. Each age will be on a single line.

1, 1	(2 children)
2, 2, 2	(3 children)
3, 3, 3, 3	(4 children)
4	(1 child)

In this case it is easy to see that there are four children that are three years old, which is the value that occurs the most times. Thus the mode is three.

The mode is the easiest of the measures of central tendency to master and apply. The next measure of to teach the child is the median.

The median is the middle value of any set of data. All that is required to determine the median is to arrange the data according to size and select the value that is in the middle of the data. This is easy when there are an odd number of data values.

Example:

There are seven gas stations near the home of the Johnson family. On a Saturday, Mr. Johnson checks the price for a gallon of gasoline at each station. The prices are $2.04, $2.26, $2.18, $2.31, $2.17, $2.01, and $2.35. What is the median price per gallon among these seven stations?

Solution:

The first step is to arrange the data vertically from greatest value to least value.

2.01
2.04
2.17
2.18
2.26
2.31
2.35

Seven there are seven different values in the data, the fourth value of data is in the middle of the data set. There are three values of data above the fourth value of data and three values of data below the fourth value of data.

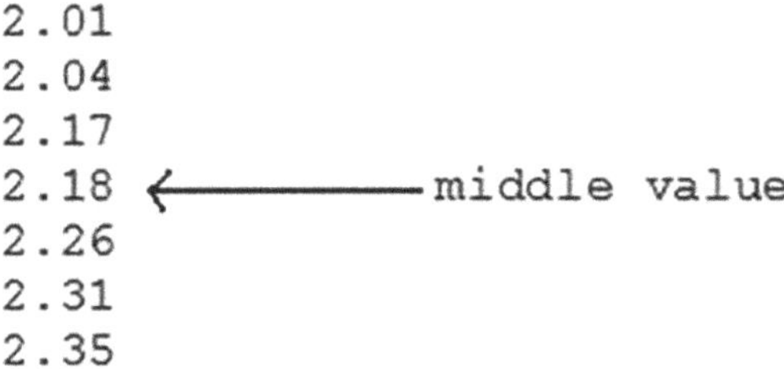

Since the middle value of data is 2.18, the median price of gasoline among the seven stations is $2.18.

When there are an even number of values in a set of data, take the sum of the two middle values and divide by two in order to find the median.

Example:

Eight houses in a neighborhood were recently purchased. The sales prices of these eight homes are listed in the table below.

$125,000	$132,000
$115,000	$105,000
$145,000	$163,000
$180,000	$150,000

Find the median homes sales price in this neighborhood.

Solution:

The first step is to list the values in order.

180,000
163,000
150,000
145,000
132,000

125,000
115,000
105,000

Since there is an even number of values in the data set, it is necessary to select the two middle values.

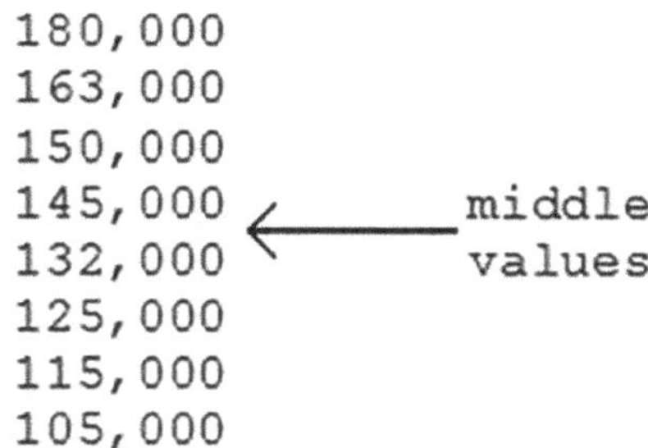

Find the sum of the two middle values.

$$\begin{array}{r} 145{,}000 \\ +132{,}000 \\ \hline 277{,}000 \end{array}$$

Divide that sum by two.

$$277{,}000 \div 2 = 138{,}500$$

He median sales price for a home in the neighborhood is $138,500.

Once the child has mastered how to find the mode and the median from a set of data, it is time for the child to learn how to find the mean value of a set of data. When people speak of an average, most of the time they are speaking about a mean. A mean is calculated by taking the sum of all the values in the data set and then dividing that sum by the number of values in that data set. A quick way for the child to remember how to calculate the mean is to remember, "add and divide."

Example:

A student has taken five exams during a semester for a math class. The student scored 83, 78, 95, 87, and 91 on these exams. What is the student's mean score?

Solution

To begin solving this problem, add the values of the data set to get a total.

$$\begin{array}{r} 83 \\ 78 \\ 95 \\ 87 \\ +91 \\ \hline 434 \end{array}$$

Since there are five values of data, divide the total by five.

$$434 \div 5 = 86.6$$

The mean score of the exams is 86.8.

Many times a mean will need to be rounded to the nearest decimal. For instance a problem could require a mean be rounded to the nearest tenth, another problem will require a mean rounded to the nearest hundredth, and still another problem will require a mean rounded to the nearest thousandth. The child has previously mastered this skill when taught to divide decimals.

Some problems will require a student to find a value to obtain a certain mean. In this case it is necessary to work backwards; instead of add and divide, the child will multiple and subtract.

Example:

A student wishes to have a mean score of 90 on exams taken during a semester of history. A mean of 90 is needed to earn an A for this class. The grade is based on four exams. The student's first three exams resulted in scores of 86, 94, and 89. What grade will the student need to achieve of the fourth and final exam, to earn an A for the semester.

Solution:

In this case the mean and the number of data values are known. What the student does not know is the total. That can be found by multiplying the mean by the number of values (including the one unknown value) in the data set.

$$90 \times 4 = 360$$

This number represents the total score on all of the exams that the student must obtain in order to have a mean of 90. The student knows the scores of the first three exams. To get the score that is necessary to achieve on the fourth exam, total the first three exams and then subtract that total from the product of the mean and the number of values in the data set.

$$\begin{array}{r} 86 \\ 94 \\ +\underline{89} \\ 269 \end{array}$$

The result of the final exam needs to get this total to 360, so subtract.

$$\begin{array}{r} 360 \\ -\underline{269} \\ 91 \end{array}$$

This result represents the score the student must earn on the fourth and final exam in order to obtain a mean of 90 for the four exams and thus earn an A for the semester.

To quickly review, in order to calculate the mean, add and divide. In order to calculate a certain value in the data set to get a known mean, multiply the mean by the number of values in the data set (including the value that is unknown) to get a product. Add all other known values to get a sum. Subtract the sum from the product. The result will be the value necessary to get the required mean.

Measures of central tendency can be observed by the child in everyday life. Median home prices are used in real estate for neighborhoods and cities. Measures of the mean are used in sports with measures such as yards per carry in football, minutes per game in basketball, and average speed per pitch in baseball. If a child is interested in sports have the child calculate the mean from raw data. In basketball select a player and look up the total of points scored and the number of games played. Take that data and have the child calculate the mean number of points scored per game. Such practice can be enjoyable and build confidence to tackle more advanced mathematical concepts.

TEACHING EXPONENTS

The concept of the exponent is very common in middle school, high school and advance mathematics. Some students experience confusion at first and will solve problems involving exponents as a multiplication problem. Once the concept is taught, practiced and finally mastered the child will have an easier time understanding and mastering more advanced mathematical concepts.

An exponent is a number that makes a certain other number multiplied by itself a certain number of times. For instance if the exponent is four, then that means that the certain number, called a base, will be multiplied by itself four times.

3^4 ← Exponent

↑ Base

In the above example the three is the base and the four is the exponent. This is vocalized as, "Three to the fourth power," and means that three is to be multiplied by itself four times as shown below.

$$3^4 = 3 \times 3 \times 3 \times 3$$

Textbooks will sometimes use the terms exponential form, expanded form and standard form in lessons. These terms should not be difficult for the child to understand once they are explained and an example is shown.

Exponential form is when there is a base and an exponent.

Expanded form is when the same factor is multiplied a certain number of times.

Standard form is how a number is normally written.

For instance:

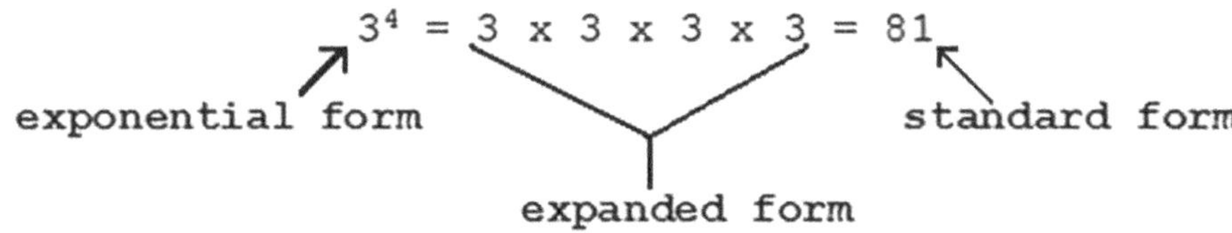

To solve a problem involving exponents, convert the problem to expanded form and then multiply to get a final product.

Example:

Solve:

$$5^3$$

Solution:

To solve five to the third power, convert form exponential form to expanded form.

$$5 \times 5 \times 5$$

Multiply five three times.

$$5 \times 5 \times 5 = 125$$

Thus:

$$5^3 = 125$$

It is possible for a child to misunderstand this process and multiply the base and the exponent, in this case multiply five and three to get a product of fifteen. This is of course incorrect and when the child makes this mistake; gently correct and explain how to get the right answer.

When a number is raised to a second power, it can also be vocalized as being squared.

For instance consider the following:

$$7^2$$

This can be vocalized as, "Seven to the second power."

This can also be vocalized as, "Seven squared."

The child needs to memorize the first twelve squares.

$$1^2 = 1$$
$$2^2 = 4$$
$$3^2 = 9$$
$$4^2 = 16$$
$$5^2 = 25$$
$$6^2 = 36$$
$$7^2 = 49$$
$$8^2 = 64$$
$$9^2 = 81$$
$$10^2 = 100$$
$$11^2 = 121$$
$$12^2 = 144$$

These squares will show up several times in the future of the child's mathematical studies.

The concept of exponents is very important for the child to understand and master. Practice by having the child do two problems that have a base that is a single digit and an exponent that is either three or four. Occasionally have the child solve a problem where the base is two and the exponent is between five and ten. The child should be able to consistently solve these problems in less than two minutes to achieve mastery.

TEACHING ORDER OF OPERATIONS WITH EXPONENTS

Once the child has mastered exponents the concept of order of operations needs to be revisited. Recall that the first order of operations was grouping symbols, then multiplication and division, followed by addition and subtraction. When exponents are included, the exponents will be completed after grouping symbols and before multiplication and division.

For instance:

$$5 \times 4^2$$

The exponent (4^2) will be completed first. Since this will result in sixteen, rewrite the problem as five times sixteen.

$$5 \times 16$$

Then multiply.

$$5 \times 16 = 80$$

It is important to teach the child to do one step at a time and rewrite the problem under the previous step.

5×4^2	Solve four squared
5×16	Multiply five and sixteen
80	Final answer

As the child completes each step the problem will become simpler until the final solution is achieved.

Example:

Solve the following:

$$4 \times (2 \times 3)^2 + 10 \div 5$$

Solution:

The first step is to look for grouping symbols in the problem. In this case there is a set of parenthesis. Inside the parenthesis is a multiplication problem. Multiply the two and the three to get a product of sis.

$$4 \times 6^2 + 10 \div 5$$

Next, look for any exponents. This problem has an exponent of two with a base of six. Since six to the second power is thirty-six, rewrite the problem with the exponent component solved.

$$4 \times 36 + 10 \div 5$$

Now comes the multiplication and division step. The problem has both multiplication and division, so from left to right the multiplication comes first. After that step is complete, then complete the division part of the problem. First multiply four and thirty-six to get a product of one-hundred forty-four.

$$144 + 10 \div 5$$

Next complete the division step with the ten and the five to get a quotient of two.

$$144 + 2$$

Finally add the final two numbers to get a sum of one-hundred forty-six.

$$144 + 2 = 146$$

To recap step by step:

$4 \times (2 \times 3)^2 + 10 \div 5$	Inside the parenthesis
$4 \times 6^2 + 10 \div 5$	Exponent
$4 \times 36 + 10 \div 5$	Multiply
$144 + 10 \div 5$	Divide
$144 + 2$	Add
146	

Have the child do one step at a time. After each step the problems smaller and simpler. It is important for the child to get into the habit of writing each step below the previous step because this is how algebra will be learned by the child.

A common mnemonic device to remember the order of operations is:

Please **E**xcuse **M**y **D**ear **A**unt **S**ally (PEMDAS)

Parenthesis (or grouping symbols), exponents, multiply, divide, add and subtract.

Mastery of the order of operations is critical to the child's success in algebra and other advanced mathematics.

TEACHING RATIOS

The definition of a ratio is the relationship that exists between the size, number, or amount of two things and this relationship is often represented by two numbers. Ratios are common in American sports.

In football a quarterback will have a touchdown to interception ratio, in baseball a pitcher will have a strikeout to walk ratio, and in basketball a point guard will have an assist to turnover ratio. Since many children follow sports, using these ratios to teach the concept might make the subject more enjoyable for the child.

Ratios can be expressed three ways. The first way is to write the word "to" between the two numbers, the second way is to write a colon (:) between the two numbers, and the third way is to write the numbers as a fraction.

For instance, if during a baseball game a pitcher struck out seven batters and walked two batters the ratio of strikeouts to walks, which is verbalized as "seven to two" can be written as:

$$7 \text{ to } 2,\ 7{:}2, \text{ or } \frac{7}{2}$$

Ratios are like fractions in that they can be reduced and expressed in simplest form. The same rules that are used to reduce fractions are used to reduce ratios.

Example:

During a football season a quarterback threw twenty touchdowns and six interceptions. What was his touchdown to interception ratio?

Solution:

Since the two numbers are twenty and six, write a ratio.

20 to 6

Now it is necessary to reduce to ratio to its simplest form. Since both numbers are divisible by two, divide both numbers by two.

$$20 \div 2 = 10 \qquad 6 \div 2 = 3$$

The new ratio is:

10 to 3

This ratio is expressed in its simplest form, therefore the quarterback's touchdown to interception ratio is: 10 to 3.

The concept of ratios is fairly simple. To practice, go to themathworksheetsite.com and under the heading, "Fractions" choose "Reduce to lowest terms." Use the fractions to assign values such as walks, strikeout, touchdowns, and interceptions and have the child express the ratio in its simplest form. Two problems once a week is sufficient practice to maintain mastery.

TEACHING UNIT RATES

A unit rate is a ratio that compares a quantity to a quantity of one unit. Many of these are seen in everyday life. When driving, speed limits (in The United States) are expressed in miles per hour. In grocery stores many items will be listed in price per ounce. Many times, a unit rates needs to be rounded to a certain decimal place.

Example:

During a basketball season a point guard had eighty-three assists and committed twenty-three turnovers. To the nearest hundred, how many assists per turnover did the point guard have?

Solution:

Since the numbers involved are eighty-three and twenty-three, write them as a ratio.

83 to 23

Recall that ratios can be expressed as a fraction.

$$\frac{83}{23}$$

Also recall that the fraction bar in a fraction can mean divide, so write the ratio as a division problem.

$$23\overline{)83}$$

Solve to three decimal places.

```
     3.608
23 )83.000
    69
    140
    138
      200
      184
       16
```

Next round the quotient to the nearest hundredth.

3.61

The point guard has 3.61 assists per turnover.

Example:

After a man filled his car's gas tank, he saw that he had driven 121.5 miles and used 4.5 gallons of gasoline. From this information, determine the gas mileage in miles per gallon to the nearest tenth.

Solution:

Set up as a ratio with the two numbers.

121.5 to 4.5

Set up the ratio as a fraction.

$$\frac{121.5}{4.5}$$

Divide.

$$4.5\overline{)121.5}$$

Solve the division problem.

```
        27.
  45. )1215.00
        90
        315
        315
          0
```

Since the problem has a zero, the division part of the problem is complete. However, since the problem stated that the answer should be stated to the nearest tenth, a decimal and a zero after the decimal needs to be annexed to show the required precision.

27.0

Thus, the car's gas mileage is 27.0 miles per gallon.

A way to practice this skill is to show the child a store receipt that has the price paid for a condiment such as ketchup, mayonnaise, or mustard. Have the child look at the label to determine the number of ounces of the condiment. Then have the child calculate the price per ounce. Once the ratio is set up have the child divide to keep in practice with long division. Doing this once every two weeks is enough to obtain and maintain mastery.

TEACHING PROPORTION

A proportion is a relationship between to ratios that are equal. This is similar to two fractions that are equivalent. These ratios must use the same units, such as boys and girls in a class.

For instance, if one class has four boys and five girls, it would be in proportion to a class that had twelve boys and fifteen girls. If the ratio of boys to girls in both of these classes were written as fractions, they would be equal.

Boys	4	12
Girls	5	15

The units are the same (boys and girls) and the ratios are equal when expressed as fractions.

It is important to notice that when two ratios or fractions are equal, the cross products will also be equal. That is when the numerator of the first fraction is multiplied by the denominator in the second fraction the product will be the same as the product of the denominator in the first fraction multiplied by the numerator in the second fraction.

4 x 15 = 60   5 x 12 = 60

4 (numerator in the first ratio)
15 (denominator in the second ratio)
5 (denominator in the first ratio)
12 (numerator in the second ratio)

Cross multiplication is often shown like this:

This concept is used when solving problems involving proportions. It will be a two-step process once the proportion is set up.

The first step is to multiply the two numbers that can be cross multiplied to obtain a product.

The second step is to divide this product by the number that cannot be cross multiplied.

A good example of this type of problem is when a recipe needs to be adjusted.

Example:

A recipe that will serve twelve needs three ounces of cream cheese. However, there are only eight people that need to be served. How much cream cheese is needed?

Solution:

Since there are two units (ounces and servings), set up the problem by writing them vertically.

Ounces
Servings

Now the original recipe calls for three ounces of cream cheese for twelve servings. Write a fraction with the three on the same line as ounces and a twelve on the same line as servings.

$$\begin{matrix}\text{Ounces} \\ \text{Servings}\end{matrix} \qquad \frac{3}{12}$$

Next, what is asked for is the number of ounces for eight servings. Write an equal sign after the first fraction and a second fraction with an eight on the line with servings and a question mark on the line with ounces.

$$\begin{matrix}\text{Ounces} \\ \text{Servings}\end{matrix} \qquad \frac{3}{12} = \frac{?}{8}$$

The proportion is set up and ready to be solved. The first step is to cross multiply the two numbers that can be cross multiplied. Since the twelve will be multiplied by the question mark, the other two numbers, which are the three and the eight, will be cross multiplied to get a product of twenty-four.

$$3 \times 8 = 24$$

The second step is to divide this product by the number that cannot be cross multiplied, which is the twelve.

$$24 \div 12 = 2$$

Rewrite the proportion with the two in place of the question mark.

$$\begin{matrix}\text{Ounces} \\ \text{Servings}\end{matrix} \qquad \frac{3}{12} = \frac{2}{8}$$

Thus, to make only eight servings, use two ounces of cream cheese.

Sometimes one or more of the numbers will not be a whole number but will be a fraction or a mixed number. Since the child has previously mastered multiplication and division with fractions and decimals, solving a proportion problem with fractions or mixed numbers should not be difficult for the child to handle. The procedure is exactly the same.

Example:

A recipe that serves six people requires one and a half pounds of ground beef. How much ground beef is required in order to make enough to serve ten people?

Solution:

Set up the proportion with a question mark as it was done in the previous problem.

$$\begin{matrix}\text{Pounds} \\ \text{Servings}\end{matrix} \qquad \frac{1.5}{6} = \frac{?}{10}$$

The first step is to cross multiply to get a product.

$$1.5 \times 10 = 15$$

The second step is to divide that product (15) by the number that was not used in the cross-multiplication process (6).

$$15 \div 6 = 2.5$$

Thus, two and a half pounds of ground beef are needed to make enough to serve ten people.

To practice, pick a recipe and change the number of servings. Pick an ingredient in the recipe and find the new amount needed by solving the proportion. This could be done once a week to obtain and maintain mastery.

TEACHING THE BASICS OF PERCENT

After the child has mastered the concepts of ratios and proportions, it will be time to teach the concept of percents. Percents and percentage are used quite frequently in daily life. Discounts on sales are displayed and computed in terms of a percent. Taxes are calculated as a percent of income or percent of sales. Therefore, an understanding of what percents are and the various ways problems involving percents are solved is necessary for the child to master before moving to more advanced mathematical concepts.

The meaning of percent is hundredths. One hundred percent is one whole, while one percent is one-hundredth. Common fractions such as one-half and one-fourth can be expressed as percents. One half is the same as fifty percent, because fifty percent is the same as fifty hundredths, which can be reduced to one-half. Likewise, one-fourth is the same as twenty-five percent.

Example:

A man has a personal library of two-hundred fifty books. Fifty percent of these books are biographies. What is the number of biographies in this man's personal library?

Solution:

Since fifty percent is the same as one-half, the number of biographies in the library if one-half of two-hundred fifty.

$$\frac{1}{2} \text{ of } 250$$

Recall that when the word "of" is used in a problem with a fraction it is the same as multiplying, so rewrite the expression with a multiplication sign.

$$\frac{1}{2} \times 250$$

Solve the problem.

$$\frac{1}{2} \times \frac{250}{1} = \frac{250}{2}$$

Recall that the fraction bar is the same as a division sign so divide and solve.

$$250 \div 2 = 125$$

Thus, the man has one-hundred twenty-five biographies in his personal library.

This is just the beginning of the subject matter of percents. It is important for the child to understand that percent means "of one hundred." As each new component of percents is introduced it is important that the child achieves mastery in the components before proceeding to the next lesson.

TEACHING CONVERTING PERCENTS AND DECIMALS

Converting percents to decimals and decimals to percents is a key skill that should be easily mastered by the child. It should take less than a day for the child to achieve mastery in this skill, and minimal practice to maintain this mastery.

The key to converting percents to decimals and decimals to percents is the movement of the decimal point. In both cases the decimal point will be moved only two places. When converting a percent to a decimal the decimal point will be moved two places to the left; likewise, when converting a decimal to a percent the decimal point will be moved two places to the right.

Example:

Convert 75% to a decimal.

Solution:

Since this is a conversion of a percent to a decimal, the decimal point must be moved two places to the left (or forward). In this case the decimal is assumed to be behind the five. Moving the decimal point one place to the left will place the decimal point between the seven and the five. Moving it two places will put the decimal point in front of the seven.

Thus:

75% converted to a decimal number is 0.75.

$$75\% = 0.75$$

Example:

Convert 0.37 to a decimal.

Solution:

Since this is a conversion of a decimal number to a percent, the decimal point must be moved two places to the right (or backwards). Moving the decimal point one place to the right will place the decimal point between the three and the seven. Moving it two places will put the decimal point behind the seven where it will not have to be written. The final step is to write the percent sign.

Thus:

0.37 converted to a percent is 37%.

$$0.37 = 37\%$$

In the case where the percent to be converted to a decimal is a single digit, a zero must be annexed in front of the number.

Example:
Convert 3% to a decimal.
Solution:
There is an assumed decimal behind the three. In order to move the decimal point two places, annex a zero in front of the three and place the decimal point in front of the zero.

.03

Write a zero in front of the decimal to complete the answer.

0.03

Thus:
3% converted to a decimal is 0.03.

3% = 0.03

In the case where there is a decimal with a single digit to the right of the decimal point to be converted into a percent, a zero must be annexed behind the number in order for the decimal to be properly converted into a percent.
Example:
Convert 0.6 to a percent.
Solution:
Since this a conversion of a decimal number to a percent, the decimal point must be moved to places to the right. However, there is only one digit so a zero must be annexed to the rear of the six before the decimal point is to be moved.

0.60

Now move the decimal point two places to the right and rewrite as a percent.

60%

Thus:
0.6 converted to a percent is 60%.

0.6 = 60%

The child should memorize these single digit equivalents.

1% = 0.01	0.1 = 10%
2% = 0.02	0.2 = 20%
3% = 0.03	0.3 = 30%
4% = 0.04	0.4 = 40%
5% = 0.05	0.5 = 50%
6% = 0.06	0.6 = 60%
7% = 0.07	0.7 = 70%
8% = 0.08	0.8 = 80%
9% = 0.09	0.9 = 90%

Children tend to get confused with the single digit equivalents of decimals and percents. Sometimes children will make them both single digits as shown below.

4% = 0.4 or 0.8 = 8%

These are both not correct.

Practice by writing a few percents to be converted to decimal numbers on a piece of paper. Then write a few decimal numbers to be converted into percents. Include single digit percents and decimal numbers in the practice. The child should be able to do each of these correctly in less than five seconds to achieve mastery.

Later, doing conversions with a number greater than one and a percent less than one will be taught. Next it is time to teach the child how to convert percents into fractions and fractions into percents.

TEACHING CONVERTING PERCENTS AND FRACTIONS

The process of converting percents to fractions and fractions to percents will combine two previously mastered skills. It will first be necessary to convert either the percent or fraction to a decimal.

In order to convert a percent to a fraction, it is first necessary to convert the percent to a decimal number. This is something that the child recently mastered. Once that is done then the decimal is to be converted to a fraction. This is a skill that the child mastered some time ago.

Percent ⟶ Decimal ⟶ Fraction

Conversely when a fraction is converted to a percent, it must first be converted to a decimal number. After that the decimal number must be converted to a percent. These are both skills that were previously mastered by the child.

Fraction ⟶ Decimal ⟶ Percent

Example:
Convert 35% to a fraction.
Solution:
The first step is to convert the percent to a decimal.

$$35\% = 0.35$$

Now convert the decimal into a fraction by writing thirty-five as the numerator and one hundred as the denominator.

$$\frac{35}{100}$$

Finally reduced the fraction to its simplest form (divide both the numerator and the denominator by five).

$$\frac{35}{100} = \frac{7}{20}$$

Thus:

35% converted to a fraction is $\frac{7}{20}$.

$$35\% = \frac{7}{20}$$

Example:

Convert $\frac{3}{4}$ to a percent.

Solution:

The fraction must be first converted into a decimal number. To do this, rewrite the fraction as a division problem.

$$4\overline{)3}$$

Divide.

$$\begin{array}{r} 0.75 \\ 4\overline{)3.00} \\ \underline{28} \\ 20 \\ \underline{20} \\ 0 \end{array}$$

$$\frac{3}{4} = 0.75$$

Now that the fraction is converted to a decimal, move the decimal point two places to the right to make the decimal number a percent.

75%

Thus:

$\frac{3}{4}$ converted to a percent is 75%.

$$\frac{3}{4} = 75\%$$

Not every fraction will convert to a percent evenly. Sometimes it is necessary to round to the nearest percent. When this is the case, the decimal must be rounded to the nearest hundredth. So, when the fraction is divided, the quotient is solved to three decimal places.

Example:

Convert $\frac{2}{3}$ to a percent to the nearest percent.

Solution:

First rewrite the fraction as a division problem.

$$3\overline{)2}$$

Since the quotient must be rounded to the nearest hundredth, which is two places after the decimal, it must have three digits after the decimal. Write a decimal point behind the two followed by three zeros.

$$3\overline{)2.000}$$

Now divide.

```
   0.666
3 )2.000
   18
    20
    18
     20
```

Next, round the quotient to the nearest hundredth.

0.67

Finally convert this to a percent.

67%

This is not exact so have the child use the word "approximately" when answering. Thus:

$\frac{2}{3}$ is approximately 67%.

To have the child practice converting percents into fractions, write a few percents on a piece of paper. Make sure at least two are divisible by either two or five, so the child will have to reduce.

To have the child practice converting fractions into percents, write two or three fractions on a piece of paper. The denominator should be less than ten. Have the child round these to the nearest percent. To achieve mastery the child should be able to consistently convert a fraction correctly in less than a minute.

TEACHING THE PERCENT PROPORTION

For most percentage problems, there are three components. The three components are the percent, the whole, and the part. These problems will give two of these components and the third component will need to be calculated.
Take the following statement:

25% of 68 is 17

In this statement twenty-five is the percent, sixty-eight is the whole and seventeen is the part. From this, three questions can be asked.

What is 25% of 68? (Answer: 17)

17 is what percent of 68? (Answer: 25%)

17 is 25% of what number? (Answer: 68)

Each of these questions can be solved by using the percent proportion.

$$\frac{\text{Part}}{\text{Whole}} = \frac{\text{Percent}}{100}$$

For instance, in the above statement:

Part = 17 Whole = 68 Percent = 25%

$$\frac{17}{68} = \frac{25}{100}$$

Some textbooks will use the word "is" for "part"; and the word "of" for "whole". This is how such a proportion will look:

$$\frac{\text{Is}}{\text{Of}} = \frac{\text{Percent}}{100}$$

To determine where the numbers are to be placed in the proportion, look at the question and see what is missing and what the child is asked to find.

What is 25% of 68?

Is = ? Of = 68 Percent = 25

When a number has a percent sign written after it (or the word "percent" in written form), that number is the percent in the proportion. If a number comes directly after the word "of", that is the whole or the "of" number. What is; signifies that this is what is asked for in the problem and what is missing, so the question mark goes in the "is" place.

17 is what percent of 68?

Is = 17 Of = 68 Percent = ?

When a number comes before is in the problem, that number will be the part in the proportion or the "is" number. This question asks, "what percent" so this signifies that the percent is missing, and this is what the child is asked to find, so the question mark goes in the "percent" place.

17 is 25% of what number?

Is = 17 Of = ? Percent = 25

When the words "what number" follow the word "of", that means the "of" number is missing. The question mark will go in the "whole" or "of" place in the proportion.

The percent proportion is one way to solve percent calculation problems. There are other methods to solve these problems. These will be learned in later lessons.

TEACHING FINDING THE PERCENT OF A NUMBER (THE "IS")

Finding the percent of a number can be found by using the percent proportion. It can also be found by multiplication. In order to find the number through multiplication the percent must first be converted into a decimal number.

The following example will be solved both ways.

Example:

What is 54% of 150?

Solution (proportion method):

In this problem the percent and the whole (of) are given. The child is asked to find the part (is). Set up the proportion with a question mark in the "is" position.

$$\frac{?}{150} = \frac{54}{100}$$

The next step is to cross multiply to get a product and then divide that product by one hundred (the number diagonally across from the question mark).

$$150 \times 54 = 8100$$
$$8100 \div 100 = 81$$

Thus:

54% of 150 is 81.

Solution (multiplication method):

To solve the problem using the multiplication method it is first necessary to convert the percent to a decimal number.

$$54\% = 0.54$$

Now multiply the decimal number by the "of" number, which in this case is one-hundred fifty.

$$0.54 \times 150 = 81$$

In both cases the answer is eighty-one. Either method can be used to solve such problems. In time the child will prefer one method over the other. This is both natural and acceptable.

In many cases the number to be calculated will not be a whole number, but a decimal number. The child should be able to manage solving these problems quite easily, since multiplying and dividing decimal number has been previously mastered.

Example:
What is 14% of 28?
Solution (proportion method):
Set up the percent proportion with the question mark in the "is" position.

$$\frac{?}{28} = \frac{14}{100}$$

Cross multiply to get a product.

$$28 \times 14 = 392$$

Divide that product by one hundred.

$$392 \div 100 = 3.92$$

Thus:
14% of 28 is 3.92.
Solution (multiplication method):
First convert the percent to a decimal number.

$$14\% = 0.14$$

Multiply this decimal number by the "of" number.

$$0.14 \times 28 = 3.92$$

Thus:
14% of 28 is 3.92.

For practice have the child do two problems about once a week. Successfully completing each problem in less than a minute is enough to achieve and maintain mastery.

TEACHING FINDING THE PERCENT

When finding the percent using the proportion method, the question mark will go above one hundred in the proportion. Another way to find the percent is to divide the part by the whole ("is" divided by "of") and then convert the quotient, which will be a decimal number into a percent. The child should have previously mastered the necessary computation skills.

Example:

18 is what percent of 75?

Solution (proportion method):

Set up the proportion with the eighteen in the "is" position, seventy-five in the "of" position and a question mark in the percent position.

$$\frac{18}{75} = \frac{?}{100}$$

Cross multiply the "is" number (18) with one hundred to get a product.

$$18 \times 100 = 1800$$

Divide this product by seventy-five.

$$1800 \div 75 = 24$$

Thus:

18 is 24% of 75.

Solution (division method):

Divide the "is" number (18) by the "of" number (75).

$$18 \div 75 = 75\overline{)18}$$

Annex a decimal point behind the eight and then annex two zeros.

$$75\overline{)18.00}$$

Divide.

```
     0.24
75 )18.00
    150
     300
     300
       0
```

$$18 \div 75 = 0.24$$

Convert the decimal number into a percent.

0.24 = 24%

Thus:

18 is 24% of 75.

Sometimes it will be necessary to round the answer to the nearest percent. In this case when using the proportion method to solve the problem, solve to the nearest tenth. When using the division method to solve the problem, solve to the nearest thousandths place (three digits after the decimal).

Example:

22 is what percent of 60?

Solution (proportion method):

Set up the proportion.

$$\frac{22}{60} = \frac{?}{100}$$

Cross multiply to get a product.

$$22 \times 100 = 2200$$

Divide that product by the "of" number to the tenths place.

$$2200 \div 60 = 36.6$$

Round that number to the nearest whole number.

37

Since this is not an exact answer, use the word approximately.

Thus:

22 is approximately 37% of 60.

Solution (division method):

Set up the division problem and annex a decimal point after the final digit of the "is" number and then annex three zeros.

$$60\overline{)22.000}$$

Divide.

```
        0.366
    60)22.000
       180
         400
         360
          400
          360
```

Next, round the quotient to the nearest hundredth.

0.37

Now, convert the decimal into a percent.

37%

Once again, use the word approximately in the answer.

Thus:

22 is approximately 37% of 60.

To give the child some problems for daily practice, go to themathworkshhetsite.com and select "Reduce to Lowest Terms" under the "Fractions" heading. Choose "20" for number of problems and vary the difficulty setting. At this time do not include improper fractions.

Select a few fractions and convert them into problems that require the child to find the percent. Make the numerator the "is" number and the denominator the "of" number.

For instance, the fraction $\frac{72}{99}$ can be converted to:

72 is what percent of 99?

Have the child round all answers to the nearest percent.

The child should be able to consistently find the correct percent of five problems in less than three minutes to achieve mastery.

TEACHING FINDING THE WHOLE (THE "OF)

To find the whole (of) A percent problem, set up the percent proportion, cross multiply the part (is) by one hundred to get a product. After that, divide the product by the percent.

Example:

27 is 60% of what number?

Solution:

Set up the percent proportion with a question mark in the "of" position.

$$\frac{27}{?} = \frac{60}{100}$$

Cross multiply to get a product.

27 x 100 = 2700

Divide that product by the percent.

2700 ÷ 60 = 45

Thus:

27 is 60% of 45.

Sometimes the problem will begin with the percent. Just remember the key phrase, "of what number" in the problem tells the child that the question mark will go in the "of" position of the percent proportion.

Example:

36% of what number is 81?

Solution:

Set up the percent proportion with a question mark in the "of" position.

$$\frac{81}{?} = \frac{36}{100}$$

Cross multiply to get a product.

81 x 100 = 8100

Divide that product by the percent.

$$8100 \div 36 = 225$$

Thus:
36% of 225 is 81.

In order to create some problems for daily practice a calculator can be used. Pick a number to be the "of" number and multiply it by a two-digit decimal number that will be the percent. The result will be the "is" number in the problem.

To see how this works, take a look at the previous two examples.

In the problem, "27 is 60% of what number"; take the answer (45) and multiply it by the percent (0.6) to get the "is" number (27). Set up the problem for the child once the three numbers of the percent problem are known.

On the calculator:

$$45 \times 0.6 = 27$$

The numbers of the problem are:

Percent	60%
Part (is)	27
Whole (of)	45

The second problem asks, "36% of what number is 81?"

On the calculator:

$$225 \times 0.36 = 81$$

The numbers of the problem are:

Percent	36%
Part (is)	81
Whole (of)	225

Another way to get some practice problems for the child is to go to themathworksheetsite.com and create a worksheet for reducing fractions. Use a calculator to find the percent and then write the problem down for the child.

For instance, the fraction:

$$\frac{27}{45}$$

Using the calculator:

$$27 \div 45 = 0.6$$

The numbers of the problem are:

Percent	60%
Part (is)	27
Whole (of)	45

A few problems once a week will be enough for the child to maintain mastery, which will be achieved by being able to consistently do such a problem correctly in less than a minute.

TEACHING PERCENT INCREASES

Another type of problem that involves the concept of percents is to find the percent or percentage increase or decrease of a number. This lesson will concern the child with the percent increase of a number.

The important thing to remember in this type of problem is that the final answer will be the sum of the whole and the part ("of" plus "is").

Example:

John makes a salary of six-hundred fifty dollars a week. His boss just gave him a raise of five percent. What is John's new weekly salary?

Solution:

In this type of problem, the "is" needs to be calculated. Once this is calculated then it will be added to the "of" amount (in this case the original weekly salary.

This could be calculated by using the percent proportion method or the multiplication method. For this example, the multiplication method will be used.

First convert the percent into a decimal number.

$$5\% = 0.05$$

Now multiply the decimal by the original salary.

$$0.05 \times 650 = 32.5$$

This product is the amount of increase. The amount of increase must be added to the original amount to calculate the new weekly salary.

$$650 + 32.5 = 682.5$$

Since this figure represents pay in dollars it can be written with a dollar sign.

$$682.5 = \$682.50$$

Thus:

John's new weekly salary is six-hundred eighty-two dollars and fifty cents.

Have the child practice by giving a number and a percent increase. Use a calculator to figure out the answer. Just remember that the child must add the "is" number to the original "of" number to obtain the final answer.

TEACHING PERCENT DECREASES

In the previous lesson, the child learned and mastered problems that involved a percent increase. Problems that involve a percent decrease are very similar. The only difference is that that "is" amount will be subtracted from the "of" amount instead of added to it. Typically, these problems involve purchasing products that are on sale at a discount.

Example:

A laptop computer that has a listed price of five-hundred fifty dollars is on sale at a fifteen percent discount. What is the new sales price of the laptop?

Solution:

To solve this problem, find the amount of discount and then subtract that from the original price.

First find the amount of discount.

What is 15% of 550?

Set up the percent proportion with a question mark in the "is" position.

$$\frac{?}{350} = \frac{15}{100}$$

Cross multiply to get a product.

$$550 \times 15 = 8250$$

Divide that product by one hundred.

$$8250 \div 100 = 82.50$$

The quotient is the amount of discount. To complete the problem, subtract this number from the original price to get the sales price.

$$550 - 82.50 = 467.50$$

Thus:

The sales price of the laptop is four-hundred sixty-seven dollars and fifty cents.

Have the child practice by giving a number and a percent decrease. Use a calculator to figure out the answer. Just remember that the child must subtract the "is" number to the original "of" number to obtain the final answer.

TEACHING PERCENTAGE INCREASES

In order to find the percentage increase of an event, a subtraction step is first required to find the part or "is" component of the percent proportion. A typical problem of this nature usually involves a price increase of an item. The original price must be subtracted from the new price to obtain the price increase. The price increase will be the "is" portion of the percent proportion.

Example:

A restaurant increased the price of a popular hamburger from four dollars to five dollars. What is the percentage increase?

Solution:

Before setting up the percent proportion, it is necessary to subtract the original price, which is four dollars, from the new price, which is five dollars to get a difference of one.

$$5 - 4 = 1$$

The difference of one will be the "is" component of the percent proportion. The original price will be the "of" component.

$$\frac{1}{4} = \frac{?}{100}$$

Cross multiply to get a product.

$$1 \times 100 = 100$$

Divide the product by the "of" number to get the percent.

$$100 \div 4 = 25$$

Thus:

The price of the hamburger was increased by twenty-five percent.

Sometimes the percentage must be rounded to the nearest percent.

Example:

A publishing company increased the price of a magazine subscription from twenty-two dollars a year to twenty-five dollars a year. What was the percentage increase of the subscription price to the nearest percent?

Solution:

The first step is to subtract the original price from the new price to obtain the amount of price increase.

$$25 - 22 = 3$$

The difference, which is three, is the amount of increase. The amount of increase will go in the "is" position of the percent proportion. The original amount, which is twenty-two, will go in the "of" position of the percent proportion.

$$\frac{3}{22} = \frac{?}{100}$$

Cross multiply to get a product.

$$3 \times 100 = 300$$

Divide this product by the "of" number to get a quotient. Since the answer must be rounded to the nearest percent, the quotient must be calculated to the tenth's digit.

```
     13.6
22 )300.0
    22
     80
     66
     140
     132
       8
```

Since the quotient must be rounded to the nearest whole number, the quotient and thus the percent will be fourteen.

Thus:

The percentage increase in the price of the magazine subscription is fourteen percent.

Have the child practice by giving an original number and a final number. The final number must be less than twice the original number. In order to ensure that this is the case, multiply the original number by two and make the final number less than this. Have the child find the percentage increase. Use a calculator to figure out the answer.

TEACHING PERCENTAGE DECREASES

Once the child has mastered solving problems that require finding the percentage increase, it should be very easy for the child to master solving problems that require finding the percentage decrease. The only difference is that the new amount must be subtracted from the original amount to find the amount of decrease. After that, use the percent proportion.

Example:

A high school sold eighty tickets for a Friday night showing of a musical. The next night the high school only sold sixty-eight tickets for the musical. What is the percentage decrease in tickets sold?

Solution:

The first step is to subtract the new amount, which is sixty-eight, from the original amount, which is eighty.

$$80 - 68 = 12$$

This difference is the amount of change and will go in the "is" position of the percent proportion. The original number will go in the "of" position.

$$\frac{12}{80} = \frac{?}{100}$$

Cross multiply to get a product.

$$12 \times 100 = 1200$$

Divide this product by the "of" number.

$$1200 \div 80 = 15$$

Thus:

There was a fifteen percent decrease in the number of tickets sold on the second night of the musical.

As with some problems where the child must find the percent increase, some problems where the child must find the percentage decrease must be rounded to the nearest percent.

Example:

The temperature in a town dropped from eighty-seven degrees to sixty-three degrees. What was the percentage decrease to the nearest percent?

Solution:

The first step is to subtract the new temperature from the original temperature.

$$87 - 63 = 24$$

The difference is the amount of decrease, which will go in the "is" position in the percent proportion.

$$\frac{24}{87} = \frac{?}{100}$$

Cross multiply to get a product.

$$24 \times 100 = 2400$$

Divide this product by the "of" number to get the percent. Compute to the tenths place so that the quotient can be rounded to the nearest whole number.

```
      27.5
87 )2400.0
    174
     660
     609
      510
      435
       75
```

Since the quotient must be rounded to the nearest whole number, the quotient and thus the percent will be twenty-eight.

Thus:

The percentage decrease in temperature was twenty-eight percent.

Have the child practice by giving an original number and a final number. The final number must be less than the original number. Have the child find the percentage decrease. Use a calculator to figure out the answer.

TEACHING PERCENTAGES GREATER THAN ONE HUNDRED

There will be many problems when a percent will be greater than one hundred percent. It is therefore very important for the child to understand and be comfortable with this concept.

Since one hundred percent is equal to one, two hundred percent is equal to two.

100% = 1
200% = 2

The child knows that when a number is multiplied by one, there is no change in value. Explain that since one and one hundred percent have the same value, and that "of" will mean multiply; one times a number is the same as one hundred percent of a number.

1 x 5 = 5
100% of 5 is 5

The same is true when two is substituted for one and two hundred percent is substituted for one hundred percent.

2 x 5 = 10
200% of 5 is 10

Once this is understood the child should quickly be able to understand greater percentages.

300% = 3
400% = 4
500% = 5
600% = 6
700% = 7
800% = 8
900% = 9
1000% = 10

Example:

After the first week of a You Tube channel, a boy had fifty subscribers. After the second week the boy had three-hundred subscribers. What was the percentage increase in subscribers?

Solution:

Since this is a percentage increase problem the first step is subtraction. Subtract the original amount, which is fifty, from the new amount, which is three hundred. This is the amount of increase and will go in the "is" position of the percent proportion.

$$300 - 50 = 250$$

Set up the percent proportion.

$$\frac{250}{50} = \frac{?}{100}$$

Cross multiply to get a product.

$$250 \text{ x } 100 = 25000$$

Divide this product by the "of" number to get the percent.

$$25000 \div 50 = 500$$

Thus:

In the week there was a five-hundred percent increase in subscribers.

As with percentage increases where the percent is less than one hundred percent, sometimes problems with a percent greater than one hundred needs to be rounded to the nearest percent. Keep this in mind as the child practices this skill.

Go back through all the lessons regarding percent and work with percents larger than one hundred percent. Solving one or two such problems a week will be enough for the child to gain and maintain mastery.

TEACHING PERCENTAGES LESS THAN ONE

Problems that have percents that are less than one percent will be solved exactly the same way as problems that have percents that are greater than or equal to one percent. To convert these percents into decimals it will be necessary to annex zeros to the left (in front of) the first digit.

Example:

Convert 0.56% to a decimal number.

Solution:

Annex two zeros to the left of the five.

$$00.56$$

Move the decimal point two places to the left.

$$.0056$$

Write a zero in front of the decimal.

$$0.0056$$

Thus:

0.56% converted to a decimal number is 0.0056.

Use the percent proportion to solve problems involving percents that are less than one percent.

Example:

6 is 0.5% of what number?

Solution:

Set up the percent proportion with six in the "is" position, the decimal in the percent position, and a question mark in the "of" position.

$$\frac{6}{?} = \frac{0.5}{100}$$

Cross multiply to get a product.

$$6 \times 100 = 600$$

Divide this product by the percent to get a quotient.

$$600 \div 0.5 = 1200$$

Thus:
6 is 0.5% of 1200.

Go back through all the lessons regarding percent and work with percents less than one percent. Solving one or two such problems a week will be enough for the child to gain and maintain mastery.

TEACHING THE METRIC SYSTEM

While the United States does not use the metric system in daily life, there is still a need for the child to understand the basics of this system. It is used worldwide and in advanced science classes. There are some aspects of American culture that has been changed to use the metric system to comply with certain international standards.

Track and field is one area that uses the metric system. In the United States tracks have been changed to meters so athletes in this field can be compared to their international counterparts. However, there is no likelihood of American football fields being converted into meters.

For the purpose of this lesson, consideration will only be given to measurements of distance, mass, and volume. In addition, the basic prefixes will be addressed.

The basic unit of measurement for distance in the metric system is the meter. The length of a meter is slightly more than the length of a yard. In track the one-hundred-meter dash has replaced the one-hundred-yard dash.

The basic unit of mass in the metric system is the gram. The mass of a gram is less than an ounce. It is used on nutritional labels for foods. Such food labels will display the amounts of fat, protein, carbohydrates, sugar, and fiber per serving in grams.

The basic unit of measurement for volume in the metric system is the liter. A liter is slightly more than a quart. Many soft drink companies sell soda in one- or two-liter bottles.

The metric system relies on prefixes to label differences in the size of the various measurements. It makes it easier to discuss units of measurements that are a lot larger or a lot smaller than the base measurement.

All of these prefixes defines increases or decreases in powers of ten. For now, teach the child the three basic prefixes that are greater than the base measurement and the three basic prefixes that are less than the base measurement. Other prefixes will be taught in high school science. The goal for now is to have the child have a basic understanding of the metric system.

The three prefixes for an amount greater than the base measurement are kilo, hecto, and deca. Kilo means one thousand, so a kilometer is one-thousand meters. Hecto means one hundred, so a hectogram is one-hundred grams. Deca means ten, so a decaliter is ten liters. It is possible that the child has been exposed to the terms kilometer and kilogram.

The three prefixes for an amount less than the base measurement are deci, centi, and milli. Deci means one-tenth, so a decimeter is one-tenth of a meter. That will also mean that ten decimeters will equal one meter. Centi means one-hundredth, so a centigram is one-hundredth of a gram. That will also mean that one-hundred centigrams will equal one gram. Milli means one-thousandth, so a milliliter is one-thousandth of a liter. That also means that one-thousand milliliters is equal to one liter. It is possible that the child has been exposed to the terms, centimeter, millimeter, and milligram.

Chart

Base Unit	Meter	Gram	Liter
1000	Kilometer	Kilogram	Kiloliter
100	Hectometer	Hectogram	Hectoliter
10	Decameter	Decagram	Decaliter
1	Meter	Gram	Liter
0.1	Decimeter	Decigram	Deciliter
0.01	Centimeter	Centigram	Centiliter
0.001	Millimeter	Milligram	Milliliter

Typical questions will require the child to convert one metric measurement into another metric measurement. This will be accomplished by either multiplying or dividing by a power of ten. Once the child understands this it will be a simple matter of moving the decimal point to the right or the left. Once the child achieves mastery in this skill, such problems can be solved in less than ten seconds.

If the child is converting a larger unit to a smaller unit, then multiplication will take place. If the child is converting a smaller unit to a larger unit, then division will take place.

Example:

How many centimeters in two-hundred fifty-seven millimeters?

Solution:

Since the problem calls for a conversion of a smaller unit (millimeters) to a larger unit (centimeters), division will take place.

The amount must be divided by a power of ten (10, 100, 1000 ...). In order to determine what power of ten to use as a divisor, look at how many steps up the chart centimeter is from millimeter.

Since it is only one place, ten will be used as a divisor.

257 millimeters

$$257 \div 10 = 25.7$$

Notice that the decimal point is moved one place to the right.

Thus:

There are 25.7 centimeters in 257 millimeters.

Once the child has mastery of this process and understands how to move the decimal point, the problem should take less than five seconds to solve.

Example:

How many centimeters in 2.46 kilometers?

Solution:

Since the problem calls for a conversion of a larger unit (kilometer) to a smaller unit (centimeter), multiplication will take place.

The amount must be multiplied by a power of ten. In order to determine what power of ten to use as a factor look at how many steps down from kilo is centi.

It is three steps from kilo to the base measurement (kilometer to meter) and another two steps from the base measurement to centi (meter to centimeter), for a total of five steps. So, the power of ten to use is one-hundred thousand.

$$10^5 = 10 \times 10 \times 10 \times 10 \times 10 = 100{,}000$$

So multiply.

$$2.46 \times 100{,}000 = 246{,}000$$

Thus:

There are 246,000 centimeters in 2.46 kilometers.

Once again, notice that the answer can be obtained by moving the decimal point five places to the right.

The concept of multiplying by powers of ten and moving the decimal point will be used in teaching scientific notation.

TEACHING SCIENTIFIC NOTATION WITH POSITIVE EXPONENTS

An important concept in higher level mathematics and science classes is the concept of scientific notation. This concept allows easy use of very large and very small numbers. Large numbers typically are the number of atoms in a certain situation, or the distance between two objects in outer space. Small numbers are typically measurements at the atomic and subatomic level. This lesson will cover very large numbers.

Begin by explaining that numbers such as ninety and nine hundred can be expressed as a single digit multiplied by a power of ten.

$$90 = 9 \times 10$$
$$900 = 9 \times 100$$

A large number such as ninety million can be expressed the same way.

$$90{,}000{,}000 = 9 \times 10{,}000{,}000$$

Now explain that the number ten million can be expressed by multiplying ten by itself seven times.

$$10{,}000{,}000 = 10 \times 10 \times 10 \times 10 \times 10 \times 10 \times 10$$

Next explain that ten multiplied by itself seven times can be expressed as an exponent as ten to the seventh power.

$$10 \times 10 \times 10 \times 10 \times 10 \times 10 \times 10 = 10^7$$

Now show that ten million is equal to ten to the seventh power.

$$10{,}000{,}000 = 10^7$$

Since ten million is equal to ten to the seventh power, and ninety million is equal to nine times ten million; that will mean that ninety million is equal to nine times ten to the seventh power.

$$90{,}000{,}000 = 9 \times 10^7$$

This is ninety million expressed in scientific notation.

In order for a number to be express in scientific notation, only one digit must be to the left of the decimal point. That number must be multiplied by ten to a power.

For instance, the distance from the sun to the earth is ninety-three million miles. In standard form the number will look like this:

93,000,000

Now it could be expressed as follows:

93×10^6

While this expression is equal to the standard form it is not in scientific notation because there are two digits (the nine and the three) that are to the left of the decimal point.

The proper way to express this number in scientific notation is to just have the nine to the left of the decimal point and the three to the right of the decimal point. To figure out the exponent, count the number of digits in the number after the first digit.

$93{,}000{,}000 = 9.3 \times 10^7$

This is proper scientific notation. The nine is the first digit, and there are seven digits after the nine (the three and the six zeros), so the exponent will be seven.

Example:

What is 274,000,000 in scientific notation?

Solution:

In this problem the first digit is a two, so write a two with a decimal point.

2.

The next digits are a seven and a four, so write then after the decimal point.

2.74

Next write times ten after the number.

2.74×10

All that is left is to figure out the exponent. Count the seven as a one, the four as two, and continue with the zeros to get a total of eight. The exponent will be eight.

2.74×10^8

Thus:

274,000,000 in scientific notation is 2.74×10^8.

It is also important for the child to be able to convert a number in scientific notation to standard notation. To do this write the numbers and omit the decimal. The exponent will determine the number of digits after the first digit. The number of digits after the first digit and the number of zeros add up to the exponent.

Example:

What is 3.875×10^{10} in standard notation?

Solution:
The first step is to write the numbers without the decimal point.

3875

The exponent is ten. That means that there must be ten digits after the first digit, which in this case is three. The eight, the seven, and the five will be part of the ten digits. Since there are three digits after the first digit, seven zeros are needed to make ten, therefore write seven zeros after the five.

38750000000

Finally work right to left and place a comma in front of every third digits.

38,750,000,000

Thus:
3.875×10^{10} in standard notation is 38,750,000,000.

Once the child has achieved mastery with scientific notation that have positive exponents, such problems will be easily solved in five to ten seconds. Such problems are common in annual testing. The use of scientific notation in calculations will be taught in high school mathematics and science classes. For now, to have the child understand what scientific notation is, and how to convert numbers between standard notation and scientific is sufficient for elementary school mathematics.

TEACHING THE BASICS OF NEGATIVE NUMBERS

Before any child begins to learn Algebra, total mastery of positive and negative numbers is a must. This topic is often confusing to elementary school students when it is first presented to them, so this concept needs to be broken down into smaller steps that must be mastered before proceeding. As these steps are mastered in turn, the child will gain confidence and mastery in all aspects of positive and negative numbers, especially computations involving positive and negative numbers.

To begin, discuss the concept of a number's opposite. This is very simple and easy to master, but very important for the child to understand.

For any positive number, its opposite will be the negative number the same distance from zero on a number line in the opposite direction. Thus, the opposite of five is negative five. The reverse is also true. The opposite of a negative number is a positive number the same distance from zero on a number line in the opposite direction. Thus, the opposite of negative seven is seven.

Negative numbers are common when dealing with cold temperatures. A temperature such as twelve degrees below zero can also be expressed as negative twelve degrees.

At this point it is important for the child to understand the concept of negative numbers. Basic operations involving numbers will be learned in later lessons.

TEACHING THE SUBSETS OF REAL NUMBERS

There are a few subsets of real numbers that are easy to understand. It is important for the child to understand this terminology. There are five subsets of real numbers, but in this lesson only four of the subsets will be covered.

The four subsets of real numbers covered in this lesson are natural numbers, whole numbers, integers, and rational numbers. The smallest of these subsets are the natural numbers while the largest of these subsets are the rational numbers. Each larger subset of numbers will contain all the numbers in the smaller subsets of numbers.

Natural numbers begin at one and continue to infinity.

1, 2, 3, 4, 5...

Whole numbers consist of all of the natural numbers and zero.

0, 1, 2, 3, 4, 5...

Integers are all of the natural numbers, their opposites and zero.

...-5, -4, -3, -2, -1, 0, 1, 2, 3, 4, 5...

Take a moment and explain to the child that a natural number, such as fifteen is also a whole number and an integer. Zero is both a whole number and an integer. The number negative twenty-four is an integer, but not a whole number or a natural number.

A rational number is defined as any number that can be expressed as a ratio of two integers. What this means is that any fraction that has an integer in the numerator and an integer in the denominator is a rational number. A natural number, such as six, can be expressed as such a fraction that has a numerator of six and a denominator of one.

$$6 = \frac{6}{1}$$

So, numbers such as one and a half and negative two and three quarters are rational numbers. The mixed numbers can be converted into improper fractions.

$$1\frac{1}{2} = \frac{3}{2}$$

$$-2\frac{3}{4} = -\frac{11}{4}$$

Another characteristic of rational numbers is that they will either be a terminating decimal or a repeating decimal.

$$\frac{1}{5} = 0.2$$

$$\frac{1}{6} = 0.1\overline{6}$$

Numbers that have neither a terminating decimal nor a repeating decimal are called irrational numbers. These numbers will be discussed later. For now, it is important for the child to understand the four subsets of numbers that were discussed in this lesson.

TEACHING THE SUBTRACTION OF LARGE NUMBERS FROM SMALL NUMBERS

Operations involving positive and negative numbers can be very confusing to children. This is especially true if the subject matter is introduced too quickly for the child to internalize and master. It is therefore necessary to breakdown the subject matter into small parts that can be easily understood and mastered. Mastery of one concept is essential before moving onto the next concept.

To start off, teach the child how to subtract a larger positive number from a smaller positive number. At first this concept will look strange because up to now the child was told that this was not done. Now that the child understands the concept of negative numbers, this can be done.

For instance, the child has memorized the following subtraction fact:

$$5 - 3 = 2$$

Now explain what happens with the following problem:

$$3 - 5$$

Use a number line to explain.

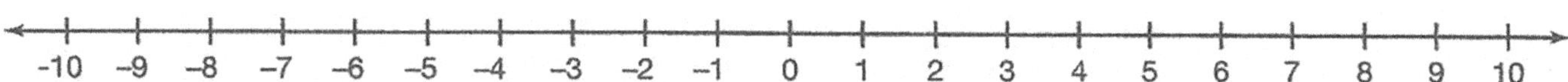

To show the first subtraction problem (5 – 3), circle the five.

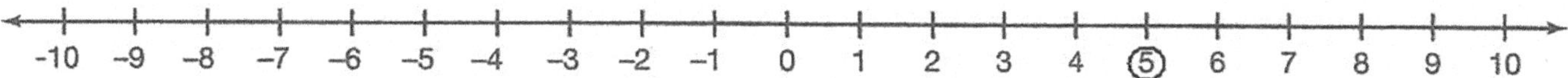

Draw a line going left three places to show that the circled number is being subtracted by three.

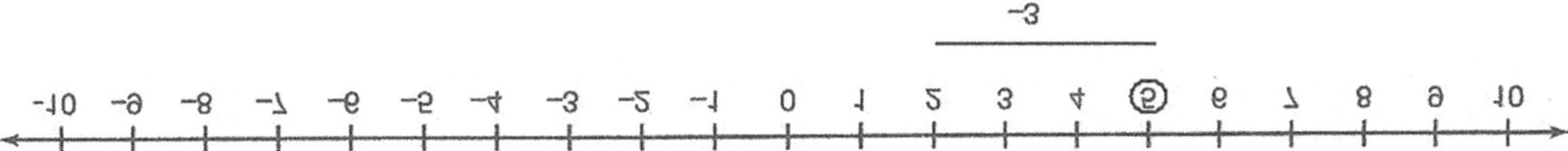

Circle the two where the line ends.

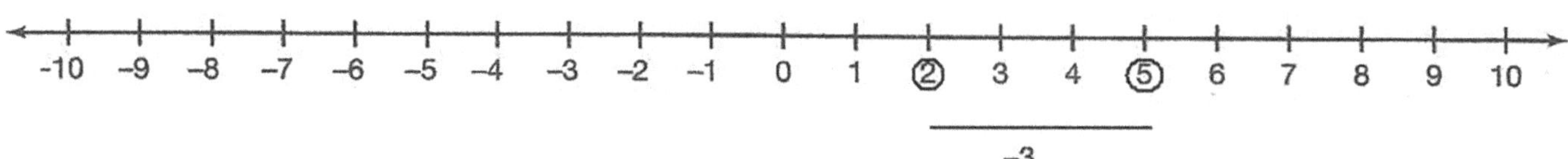

This picture shows how subtraction works. Now use another number line to show the second subtraction problem (3 – 5)

Start off by circling the three.

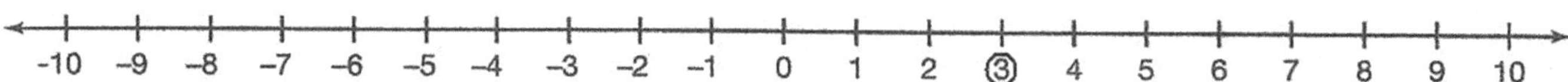

Draw a line going left five places to show that the circled number is subtracted by five.

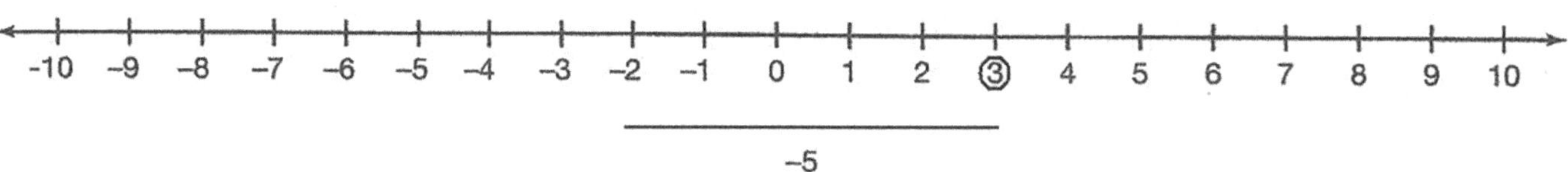

Circle the negative two where the line ends.

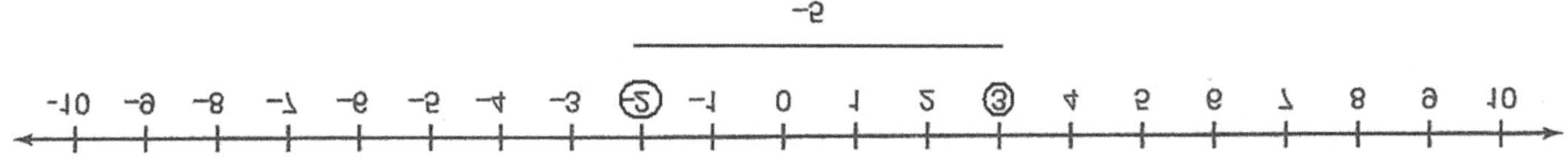

Thus:

$$3 - 5 = -2$$

Obviously, it is not practical to use a number line when subtracting very large numbers. Fortunately, it is only necessary to do this a few times to establish a pattern that the child can understand and memorize.

$$5 - 3 = 2$$
$$3 - 5 = -2$$

This will be the case when a larger number is subtracted from a smaller number. State the following rule to the child.

The difference when a large positive number is subtracted from a small positive number is the opposite of the difference when the same small positive number is subtracted from the same large positive number.

Example:

What is 8 – 17?

Solution:

Since 17 − 8 = 9
The opposite of 9 is −9
Thus:
8 − 17 = −9
Example:
Solve the following:

$$\begin{array}{r} 236 \\ \underline{-579} \end{array}$$

Solution:
Rewrite the problem with the larger number on top and subtract.

$$\begin{array}{r} 579 \\ \underline{-236} \\ 343 \end{array}$$

Since the opposite of 343 is −343, the answer is −343.
Thus:

$$\begin{array}{r} 236 \\ \underline{-579} \\ -343 \end{array}$$

For practice go to themathworksheetsite.com and make a worksheet. However, the parent will have to rewrite the problems on the worksheet so that the larger positive numbers are subtracted from the smaller positive numbers.

Under the "Subtraction" heading select "Single Digit, Horizontal." This will create a worksheet with ten problems. On the back of the paper rewrite the problems.

For instance:

14 − 8

Rewrite as:

8 − 14

The child should be able to correctly do these problems in less than two minutes to achieve mastery.

Also have the child practice subtraction problems with large numbers.

For instance:

$$\begin{array}{r} 724 \\ \underline{-368} \end{array}$$

Rewrite as:

$$\begin{array}{r} 368 \\ \underline{-724} \end{array}$$

Have the child do a few of these problems daily for practice. The child should be able to do two such problems correctly in less than two minutes to achieve mastery with this skill.

This is the first skill among many for the child to learn when it comes to operations with positive and negative numbers. Each lesson will introduce just one change to what the child previously has mastered. Patience is very important when teaching and learning these concepts. However, once these skills are mastered, algebra and other advanced subjects in mathematics will be easier for the child to master. The child's confidence in being able to learn advanced mathematics will increase, which is extremely important.

TEACHING ABSOLUTE VALUE

The concept of absolute value is both extremely simple and important. The child needs to learn this because it is used to explain how to correctly do operations involving positive and negative numbers.

Absolute value is defined as the distance a number is from zero on the number line. To show this, take a number line and circle both the four and the negative four.

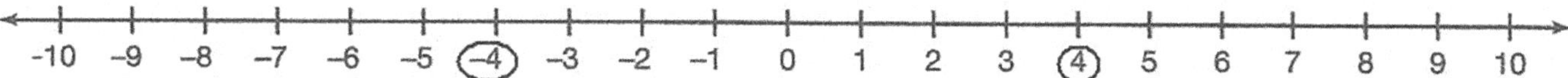

Now for each number, draw a line from zero to each number.

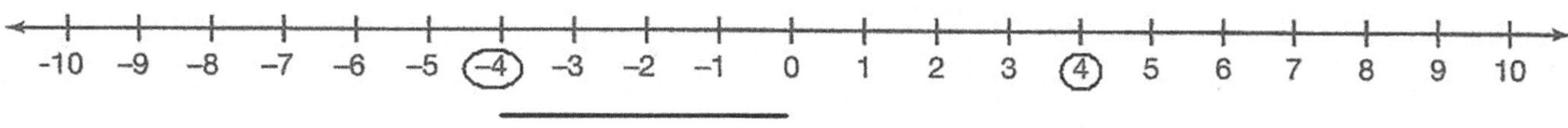

In each case the distance is the same, which is four. So, the absolute value of both numbers is four.

The absolute value of a number is written with the number between two vertical lines.

$$|4| \qquad\qquad |-4|$$

The absolute value of a number is always positive.

$$|4| = 4$$
$$|-4| = 4$$

That is how simple absolute value is.

TEACHING THE ADDITION OF TWO NEGATIVE NUMBERS

The addition of two negative numbers is a fairly straightforward process. All that is required is to add the absolute value of both numbers and make the result a negative number.

Most math textbooks display a negative number between two parentheses.

$$(-8)$$

So, an addition problem involving two negative numbers would look like this:

$$(-8) + (-6)$$

The first step to solve this problem is to add the absolute values of the two numbers, which are eight and six.

$$8 + 6 = 14$$

The second and final step is to rewrite the sum as a negative number.

$$-14$$

Thus:

$$(-8) + (-6) = (-14)$$

Example:
Solve $(-32) + (-17)$
Solution:
Since this problem is the addition of two negative numbers, the first step is to add the absolute values of both numbers to get a sum.

$$32 + 17 = 49$$

The second step is to change the sum to a negative number.

$$-49$$

Thus:

$$(-32) + (-17) = (-49)$$

For practice give the child a few problems each day. Being able to correctly solve five problems with one or two digits in less than a minute is enough to ensure mastery.

TEACHING THE SUBTRACTION OF A POSITIVE NUMBER FROM A NEGATIVE NUMBER

Use a number line to teach the subtraction of a positive number from a negative number. The movement will be toward the left.

For instance, show a child the following problem:

$$(-3) - 5$$

To begin, circle the negative three on the number line.

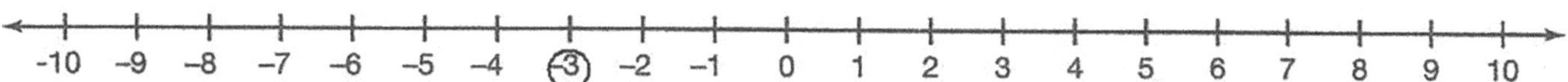

Next draw a line five spaces to the left to show the subtraction of five.

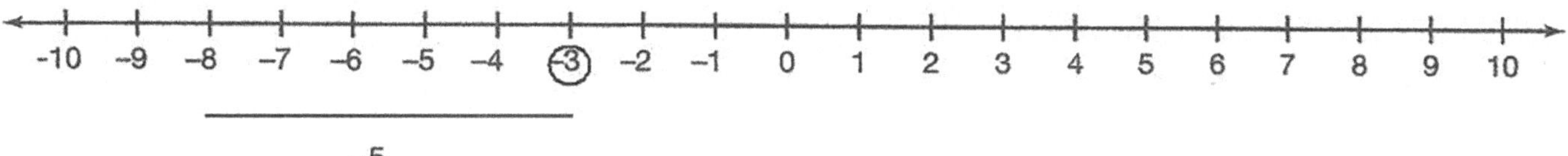

Finally circle the negative eight.

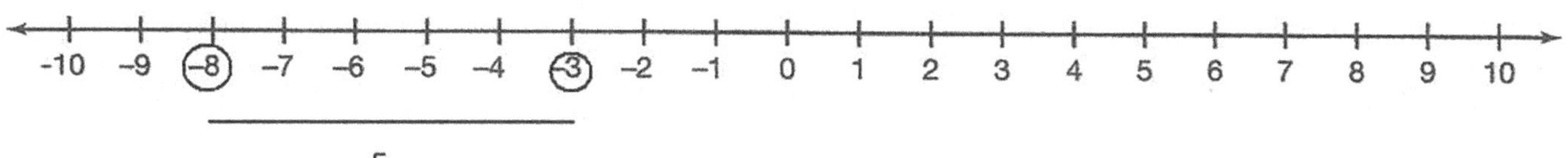

Thus:

$$(-3) - 5 = (-8)$$

Notice that this will be the same answer as if negative five were added to negative three.

$$(-3) - 5 = (-8)$$
$$(-3) + (-5) = (-8)$$

So, tell the child that subtracting a positive number from a negative number is the same as adding a negative number to a negative number. The first step is to convert the positive number to a negative number and change the operation from subtraction to addition. The second step is to add the two absolute values to get a sum. The third step is to change the sum to a negative number. Notice how the second and third steps are exactly the same as the first and second step of the previous lesson. This is why it is important for the child to master a lesson before proceeding.

Example:

$$(-13) - 26$$

Solution:

First rewrite the problem as an addition problem with two negative numbers.

$$(-13) - 26 = (-13) + (-26)$$

Solve the addition problem by adding the absolute values of both numbers and change the sum to a negative number.

$$13 + 26 = 39$$
$$39$$

Thus:

$$(-13) - 26 = (-39)$$

It is possible after practicing several problems the child will be able to skip the step of re-writing the problem as an addition problem. This is natural and should be allowed.

Once the child has mastered this skill by being able to do five single- or double-digit problems correctly in less than a minute, have the child practice doing a mix of five problems from the previous lessons. Once the child can do the different type of problems at the same level of mastery as problems of the same type, it will by time to move on to the next lesson.

TEACHING THE ADDITION OF A POSITIVE NUMBER AND A NEGATIVE NUMBER

It is important for the child to understand what is taking place when a positive number is added to a negative number. A number line will be used to explain the process. Once the process is understood, then the rule should be explained.

Use the numbers five and three. In the first case have the five negative and the three positives, and in the second case have the five positive and the three negative.

In the first case explain:

$$(-5) + 3$$

Use the number line and circle the negative five.

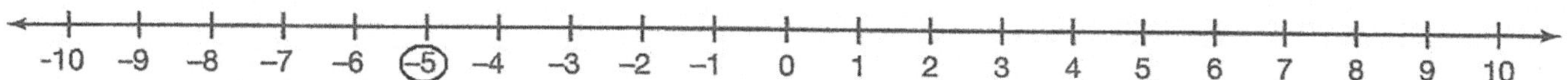

Draw a line to the right three places to show the addition of three.

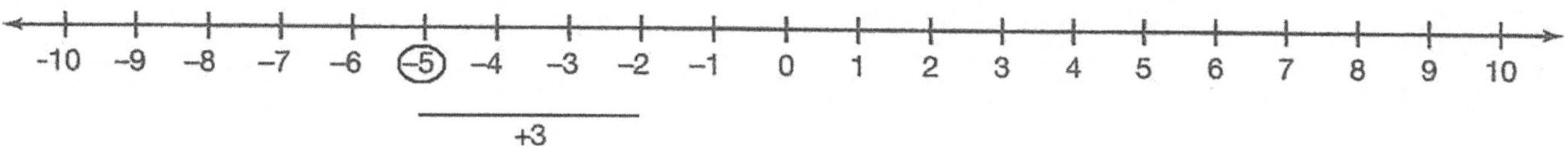

Circle the negative two.

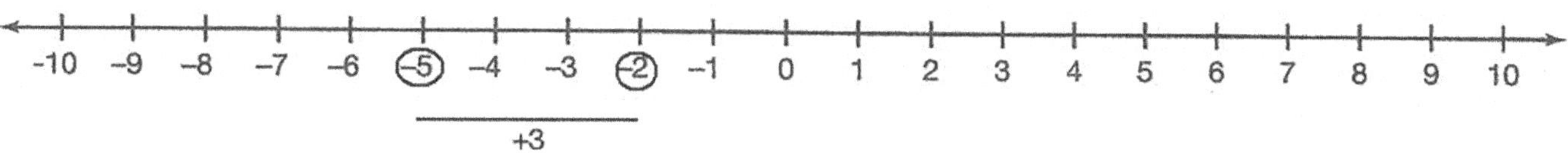

Thus:

$$(-5) + 3 = (-2)$$

Now use another number line to do the second problem.

$$(-3) + 5$$

Circle the negative three.

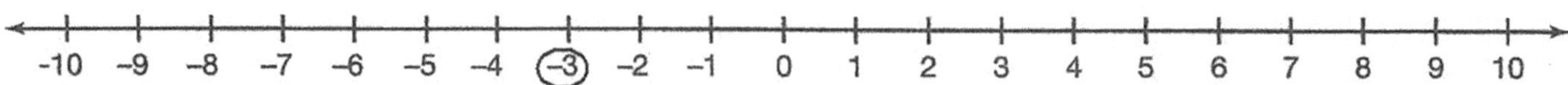

Draw a line to the right five places to show the addition of five.

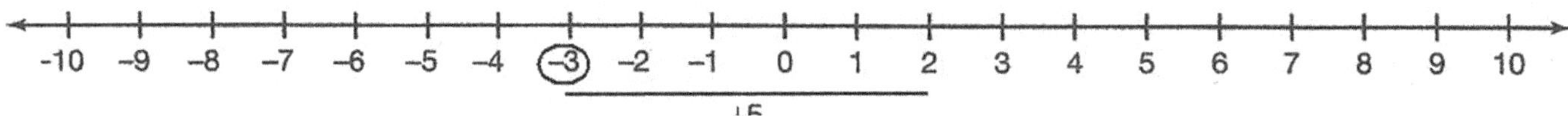

Circle the two.

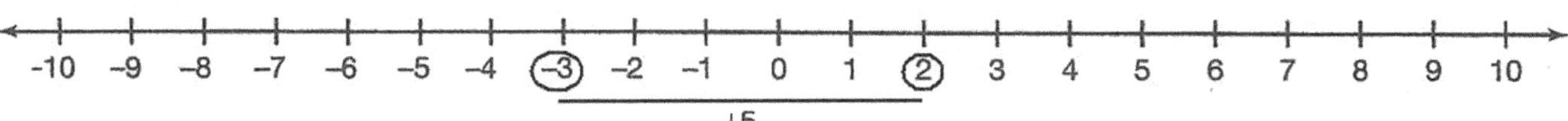

Thus:

$$(-3) + 5 = 2$$

Example:
What is the sum of eighteen and negative thirty-five?
Solution:
First set up the problem.

$$18 + (-35)$$

Find the absolute value of both addends.

$$|18| = 18 \qquad |-35| = 35$$

Thirty-five is the larger absolute value. Subtract.

$$35 - 18 = 17$$

The final step is to determine the sign of the answer. Since the sign of the thirty-five is negative, the sign of the answer is negative.
Thus:

$$18 + (-35) = (-17)$$

Example:
What is the sum of forty-two and negative twenty-six?
Solution:
First set up the problem.

$$42 + (-26)$$

Find the absolute value of both addends.

$|42| = 42$ $|-26| = 26$

The larger absolute value is forty-two. Subtract.

$$42 - 26 = 16$$

The final step is to determine the sign of the answer. Since the sign of forty-two is positive, the answer is positive.

Thus:

$$42 + (-26) = 16$$

Point out to the child that because these are addition problems, that it does not matter the order that the numbers are added. This is due to the commutative property of addition.

$18 + (-35) = (-17)$	$(-35) + 18 = (-17)$
$42 + (-26) = 16$	$(-26) + 42 = 16$

Once again have the child practice doing these problems until mastery is achieved. Mix up the type of problems from previous lessons so that the child must determine what method to use to solve the problem. Once the child is able to consistently do ten problems correctly in less than two minutes, mastery will be achieved.

TEACHING THE SUBTRACTION OF A NEGATIVE NUMBER FROM A POSITIVE NUMBER

Subtracting negative numbers can be confusing to children and unless it is mastered the child will experience difficulty and frustration when learning algebra and other higher-level mathematics. It is important that the child master all the previous lessons regarding the addition of positive and negative numbers before attempting subtraction.

Once again use the number line to explain to the child how this operation is accomplished. Use the number five and negative three. The negative three will be subtracted from the positive five.

$$5 - (-3)$$

Begin by circling the five on the number line.

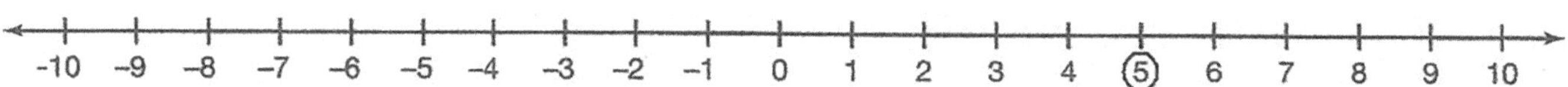

Now draw a line three places to the left to show what happens when a positive three is subtracted.

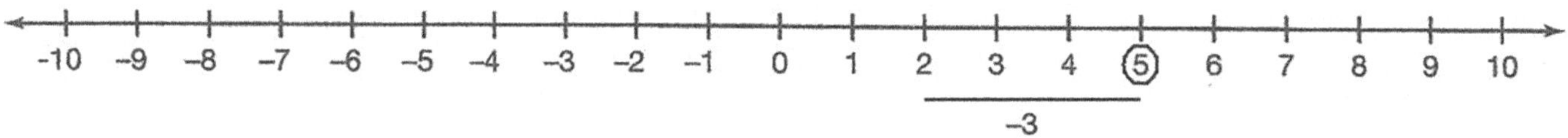

Remember that negative three is the opposite of positive three, so in order to subtract a negative three draw a line three places in the opposite direction of the previous line.

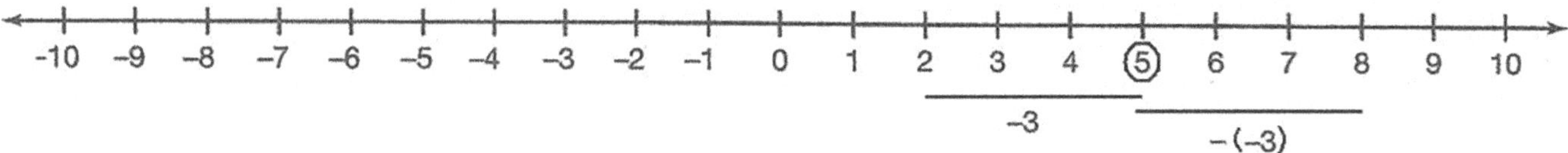

Finally circle the eight.

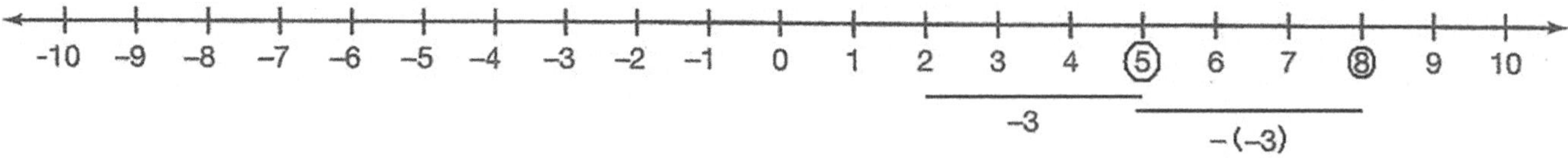

Thus:

$$5 - (-3) = 8$$

This is the same result if a positive three was added to the five.

$$5 + 3 = 8$$

When a negative number is subtracted from a positive number, the result would be the same as the opposite of the negative number was added to the positive number.

$$5 - (-3) = 8 \qquad 5 + 3 = 8$$

Other examples:

$$6 - (-4) = 10 \qquad 6 + 4 = 10$$
$$32 - (-12) = 44 \qquad 32 + 12 = 44$$

Example:
Solve: $48 - (-35)$
Solution:
Rewrite the problem as an addition problem.

$$48 - (-35) = 48 + 35$$

Add the two addends.

$$48 + 35 = 83$$

Thus:

$$48 - (-35) = 83$$

For practice, use themathworksheetsite.com to create problems for the child to solve. Rewrite the problems so that a negative number is subtracted from a positive number.
Example:
The worksheet shows the following problem:

$$\begin{array}{r} 26 \\ \underline{+53} \end{array}$$

Rewrite the problem like this:

$$26 - (-53)$$

Give the child five problems. Once the child is able to consistently answer five problems correctly in less than two minutes, mastery will be achieved.

TEACHING THE SUBTRACTION OF A NEGATIVE NUMBER FROM A NEGATIVE NUMBER

Subtracting a negative number from a negative number will be the same as adding a negative number to a positive number. If the previous lessons have been mastered, then this should be fairly easy for the child. However, if all of these lessons are taught at once, then the child could be easily confused, and frustrated when trying to learn these concepts.

Once again explain that the first step is to rewrite the problem from a subtraction problem to an addition problem. When the problem is rewritten, then use the rules for adding a positive number and a negative number to solve the problem.

Example:
Solve: (-13) - (-38)
Solution:
The first step is to rewrite the problem as an addition problem.

$$(-13) + 38$$

Now solve the problem as an addition problem of a negative number and a positive number.

$$|-13| = 13 \qquad |38| = 38$$

$$38 - 13 = 25$$

Thus:

$$(-13) - (-38) = 25$$

Example:
Solve: (-82) - (-47)
Solution:
First rewrite as an addition problem.

$$(-82) + 47$$

Now solve as an addition problem of a negative number and a positive number.

$$|-82| = 82 \qquad |47| = 47$$
$$82 - 47 = 35$$
Thus: $(-82) - (-47) = (-35)$

For practice go to themathworksheetsite.com and make a subtractions worksheet. Rewrite the problems so that they look like problems learned in this lesson.

For instance, the problem:

$$\begin{array}{r} 94 \\ \underline{-41} \end{array}$$

Can be rewritten the following ways:

$$(-41) - (-94)$$
$$(-91) - (-41)$$

Once the child is able to consistently answer five problems correctly in two minutes, mastery will be achieved. It will then be important for the child to solve a set of problems that are mixed, so that the child understands when to use the various techniques discussed in previous lessons.

TEACHING THE MULTIPLICATION OF A POSITIVE NUMBER AND A NEGATIVE NUMBER

The multiplication and division of positive and negative numbers will be easier for the child to master compared to the addition and subtraction of positive and negative numbers. However, if the addition and subtraction of positive and negative numbers is not mastered, the child can easily get confused by applying rules of multiplication and division to addition and subtraction. It is important for the child to understand mathematically what is taking place as opposed to just memorizing rules.

Consider the following simple multiplication fact:

$$3 \times 5 = 15$$

Remember that negative five is the opposite of positive five. That means that when three is multiplied by the opposite of a positive five, the product must be opposite of a positive fifteen.

$$3 \times (-5) = (-15)$$

Explain this to the child before telling the child the rule.

If a positive number is multiplied by a negative number, then the product will always be a negative number.

Observe the following:

$3 \times 5 = 15$	$3 \times (-5) = (-15)$
$6 \times 8 = 48$	$(-6) \times 8 = (-48)$
$11 \times 12 = 132$	$11 \times (-12) = (-132)$

When multiplying larger numbers, do not worry about the sign until the calculation has taken place. The sign will be the final step when solving the problem.

Example:

What is the product of (−78) and 29?

Solution:

Setup the problem, but do not worry about positives and negatives.

```
  78
x 29
 702
156X
2262
```

The final step is to determine the sign of the product. Since one factor is a positive number and one factor is a negative number, the product must be a negative number.

Thus:

(-78) x 29 = (-2262)

It is important to show the child the difference between adding a positive number and a negative number and multiplying a positive number and a negative number. Many children remember, "A positive and a negative make a negative," which is a rule for multiplication and apply it to addition. This can lead to confusion and mistakes.

(-3) + 5 = 2	(-3) x 5 = (-15)
3 + (-5) = (-2)	3 x (-5) = (-15)

Practice by giving the child a few multiplication problems with one positive number and one negative number. Once the child has mastered this, then have the child do several single digit addition and multiplication problems with a positive integer and a negative integer. The child will have to quickly determine how to solve these problems. Doing ten such problems correctly in a minute is enough to achieve mastery.

TEACHING THE MULTIPLICATION OF TWO NEGATIVE NUMBERS

Recall in the previous lesson that when a negative number is multiplied by a positive number, that the product will be a negative number.

$$(-3) \times 5 = (-15)$$

That means that if a negative number is multiplied by a negative number, then the product must be the opposite of a product when a negative number is multiplied by a positive number, which would be a positive number.

$$(-3) \times (-5) = 15$$

One of the challenges in dealing with operations regarding positive and negative numbers is that students will remember the rule, "Two negatives make a positive," and apply it to addition. It is important that the child understand the difference between multiplying two negative numbers and adding two negative numbers. Use negative three and negative five to show the child the difference.

$$(-3) + (-5) = (-8) \qquad (-3) \times (-5) = 15$$

Practice by having the child add and multiply two single digit integers. Vary the problems with either two negative integers or a positive integer and a negative integer. If the child is experiencing difficulty with this, use the same integers and their opposites, such as a positive and negative four and six.

$$(-4) + 6 = 2$$
$$4 + (-6) = (-2)$$
$$(-4) + (-6) = (-10)$$
$$(-4) \times 6 = (-24)$$
$$4 \times (-6) = (-24)$$
$$(-4) \times (-6) = 24$$

Once the child achieves thorough understanding and mastery with this material, continue to the next lesson, which will cover division.

TEACHING THE DIVISION OF A POSITIVE NUMBER AND A NEGATIVE NUMBER

Recall that when two negative numbers are multiplied together the product is a positive number.

$$(-3) \times (-5) = 15$$

Since the product in a multiplication problem is the dividend in a division problem, if the dividend is a positive number and the divisor is a negative number, then the quotient must be a negative number.

$$15 \div (-3) = (-5)$$
$$15 \div (-5) = (-3)$$

Now recall that in a multiplication problem where one factor is a positive number and one factor is a negative number, the product is a negative number.

$$(-3) \times 5 = (-15)$$
$$3 \times (-5) = (-15)$$

In a division problem where the dividend is a negative number and the divisor is a positive number the quotient must be a negative number.

$$(-15) \div 3 = (-5)$$
$$(-15) \div 5 = (-3)$$

After showing the child these examples, explain that in multiplication and division, if the signs are different, then the answer is a negative number. Also stress that this rule applies only to multiplication and division and not addition or subtraction.

TEACHING THE DIVISION OF TWO NEGATIVE NUMBERS

The rule for dividing two negative numbers is the same as multiplying two negative numbers. In each operation the answer will be a positive number.

Once again look at the multiplication of a positive number and a negative number.

$$(-3) \times 5 = (-15)$$
$$3 \times (-5) = (-15)$$

Now when the product in the multiplication problem is the dividend in a division problem with the negative factor in the multiplication problem as the divisor, the result is that the positive factor in the multiplication problem will be the quotient.

$$(-15) \div (-3) = 5$$
$$(-15) \div (-5) = 3$$

It is important for the child to understand the mathematical reasoning of the operation. Many children remember, "Two negatives make a positive," and will make computational errors by applying that rule to addition and subtraction problems.

Have the child practice completing problems involving positive and negative numbers with all four operations at the same time.

REVIEW OF OPERATIONS WITH POSITIVE AND NEGATIVE NUMBERS

Now that the child has learned all of the different aspects of operations involving positive and negative numbers, it is time for a review. This review can also be a study guide for the child to go over every night for a few minutes in addition to daily practice.

Use the numbers three, five and their opposites.

Addition:

$$3 + 5 = 8 \qquad (-3) + 5 = 2$$
$$3 + (-5) = (-2) \qquad (-3) + (-5) = (-8)$$

Notice that the sum of two positive numbers is the opposite of the sum of two negative numbers. Since five is a larger absolute value than three, its sign will dictate the sign of the sum when one addend is positive, and one addend is negative. When five is positive the sum is positive and when five is negative the sum is negative.

Subtraction:

$$5 - 3 = 2 \qquad 3 - 5 = (-2)$$
$$5 - (-3) = 8 \qquad 3 - (-5) = 8$$
$$(-5) - 3 = (-8) \qquad (-3) - 5 = (-8)$$
$$(-5) - (-3) = (-2) \qquad (-3) - (-5) = 2$$

Subtraction is often the most confusing operation involving positive and negative numbers. In the first row both numbers are positive, and the result is based on the order of the numbers in the subtraction problem.

$$5 - 3 = 2 \qquad 3 - 5 = (-2)$$

In the second row the results are the same. This is because subtracting a negative number is the same as adding a positive number, and the order that two numbers are added will not change the sum.

$$5 - (-3) = 8 \qquad 3 - (-5) = 8$$

The answers are also the same in the third row because this subtraction problem is just like adding two negative numbers.

$$(-5) - 3 = (-8) \qquad (-3) - 5 = (-8)$$

In the fourth row the results are similar to the first row, which is also similar to adding a positive number to a negative number.

(-5) - (-3) = (-2)   (-3) - (-5) = 2

Multiplication:

5 x 3 = 15   (-5) x 3 = (-15)
5 x (-3) = (-15)   (-5) x (-3) = 15

Multiplication is less confusing than subtraction. In each case the answer is either a positive fifteen or a negative fifteen. If the signs are the same, then the answer is a positive number. If the signs are different then the answer is a negative number.

Division:

15 ÷ 5 = 3   15 ÷ 3 = 5
15 ÷ (-5) = (-3)   15 ÷ (-3) = (-5)
(-15) ÷ 5 = (-3)   (-15) ÷ 3 = (-5)
(-15) ÷ (-5) = 3   (-15) ÷ (-3) = 5

Just as with multiplication if the signs are the same, then the answer will be a positive number; and if the signs are different, then the answer will be negative.

It is extremely important that the child master all of these types of problems. If mastery is not achieved, then algebra will be extremely difficulty. Many children (and adults) frustrations and hardships with advanced concepts in mathematics can be traced to the lack of mastery with operations involving positive and negative numbers.

TEACHING SQUARE ROOTS

An important concept is the square root. It is the reverse of a number squared, which is a number multiplied by itself.

By now the child should know the following perfect squares:

1 x 1 = 1
2 x 2 = 4
3 x 3 = 9
4 x 4 = 16
5 x 5 = 25
6 x 6 = 36
7 x 7 = 49
8 x 8 = 64
9 x 9 = 81
10 x 10 = 100
11 x 11 = 121
12 x 12 = 144

Once operations with negative numbers has been taught to and mastered by the child, a key concept is that this also works for negative numbers as well.

(−1) x (−1) = 1
(−2) x (−2) = 4
(−3) x (−3) = 9
(−4) x (−4) = 16
(−5) x (−5) = 25
(−6) x (−6) = 36
(−7) x (−7) = 49
(−8) x (−8) = 64
(−9) x (−9) = 81
(−10) x (−10) = 100
(−11) x (−11) = 121
(−12) x (−12) = 144

Since 2 x 2 = 4, the square root of four is two. Also, since (−2) x (−2) = 4, the square root of four is also negative two. Every perfect square will have one positive and one negative square root.

Most problems involving a square root will use the radical sign.

A button will be on most calculators to calculate the square root of a number. This answer will usually be displayed as a positive number. It is important for the child to remember that the opposite of what is displayed one the calculator (the negative number), will also be the square root of that number.

Example:

Solve: $\sqrt{36}$

Solution:

Since 6 x 6 = 36

$\sqrt{36} = 6$

Also $\sqrt{36} = (-6)$

This will often be written as $\sqrt{36} = \pm 6$

This is usually verbalized as, "Plus or minus six."

Most numbers are not perfect squares. The square root of these numbers will be irrational numbers. An irrational number is a number that has neither a terminating nor repeating decimal.

For instance, on a calculator take the square root of two. ($\sqrt{2}$)

$$\sqrt{2} = 1.4142136237..........$$

The decimal will go on forever.

The child should have the following square roots memorized before beginning algebra:

$$\sqrt{1} = \pm 1$$
$$\sqrt{4} = \pm 2$$
$$\sqrt{9} = \pm 3$$
$$\sqrt{16} = \pm 4$$
$$\sqrt{25} = \pm 5$$
$$\sqrt{36} = \pm 6$$
$$\sqrt{49} = \pm 7$$
$$\sqrt{64} = \pm 8$$
$$\sqrt{81} = \pm 9$$
$$\sqrt{100} = \pm 10$$
$$\sqrt{121} = \pm 11$$
$$\sqrt{144} = \pm 12$$

Memorization of these square roots will make certain problems in algebra extremely easy for the child to solve. If these are not memorized, the child will find the same problems difficult and extremely frustrating.

TEACHING SCIENTIFIC NOTATION WITH NEGATIVE EXPONENTS

Recall that very large numbers can be written in scientific notation with a positive exponent. Very small numbers can be written with a negative exponent. It is important to stress that a negative exponent does not mean a negative number.

Remember that the distance from the earth to the sun is ninety-three million miles. Compare the numbers in standard form and scientific notation.

93,000,000

9.3×10^{7}

Since a negative number is the opposite of a positive number, a negative exponent in scientific notation moves the decimal in the opposite direction.

$0.1 = 10^{-1}$	One tenth
$0.01 = 10^{-2}$	One hundredth
$0.001 = 10^{-3}$	One thousandth
$0.0001 = 10^{-4}$	One ten thousandth
$0.00001 = 10^{-5}$	One hundred thousandth

Something that is very small would be a transistor. The width of a transistor is forty-five billionths of a meter. In standard form that number would look like this.

0.000000045

In scientific notation it would look like this:

4.5×10^{-8}

Since the number in standard form is less than one, the exponent will be negative. To determine the value of the exponent, count how many places to the right that the decimal must be moved before the first non-zero number is to the left of the decimal.

To convert a number written in scientific notation to standard notation will take a few steps.

The first step is to write the base in order without the decimal.

The second step is to take the absolute value of the exponent and write that many zeros to the left (in front of) the first number of the base.

The third step is to write the decimal in the proper place. To do this, count the spaces from the rear of the first number of the base to the absolute value of the exponent. This should leave one zero to the left of the decimal.

Example:

Convert 3.64×10^{-6} to standard notation.

Solution:

The first step is to write the base without the decimal.

364

The second step is to take the absolute value of the exponent, which is six ($|-6| = 6$), and write that many zeros to the left of the first number of the base.

000000364

Finally write the decimal. Count between the numbers to the left. Start behind the three and count to six.

0.00000364

Thus:

3.64×10^{-6} in standard form is 0.00000364

To convert a number in standard notation to a number in scientific notation will require a few simple steps.

The first step is to write the number without the zeros that are to the left of the first non-zero digit.

The second step is to multiply the number written by ten to a negative exponent.

The third step is to determine the value of the exponent. To do this, count the spaces from where the decimal is when the number is written in standard notation to the space just to the right of the first non-zero number.

Example:

Convert 0.000000704 to scientific notation.

Solution:

The first step is to write the number without the zeros and with the decimal point to the right of the first non-zero number, which is seven.

7.04

Next write a multiplication sign and ten to a negative exponent.

$7.04 \times 10^{-}$

To determine to value of the exponent, count the spaces between the numbers from where the decimal is when the number is written in standard notation to where the decimal will be when the number is written scientific notation. In this case it is seven spaces, so the exponent is a negative seven.

Thus:

0.000000704 written in scientific notation is 7.04×10^{-7}

Remember that any number written in scientific notation will only have one number to the left (in front of) the decimal point.

This is a quick overview of scientific notation. The child will learn how to complete operations involving numbers in scientific notation in more advanced mathematics classes.

TEACHING THE BASICS OF CIRCLES

In this final lesson, a few things about circles will be discussed to prepare the child for hire level mathematics. These will include some definitions, measurements and calculations.

The definition of a circle is all of the points that are an equal distance from the same point, called the center, on the same plane. While this seems complicated, the child will revisit this definition in geometry. For the purposes of this lesson, it is important to know that a circle has a center, because the other definitions in this lesson involve the center of the circle.

The first definition is the diameter. The diameter is a line that touches two points on the circle that passes through the center of the circle.

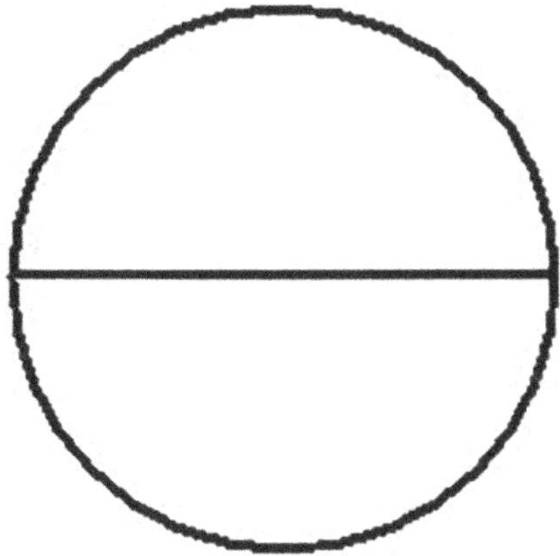

The second definition is theg radius. The radius is a line from the center of the circle to a point on the circle.

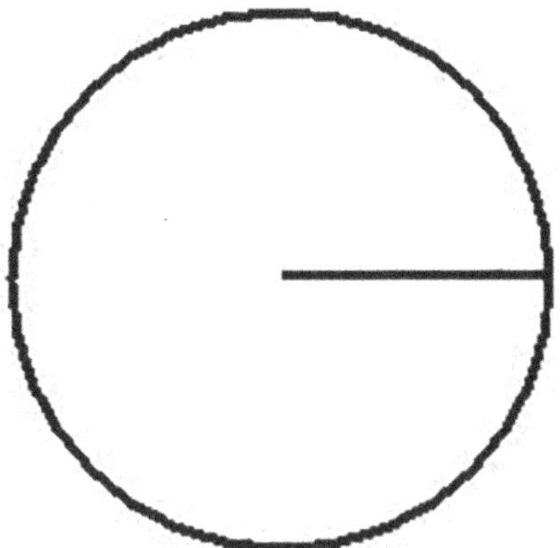

The length of the diameter of any given circle will always be twice the length of the radius of that circle. The length of the radius of any given circle will always be one-half the diameter of that circle.

Circumference is the distance around a circle. The ratio of the circumference to the diameter is represented by the Greek letter pi (Π). This is an irrational number that is usually rounded to 3.14. To find the circumference of a circle, multiply the diameter by pi.

Example:

What is the circumference of a circle that has a diameter of twelve inches?

Solution:

This problem is solved by multiplication. Take the diameter, which is twelve and multiply it by pi.

$$12\Pi$$

Substitute 3.14 for pi. This is an approximation.

$$12 \times 3.14$$

Multiply.

$$12 \times 3.14 = 37.68$$

Thus:

The circumference of a circle with a diameter of twelve inches is approximately 37.68 inches.

This can be displayed using the approximate sign.

$$12\Pi \approx 37.68$$

Sometimes such problems will give the radius instead of the diameter. In this case double the length of the radius to get the length of the diameter.

Example:

Find the circumference of a circle that has a radius of fifteen feet.

Solution:

The first step is to double the radius to get the diameter.

$$15 \times 2 = 30$$

Now multiply the diameter by pi.

$$30\Pi$$
$$30 \times 3.14$$
$$30 \times 3.14 = 94.2$$

Thus, the circumference of a circle with a radius of fifteen feet is approximately 94.2 feet.

Pi is also used to find the area of a circle. This is done by multiplying pi by the radius squared.

Example:

What is the area of a circle that has a radius of four feet?

Solution:

It should not take long to solve this type of problem. The first step is to square the radius.

$$4^2 = 16$$

Now multiply by pi.

$$16\pi$$
$$16 \times 3.14$$
$$16 \times 3.14 = 50.24$$

Thus:

The area of a circle with a radius of four feet is approximately 50.24 square feet.

To find the area of a circle when the diameter is given, it is necessary to first divide the diameter by two.

Example:

What is the area of a circle that has a diameter of eighteen inches?

Solution:

First divide the length of the diameter by two to get the length of the radius.

$$18 \div 2 = 9$$

Now square the length of the radius and multiply by pi.

$$9^2 = 81$$
$$81\pi$$
$$81 \times 3.14$$
$$81 \times 3.14 = 254.34$$

Thus:

The area of a circle that has a diameter of eighteen inches is approximately 254.34 square inches.

Finally, the child needs an overview of angles. This will be covered more thoroughly in geometry, but a quick overview at this time is helpful.

A circle has 360 degrees. The measurement of an angle is proportionate to the fraction of the circle it contains.

Consider the following picture:

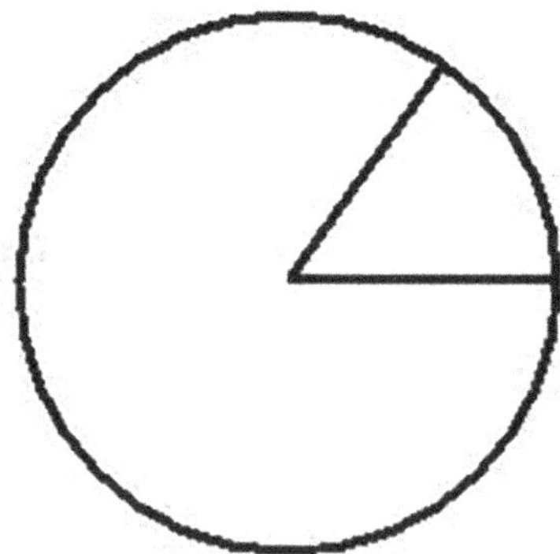

Since the angle is one-eighth of the circle, the measurement of the angle will be one-eighth of 360 or forty-five.

Without the circle the forty-five-degree angle looks like this:

Two types of angles that are of particular importance for the child to understand are right angles and straight angles. A right angle is an angle that measure ninety degrees.

A straight angle is an angle that measures one-hundred eighty degrees. It is a line. When someone is said to do a "one eighty", it means to reverse direction.

Once the child understands the concept of right angles and straight angles, two definitions should be learned. These are complimentary angles and supplementary angles.

Complementary angles are two angles that when their measurements are added result in a sum of ninety degrees.

Supplementary angles are two angles that when their measurements are added result in a sum of one-hundred eighty degrees.

These concepts will be taught in greater detail in high school geometry classes. Giving the child awareness of these concepts before middle school and high school will serve to both demystify advanced mathematics and to increase confidence in being able to learn and master advanced mathematics. Daily practice with different concepts will ensure that math skills will be constantly improved.

AUTHOR'S NOTE

Math skills will become increasingly important to a person's success in the future as the world transitions to a knowledge-based economy. Unfortunately, school districts in the United States are graduating students with relatively mediocre math skills. It is sad because this does not have to happen.

I have written this book after several conversations with parents who have told me that they are frustrated because they cannot help their children with elementary school math, with students who have told me that they that math is something that they struggle through just to get by in order to graduate, and with teachers who have become jaded because the bureaucrats in education prevent children from coming to high school properly prepared to enroll in high school mathematics. Add to this my own experience teaching and tutoring children led me to the conclusion that mathematics was not being taught properly.

I was fortunate to have great teachers in elementary school coupled with relatives to instill in me the fascination, curiosity and confidence to learn math. I sincerely believe that if math is taught correctly, it can not only be learned but enjoyed by all students.

It is sad that so many students see math as something to struggle through and overcome in order to graduate, instead of something to learn, master and explore. For many of these students this frustration begins in elementary school, where at some point they get so confused that to them math is something so difficult and complex that only a select few are able to understand.

I want all parents to understand that they have the power to teach their children math. It is not important just to go over how to solve problems. Instilling a fascination of math, and the confidence in their ability to do math is just as important but often neglected.

Once children are fascinated by math and confident in their math skills, they will then experience something that they felt was previously unattainable. When this happens, they will have more options and be able to pursue any endeavor that they wish to pursue.

I wrote this book because I want every child to be able to achieve greatness. Most parents want this for their children, and this book will help parents help their children to pursue their dreams and become great.

www.ingramcontent.com/pod-product-compliance
Lightning Source LLC
LaVergne TN
LVHW060617110826
845147LV00019B/1038
* 9 7 8 1 9 6 7 3 8 6 4 8 2 *